you&**your**
Jaguar **XJ40**

you & your
Jaguar XJ40

Nigel Thorley *Buying, enjoying, maintaining, modifying*

© Nigel Thorley 2002

First published in 2002

Nigel Thorley has asserted his right to
be identified as the author of this work.

All rights reserved. No part of this publication may be reproduced or
transmitted in any form or by any means, electronic or mechanical,
including photocopying, recording or by any information storage or
retrieval system, without permission in writing from the publisher.

British Library cataloguing-in-publication data:
A catalogue record for this book is available
from the British Library

Published by Haynes Publishing,
Sparkford, Yeovil, Somerset BA22 7JJ, UK

Tel: 01963 442030 Fax 01963 440001
Int. tel: +44 1963 442030 Fax +44 1963 440001
E-mail: sales@haynes-manuals.co.uk
Web site: www.haynes.co.uk

ISBN 1 85960 862 0

Library of Congress catalog card no. 2001099282

Haynes North America, Inc.,
861 Lawrence Drive, Newbury Park,
California 91320, USA

Printed and bound in Great Britain by
J. H. Haynes & Co. Ltd, Sparkford

Jurisdictions which have strict emission control laws may consider any modification to a vehicle to be an infringement of those laws. You are advised to check with the appropriate body or authority whether your proposed modification complies fully with the law. The publishers accept no liability in this regard.

While every effort is taken to ensure the accuracy of the information given in this book, no liability can be accepted by the author or publishers for any loss, damage or injury caused by misuse of, errors in, or omissions from, the information given.

Contents

	Acknowledgements	6
	Introduction	7
Chapter 1:	The birth of an entirely new car	9
Chapter 2:	Technology to the fore	20
Chapter 3:	The launch of a new car with an old name – XJ6	35
Chapter 4:	2.9-litre and 3.6-litre models – 1986 to 1990	40
Chapter 5:	Times of change – 1990 to 1991	56
Chapter 6:	Mid-life crisis	67
Chapter 7:	The revitalisation years – 1993 to 1994	76
Chapter 8:	Variations on a theme	94
Chapter 9:	Choosing and buying an XJ40	118
Chapter 10:	Owning, running and maintaining your XJ40	130
Chapter 11:	Modifications and improvements	146
Appendix A:	Specifications	153
Appendix B:	Model history	154
Appendix C:	Total production figures	155
Appendix D:	Factory options listing from 1986 to 1994	156
Appendix E:	Regular maintenance schedule	157
Appendix F:	Engine management system fault codes	158
	Index	159

Acknowledgements

It is only fitting that I should thank all those who have helped me in the preparation of this book, and I apologise now if anyone has been left out; this is certainly not intentional.

First, I must acknowledge Jaguar Cars Limited, because if they had not produced the XJ40, then I would have had nothing to write about. Fortunately, although the company has moved on to other models since that time, there were still plenty of people around who had worked on the car and were able to provide valuable information. A close second is the Jaguar Daimler Heritage Trust which has over the years provided me with a lot of background information and detail aspects of the model as it is now custodian of Jaguar Cars' material on this model. It is a tribute to Jaguar and the JDHT that such items have been saved for posterity and I would particularly like to thank Curator Tony O'Keeffe and Archivist Julia Simpson.

I must also give special thanks to a personal friend and someone who is arguably the greatest expert on the model technically, David Marks from David Marks Garages in Nottingham. He freely provided his time to help me with this project and his in-depth knowledge on the cars was invaluable.

Thanks are due to the Jaguar Enthusiasts' Club and in particular many of their members who provided cars for me to photograph and lastly, thanks to Haynes Publishing and their Publishing Director, Mark Hughes, for having faith in the saleability of this publication. The XJ40 has been much maligned over the years and it was encouraging to find someone else who was as interested in pursuing this project as much as I have been.

Nigel Thorley
Doncaster
January 2002

Introduction

The Jaguar name is associated with prestige luxury motor cars. This is an image which has been built up over the years, for although Jaguar has produced many fascinating sports and sports/racing cars in its time, it is the saloons sold into the luxury sector of the market that have arguably made the most impact long term for the company, both financially and in other ways.

Started in 1922 in the town of Blackpool on the north-west coast of England, the company was founded by William Lyons with partner William Walmsley, initially to produce sidecars for motorcycles. This led to the design and building of bespoke bodies on cars, like the little Austin 7, up to the Swift, which was prestigious in its day. A move to Coventry in 1928 led to the introduction of their own motor cars in 1931, which were built in the name of SS, around mechanics supplied by the Standard Motor Company.

It wasn't until late in 1935 however, that there was the first sight and sound of a 'Jaguar' in the form of the SS Jaguar 2½-litre saloon. At £385 it was to set the scene for many future models, all built to a luxury standard, but at an affordable price. This first Jaguar remained in production until the outbreak of the Second World War and then continued, without the SS name, from 1946 until 1948 when it was replaced by a much improved Mark V model.

Although very successful the early pre and post-war pushrod-engined cars were to be eclipsed by the brand-new Mark VII from 1950, the first saloon Jaguar to feature the company's own XK twin-overhead camshaft six-cylinder engine of advanced design. This car put the company on the map, particularly in valued export markets and remained in production, in various guises, until 1961 when it was replaced by the Mark X.

This later model, which was not as sporty as the earlier cars, offered enormous interior accommodation, mated to the latest triple-carburettor version of the XK engine, refined independent rear suspension, and was to carry the accolade of being the widest production car produced in the UK for many years. This model remained in production until 1970.

It was in 1968 that we first saw the designation 'XJ6' used by Jaguar with the launch of their entirely new saloon model, a car destined to replace the other medium-sized saloons produced in the Sixties and the large Mark X/420G design, effectively taking the company into a one-model policy at the time. The XJ6 concept, initially with just two engine sizes (2.8 litre and 4.2 litre) still used the XK power unit but with much improved front suspension, better brakes, specially designed tyres and a very well engineered bodyshell.

The XJ was developed later to feature the famed V12 engine as well as the six-cylinder, short and long wheelbase body lengths, and Daimler derivatives. Upgraded to the Series 2 models from 1973, the design changed to meet the demands of technology and legislation and then in 1978 to its final, Series 3 guise, by this time with fuel injection, redesigned interior and exterior, new gearboxes, and much more.

These XJ6 and XJ12 models were to become the most prolific cars to be built by Jaguar up to that time with a total of over 402,000 examples, the car remaining in production until 1987 in six-cylinder form, 1991 in V12 Jaguar form, and 1992 in V12 Daimler form; a hard act for any new Jaguar model to follow.

Successful though the Series 3 models were, they were not without their problems, even towards the end of production. Assembly costs were great, the body being produced by old technology, and warranty problems on new cars averaged 15 per car, despite the hard work put in by the new Jaguar boss, John Egan.

DID YOU KNOW?

When is an XJ an XJ?
There has always been confusion about the coding given by Jaguar to development projects. The following throws no new light on the subject, but merely indicates that confusion reigns!

X	–	experimental
XB	–	military chassis project
XF to XK	–	engine designations
XJ4	–	the eventual XJ6 project introduced in 1968
XJ5	–	structural changes to the Mark X
XJ6	–	the 4 ohc V12 racing engine
XJ8	–	E-type 2 + 2
XJ16	–	420 saloon
XJ27	–	XJ-S V12 Coupé from 1975
XJ50	–	Series 3 V12 saloon
Etc.!		

XJ heritage
1968 – First use of the insignia publicly for a Jaguar saloon car.
1973 – Second use in the XJ Series 2 saloons.
1978 – Third use in the XJ Series 3 saloons.
1986 – Fourth use in the XJ40 saloons.
1994 – Continued (fifth) use for the New Series XJ (X-300) saloons.
1997 – Sixth use for the XJ8 (X-308) saloons.
2002 – Latest model code-name X-350 destined to continue the heritage of the XJ insignia into the future.

The XJ Series 3 was a car of its day, peoples' aspirations of quality had moved on and technology had not only caught Jaguar up but passed it, so something entirely new was needed.

Although much has and will continue to be said about the British Leyland era, it is of some mark of tribute that BL allowed an investment of over £100 million into Jaguar at a time when it was haemorrhaging money at an alarming rate. Without that investment the new car, and perhaps subsequent Jaguar developments, might not have taken place. The replacement model for the Series 3 (coded during development as XJ40), and in the end to be still designated XJ6, was finally launched in 1986 at a total cost of some £200 million, a virtually all-new concept with nothing carried over from the previous model except its name. It met with instant acclaim. The new model was badly needed by Jaguar to survive and was launched just two years after the company returned to the private sector.

Despite an elongated gestation period hampered by BL involvement, the new car was to put right many of the criticisms laid at previous Jaguar models and as such, sales of the XJ40 boomed. By the end of the 1980s, the car had increased Jaguar's production several fold, in fact, the company's best ever sales year was 1989, primarily due to the success of the XJ40, and it would be 1998 before that figure was exceeded. The new car was constantly developed and upgraded with larger engines providing better torque, eventually receiving the V12 power unit in uprated, 6.0-litre form.

Although only in production until 1994, over 200,000 XJ40s were produced and many aspects of the car were carried forward into the X-300 (New Series XJs) from September 1994 and it could be said fairly that many aspects of the XJ40 have followed through into the XJ8s.

Despite being much maligned in later years, the XJ40 was arguably one of the most important models ever in Jaguar's history and so it is time to pay tribute to a car which is worthy of praise and, I am sure, will one day become a classic, like all other Jaguar saloon models.

Chapter **One**

The birth of an entirely new car

Although the XJ40 was launched in 1986, its origins go way back to the British Leyland era. In fact, the XJ40 was under development before the Series 2 XJ6 had arrived on the scene for the 1974 model year, such was the timescale necessary to produce a new car in those days. The XJ Series 1 had been a phenomenal success for Jaguar and, although they anticipated a longer lifespan for this model, it was inevitable that a new car would be needed within the next few years. However, we must pay tribute to the stamina of the Series models as nobody could have foreseen the extended lifespan and popularity they would eventually endure.

The true significance of the XJ40 wouldn't be realised until the early 1980s, when the ethos of the car would be to put right everything that had gone wrong at

Sir William Lyons, still active in his later years, had a keen interest and involvement in the XJ40 project.

John Egan, later knighted for his work in the motor industry, was the one man who saw the Jaguar XJ40 project through to its successful conclusion.

Jaguar during the intervening years. Those problems wouldn't just relate to the cars but the whole attitude within the organisation.

It should also be remembered that the XJ40 was the last design with which Sir William Lyons (founder of the company) had had a connection. Although he retired in 1971 he remained fairly active and visited the factory regularly, not least to see how the XJ40 design was progressing. Later in the Eighties, examples of prototypes were taken to his own home at Wappenbury Hall for his inspection – a principle that went back to the early post-war years.

John Egan took over the helm of the company in April 1980 when it was loosing money at the rate of £4 million a month, it had a bad reputation with its customers on quality and reliability issues, and was in danger of becoming just another part of the once great British motoring industry to die. His significant role in bringing the company back to profit, improving quality control and customer satisfaction cannot be overstated. Nor can we ignore his major contribution to the development of and success for the XJ40.

John Egan's first task, after assuring the workforce of his commitment to them and the company's future, was to attack the build quality of the cars and the parts that went into them, rather than giving priority to the development of new models. This subsequently proved to be the right move as the existing XJ-S and XJ6/12 Series models improved dramatically with demand still high when the latter ceased production in favour of the XJ40.

XJ40 – development

Returning to the gestation period of the XJ40, there were quarter scale models produced of the concept as early as 1972, although at that time, the board had not approved the finance required for a new model. It should be remembered that the Series 1 XJ6 had only been launched in 1968, the Series 2 was under development, the E-type Series 3 was still current, and the next brand-new model, the XJ-S wasn't to show its face until 1975. The concept for the next-generation saloon was gaining momentum and early in 1973 a full-size clay model of the XJ40 was produced, although in truth, it bore little resemblance to the production design save for the squared-off rear-end styling.

In those early days of development there were actually three evaluation projects from which to determine the future direction the company might take with a new saloon model. The first and easy option was to introduce the Rover (ex-Buick) V8 engine in a Jaguar, eventually to replace their own engines. To BL this made sense in cutting overheads, producing economies of scale production and, not least, savings in development. Such a move was out of the question as far as Jaguar was concerned, but inevitably the principle would raise its ugly head later but in the end, fortunately, it would never reach production.

Secondly, there was an option to commit new finance to effectively reskin the existing XJ model which would have meant using the then current floorpan, arguably the most vital part of any car. This would have kept costs down again in development, but was to lose

DID YOU KNOW?

When is an XJ40 an LC40?
Jaguar gave their new saloon car project the in-house code designation XJ40. In the mid-Seventies with British Leyland in control, this was changed to LC40 (for Leyland Cars). The term was used by BL staff but rarely at Jaguar resulting in it being dropped in May 1979 in favour of XJ40 again!

Ideas for the XJ40 came early on in 1972 and '73 and here, a quarter scale clay model was produced of a design by Jaguar man George Thomson, taken from an earlier sketch.

Outside assistance in the design of the new car was considered. This is a Pininfarina design called the XJ12-PF, dating from 1973.

What must be termed the first full-size clay model of Jaguar's interpretation of the XJ40 – at this point, with a frontal view similar to the forthcoming XJ-S and even at this stage, the sixth (quarter light) window had appeared.

Still in 1973, and a later version of the original Jaguar design showing a close resemblance at the rear to the final concept. Note also the typical XJ sloping style over the rear wing and the thoughts on through-flow ventilation with the extractor grids in the rear quarter. Eyeing up the car here, are Cyril Crouch (Jaguar's chief body designer at the time), and 'Lofty' England.

Another styling idea from an outside coachbuilder, this time Ital, seen here lined up for inspection with other concepts. Although the rear quarters bear a similarity to the then unreleased XJ-S, this design was never considered seriously and was later used as a concept for the Maserati Medici.

The year 1976 and yet another concept for the XJ40, working with very angular and stark lines.

Into mid-1977 and the final form starts to show through. Still undecided about the rear end the side view is similar to the production car. Note the 'XJ' badging on the front wing.

Now it is 1979 and yet more change, almost reverting back to Series 3 aspects with the window frames (and lack of the sixth rear window), but the frontal view is almost there.

The birth of an entirely new car

DID YOU KNOW?

Important dates involved in the XJ40 project

1973–75 — Geoffrey Robinson, chief executive of the company.
1974 — 'Lofty' England retires from chairmanship of the company.
1978–80 — Bob Knight, managing director.
1980 — Jaguar takes control of Castle Bromwich body plant.
1981 — Finance approved for the XJ40 project.
1983 — Launch of AJ6 engine in XJ-S models.
1984 — Jaguar privatised.
1985 — Sir William Lyons died.
— Mike Beasley appointed asstistant managing director.
1986 — John Egan knighted.
— Launch of XJ40 models.
— XJ40 voted Top Car by Guild of Motoring Writers UDT.
1987 — Whitley Research & Development Centre opened.
— XJ40 launched in the USA.

favour through the desperate need to upgrade manufacturing techniques, improve build quality and not least, move forward in terms of chassis design to keep a new car ahead of the competition.

This left the third and successful option – to invest over £70 million in a brand-new car, code-named XJ40.

By late 1973, a second full-size mock-up had been built taking cues from many different sources. Although the angular approach to styling had already been established, it was generally felt by the BL board that the design for such a new car should be totally devoid of any connection with previous Jaguars. This, fortunately, later changed as those who mattered felt the new car should retain touches from previous designs to create something of an evolutionary design rather than be too radical.

Jaguar styling gurus were also to take note of Italian coachbuilders. It was certainly not Jaguar's normal practice to involve outside coachbuilders in their designs, but a strong bond would eventually be struck with Pininfarina who were to significantly update the XJ Series 3 model in the late Seventies, to maintain the car's appeal during the development of the XJ40.

For the XJ40, Pininfarina had first produced their own concept design based on the XJ6/12 Series 1, a car that Jaguar had 'borrowed' to compare with and evaluate against their own designs. Two other Italian styling houses became involved with their own ideas on what the next Jaguar saloon should look like at the behest of Geoffrey Robinson, at the time one of the prime movers in Jaguar. Bertone and Ital produced examples which were also brought over to Coventry and from which further ideas would develop. Bertone had two different approaches which were cleverly sculpted into one body (right and left sides) while Ital completed one car and then also supplied another design, which was eventually used as a Maserati prototype. The latter, as a matter of interest, showed clear signs of the XJ-S with its 'flying buttresses' at the rear.

Frontal styling treatment went through many phases, this being the Ital design.

From several ideas, the transition from conventional lighting to rectangular units came early on.

A modernistic approach to the traditional XJ grille lead to this bonnet style which virtually stayed with the design through to production.

Back to the Pininfarina design again, with just a hint of old Series XJ styling to the wing tips and lights.

In 1979, the grille still needed some reshaping, although the frontal concept is almost complete, but as yet, the lighting is undecided.

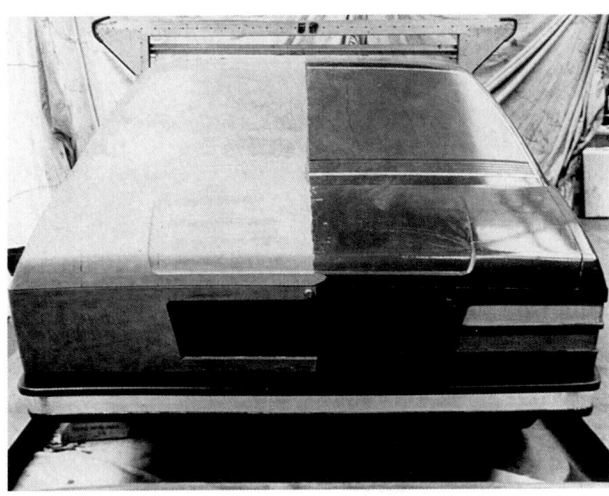
The 1973 ideas, and the truly angular approach takes hold.

The rear end of the XJ40 seemed to cause more problems as this early design shows signs of the angular style with a slight leaning towards Series XJ lighting.

By 1979, the rear-end style had almost been achieved although the boot 'lip' had not been considered at this time. The lighting perhaps, owes more to the later Rolls-Royce Silver Spirit than Jaguar.

The birth of an entirely new car

Throughout the early years of XJ40 development changes came and went like the wind. Here, an early consideration to a very untraditional interior was soon abandoned.

By June 1974, the Jaguar stylists had produced another of what would turn out to be numerous full-size mock-ups, this time leaning heavily towards Italian styling, but with a frontal aspect not unlike contemporary cars such as the Vauxhall Cavalier! The major flaw with this design was that from the side elevation it had lost all connection with previous models, and so was not instantly recognisable as a Jaguar. It was now considered vital that there should be a family resemblance between old and new models.

The number of viewings given to XJ40 concepts and progress were so numerous, that Jaguar people began to comment it was like working with an ever-expanding committee where the members changed regularly. This resulted in a lack of effective decision making which delayed the project. At this time, it should be pointed out, the massive financial investment needed for the project had still to be sanctioned.

It was agreed that the new car should retain some of the Jaguar features, and subsequent designs therefore retained the 'haunch' over the back doors into the rear wing, a feature from the then current models. However, there was a major problem as it was vital the new car should be more aerodynamic and fuel efficient than previous Jaguars, yet it was established that the most traditional aspect of the Jaguar saloon, the forward slope frontal aspect with peaked headlights, was the largest contributory aspect to a high drag factor. An opposing problem came at the rear of the car where Jaguar's traditional slope in the boot level was good for aerodynamics, but poor for luggage capacity.

The net result from the above involved the greatest design work on the front of the new car. The forward slope of the radiator grille was almost completely removed and out went the eyebrows over the headlights. Although serious consideration was given to an XJ-S-style frontage (which would have been aerodynamically acceptable), it was considered important to retain some resemblance of the previous models and an element of commanding image, hence the retention of a chromed radiator grille.

The jury was still out on the use of four headlights or new technology rectangular units, although most of the

Outside coachbuilders sometimes have a lot to answer for and this one surely had little comprehension of what constituted a Jaguar.

designs modelled used the latter which would finally win out, for the superior models at least. Significant wind tunnel testing was carried out on the designs which led to the fitment of a front air dam as well.

The designers still had to address the rear and the necessity for good luggage accommodation, which meant a raised line of the boot which in turn demanded a more angular approach, a feature which had shown through on all styling mock-ups of the car. To meet the demands of aerodynamics, however, a rear spoiler would assist in bringing down the drag factor, but this was thought unacceptable on a Jaguar – that traditional image again! Instead, Jaguar came up with a neat alternative in the form of a slightly raised lip to the boot lid which was continued to the rear wings, subtle but effective.

The threat of a BL (Rover) engine finding its way into the new Jaguar was still present which encouraged Jaguar engineers to design the inner panels and structure of the bodyshell in such a way that it would be impossible to fit a V-configuration engine! This action proved very useful at the time, but later would cost Jaguar dearly when re-engineering the car to take its own V12 power unit.

Through the mid-Seventies and into 1979, models were still being produced to indicate major changes and later finely hone the styling. By this time, the front end would almost match the production design, as would the bonnet shape, style and features. The car now featured the familiar six-light side window style (new to Jaguar) with its neatly designed additional windows in the rear quarter to improve vision. Even the lower swage line along the side of the body had been determined at this stage.

Full-size painted glass-fibre models of the car were now prepared for display at Jaguar for further detailed evaluation although lots of details still needed confirmation like lighting, trim and even the shaping to the sill areas.

Just before John Egan joined the company the BL board approved a £32 million investment in a new engine for Jaguar that would ultimately power the XJ40. Later, in 1981, the BL board also finally approved the £80 million investment in the XJ40 project. This sanction was given on the understanding that the new car would be launched in the autumn of 1983 for the UK market and spring of 1984 for export. Now the company had to produce the car in time and also ensure that the existing Series models would hold out long enough.

Their sanction was based on full-size glass-fibre

Now it is early in 1980 and this full-sized glass-fibre mock-up of the XJ40 shows the design almost completed. The sill line has still to be finalised as has the front valance, and at this time it is sitting on conventional steel wheels with XJ Series rimbellishers.

The birth of an entirely new car **15**

> **DID YOU KNOW?**
>
> **XJ40 test of strength**
> The depth of testing involving XJ40 was the most significant ever carried out by Jaguar:
>
> | | |
> |---|---|
> | Heat of Arizona | 1.25 million miles |
> | Winter in Canada | 1.1 million miles |
> | Australian heat and dust | 1.8 million miles |
> | Nardo high-speed circuit | 3/4 million miles |
> | Plus general road testing | |

mock-ups of the car produced in 1979 and '80, which by then were remarkably close to the final design. In July, one of these models appeared in Harrogate, Yorkshire at a special clinic set up by Jaguar for selected members of the public to view the car and compare it to Jaguar's own then-current Series 3 saloon, the equivalent Mercedes S Class and BMW 7 Series. Another clinic was held in Effingham, Surrey and later, another in Knutsford, Cheshire, this time with a second XJ40 design with revised exterior trim.

A first for Jaguar was the building of a special interior styling 'buck' to evaluate the layout, design of the seats and even visibility in the new car. Jaguar had previously decided to include the latest electronic technology with the car to keep it ahead of the competition. Ideas of multi-function electronic circuitry with touch-sensitive switches, however, were somewhat toned down by the need to retain some traditionalism and, perhaps reliability. The seating was another area that didn't find total approval and was altered to a more sombre design, again in keeping with the marque generally.

Another interesting aspect of the thinking behind the XJ40 was that the steering wheel was always designed to take an air bag, a feature that wouldn't see the light of day until the early 1990s, even then, Jaguar being one of the first to fit them in the luxury sector of the market. Now into the early Eighties, with the design almost finalised and the financial backing secured, it was 'all systems go'. By now, John Egan was well established and had gained the confidence of the workforce as well as Jaguar's customers. The quality of

It's 1981 and another full-sized mock-up of the XJ40 is ready for clinic review, at this point with alternative styles of bumper bar fitted.

A pre-production 'real' car in the photo studio.

the existing models had improved so much and sales had increased accordingly that this gave Egan and Jaguar the breathing space to ensure that XJ40 would be right by the time of launch. Hence the launch date for the car was put back to 1985.

The position was that the body structure had been signed off by October 1980, in November the interior styling and layout had been approved, and the AJ6 engine installation had also been confirmed. By December, the body skin panel design had been signed off, the first semi-engineering prototype had been successfully crash tested at 40mph and drawings had been completed to produce the first running prototype. Aerodynamic testing had also commenced. In January 1981 the first front and rear suspension modules had been built.

The most stringently tested car ever produced by Jaguar, up to this time.

The birth of an entirely new car 17

For most of the time testing was carried out in secret with cars heavily disguised from prying eyes.

Things were moving apace and the most significant aspect came in July 1981 when the first prototype was driven under its own power around the Browns Lane complex by Jim Randle. It followed that in April of 1982 the first fully engineered bodyshell for the XJ40 was received at Browns Lane from the supplier Pressed Steel Fisher.

The XJ40 would become the most tested car ever produced by Jaguar. One hundred prototypes were produced for testing during which a distance of some 5 million miles was covered, spread across the UK, the heat of the Arizona Desert, the extreme cold of Timmins in Canada (in both cases Jaguar having permanent facilities there), the rough roads of the Australian outback, and the intense traffic conditions of Manhattan.

Some examples of the extent of the testing included 25,000 miles at near flat-out speeds on the Nardo high-speed test circuit in Italy, 35,000 miles of Third World-type test circuits at Gaydon in Warwickshire, and 1,250 miles on the MIRA paved track in Nuneaton. Engines had to complete 400 hours of BL technology test cycles running at varying temperatures from –30 C to +52 C.

By 1982, Jaguar testers were very pleased with the car, not least its handling capabilities. At the start of 1983, two XJ40s commenced 24-hour running in the cold conditions of Timmins, based at their own garage facility there. This was followed in the summer by the delivery of two other cars to Arizona for hot weather testing. After this other cars were made available, some were moved around and testing continued at a major pace.

During this period, inter-departmental and overall planning meetings were held weekly at the Jaguar, Browns Lane factory to keep abreast of changes and amendments to the project. Also by this time, special test rigs had been set up to operate suppliers parts to destruction in an attempt to iron out previous problems of reliability with components.

At the end of 1983, the first production-built cars (Specially Designated Vehicles) were finished and handed over for further assessment, the cars being heavily disguised to hide their true identity. Disguise as such had first started with the Mark X saloon back in the late Fifties, early Sixties and had been developed into quite an art in its own right. Rubberised over-bodies were produced to clip over the whole front of the car from the scuttle forward. Similar treatment at the rear included the XJ-S feature of flying buttresses to hide the rear roof line and window features. Separate lighting was wired up to the car and by cleverly painting the cars in dull finish to match the rubberised 'hoods', most of the detail features of the car were hidden from prying eyes.

During 1984, testing continued with more cars made available, but even so, the proposed launch date of 1985 was to be put back again, now to the autumn of 1986. Jaguar had so much going for it at this time and, in 1983, had successfully launched the new AJ6 3.6-litre engine in the XJ-S, introduced the Cabriolet version of the same car, in 1984 Tom Walkinshaw had finally won the European Touring Car Championship for Jaguar in the XJ-S, Jaguar was also launching the new, highly specified XJ Series 3 Sovereign models and, not least, the company was successfully privatised to become Jaguar Cars Limited once more.

Jaguar had enough good publicity and reputation to hold off the XJ40 launch a little longer. The testing programme continued into 1985 and at this time the final launch specifications for the models were signed off. Jaguar was on the home run.

It was a most significant year for Jaguar in 1986. After the continued success of the Series 3 XJs and the revitalised fortunes of the XJ-S, it was still important that the XJ40 was not delayed further. As if to compliment this momentous year for a new-model Jaguar, John Egan was knighted by the Queen for his work in the motor industry, a fitting gesture for the man who had saved Jaguar from extinction.

During that spring and summer, final arrangements were being made for the UK launch at the Earls Court Motor Show in London. During the factory summer shutdown, one assembly track was converted to produce the new model and in August, the first full month of use, 327 cars came off the line in readiness for the launch.

Numbers were built up to have cars available at the dealerships for the launch, details of which will be found in a later chapter. Interestingly the 'old' XJ6 Series 3 saloon soldiered on in production until April 1987 as demand was still strong.

Concept ideas of how the XJ40 might have looked throughout various stages of development, the bottom right image being the final outcome.

The birth of an entirely new car **19**

Chapter **Two**

Technology to the fore

The amount of development work that took place behind the XJ40 project, and the car's subsequent importance to the company cannot be over-stated. Therefore, in this chapter we concern ourselves with the detailed technical aspects of the model by the time of launch in 1986.

Seven years of intensive development work, £200 million-worth of investment (more than ever put into any previous model) and the most tried and tested model ever produced by the company up to that time, all contributed to create what Jaguar called 'a world class car'. Part of the anticipated success of the XJ40 model was due to improved research and development, the application of advanced technology in manufacture and assembly, improved productivity, and not least, significantly enhanced quality.

Financial investment in the XJ40 project

XJ40 Research & Development of model	– £50 million
Tooling at Austin-Rover in Swindon and other component suppliers	– £70 million
Building work and new transfer line for the AJ6 engine at Radford	– £35 million
Building work for the manufacture of axles, etc. at Radford	– £10 million
New body-in-white facilities at Castle Bromwich	– £10 million
Clear over-base paint plant at Castle Bromwich	– £15 million
Pilot assembly plant at Browns Lane to trial build the new model	– £10 million

A trial build facility for the XJ40 was a significant move forward for Jaguar. As Derek Waeland (project director) put it in his own words: 'We have been able not only to try out the new assembly system extensively and iron out any problems in their infancy, but we have been able to check the build of the car itself. In addition, we have had a comprehensive training programme for the assembly workers. A further benefit is that, if necessary, this pilot line can build up to 20 per cent of our present production requirements.'

Once production of the XJ40 was fully underway, this trial assembly area was diverted to build the remaining V12 Series 3 models. The ultimate goal of the new model, as defined by Jim Randle at the time was:

1. To reduce manufacturing complexity and improve productivity and quality.
2. Improve standards and procedures to enhance quality.
3. Improve economy through lower weight, improved aerodynamics and engine management.
4. To at least equal the previous model in style and refinement with better performance.

Body assembly and design

Although initially there were plans for the XJ40 to be entirely new in *all* respects, including body styling, it soon became clear that the new car had to deploy certain characteristics of previous Jaguars, many of which would ultimately differentiate the car from the competition. From this the following prime objectives came to bear on the engineers and stylists:

1. To maintain Jaguar's graceful styling heritage whilst being aerodynamically efficient and stable.
2. To stay within broadly similar exterior dimensions to the Series 3, but more spacious inside.
3. To maintain and improve Jaguar's international reputation for refinement and silence.
4. For the body to be better protected against corrosion.
5. The paint quality to be outstanding.

The inevitable conflict between body styling and aerodynamics was addressed quite successfully. As mentioned in the previous chapter, the removal of the eyebrows over the headlights, reduction of the forward lean of the radiator grille and adding curvature to the top and bottom of the foremost edges of the front wings helped enormously. Other actions included the use of a near flush-bonded windscreen, rounded A post pillars and a new design of door mirror mounted on what Jaguar called a 'chester panel'.

Greater attention to door, bonnet and boot gaps also reduced drag and the retention of the inward sloping rear wings mated to the lip on the boot lid all improved aerodynamics. A specially designed front air dam improved high speed stability, and again, as with all other areas of the design, were compared to the old Series 3. A slightly larger frontal area compared with the previous model also did its bit in improving high speed stability. The fitment of a single, centrally mounted windscreen wiper, an idea taken from contemporary Mercedes models, also reduced drag as well as helping to stop the wiper lifting at high speed. All this contributed to the lowest Cd factor available on a comparable saloon at that time.

Drag factor comparison
XJ40	0.762
Series 3	0.849

Aerodynamics and body style progressed side by side, always remembering that the latter had to reflect previous Jaguar points of reference, yet be modern and meet all the other requirements of the new car. Hence the final outcome achieved a style that merely moved the traditional Jaguar look forward.

Once the body design had been finalised the entire clay structure surface was gauged and recorded digitally on a central computer database. This was to be the single source of engineering dimensions for the final skin as well as for the presses and other tools needed to make the car. By this time Jaguar were able to use of the latest CAD technology to provide different perspective views of any aspect of the design including cross sections.

One of the biggest concerns was to reduce the time and cost of producing and assembling the bodyshell, which resulted in the need to reduce the number of panels to build it. The Series 3 XJ bodyshell was particularly labour intensive, it being derived from a design at the turn of the Sixties, and the number of

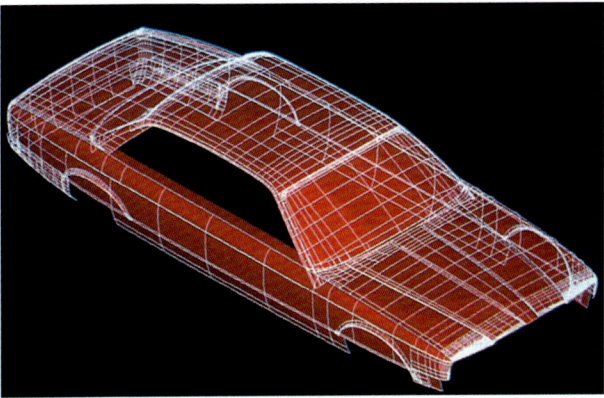

This was the first time Jaguar had used digital encoding for the design structure.

panels involved also led to inconsistent build standards. Therefore, for the XJ40, ideas that today are commonplace were put into action for the first time.

For example, whereas the Series 3 body side was made up of 20 separate steel panels welded together, the XJ40 would use one major pressing called a 'monoside' which covered the windscreen base to the rear E post. Similarly the inner door panels, three pressings on the Series 3, were reduced to one on the XJ40. In total, Jaguar engineers were able to reduce the number of individual panels by 25 per cent, a massive 136 pressings over the outgoing model.

Another advantage of this method of construction was that fewer joints and seams were called for which not only reduced the amount of hand finishing (lead loading had been a common practice at Jaguar for many years), but in turn meant a stiffer structure. The

One of the most important developments in reducing the number of panels in the bodywork was the one-piece bodyside, shown here in pink, a single pressing from A post to E post.

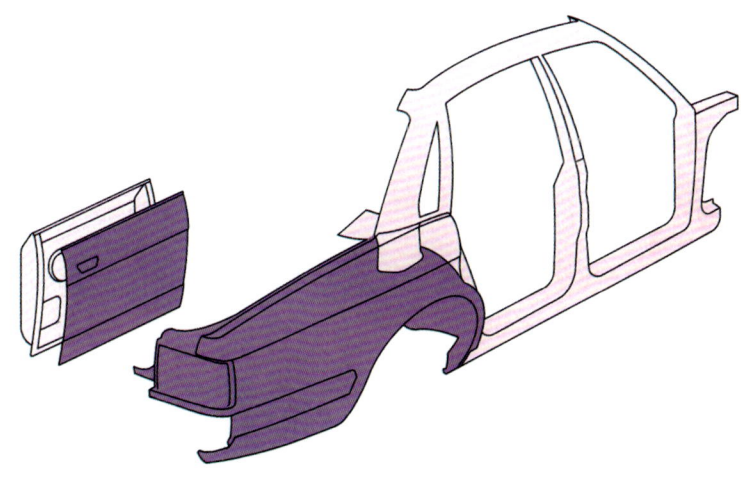

end result was more consistent quality, strength, ease of assembly and, of course, reduced costs.

The rest of the bodyshell followed normal practice for monocoque construction with a strengthened floorpan stiffened by large sill sections that provided torsional strength. The XJ40 floorpan had two crush tubes which ran the length of the engine bay and contained small 'notches' to allow them to crumple in a controlled manner during an impact. This had the effect of dissipating impact energy with the force transmitted from the crash tubes around, instead of into the passenger compartment. For further strength two box sections continued from the sills rearward (also protecting the centrally mounted fuel tank) to protect against impact. The sills themselves were particularly large and stiff and interlocked with the doors to form part of the package. The overall structure became far more rigid than the Series 3.

Corrosion protection was another major area of concern following the experience of previous Jaguar models, and for the XJ40, protection had to be effectively engineered into the new bodyshell. This started with the careful design of panel split lines together with accurate pressing and assembly of the body which eliminated the need for lead filler prior to painting, as described earlier. The bodywork seams in the main shell and doors, bootlid and bonnet were sealed with a smooth robot-supplied compound, to avoid any tendency for corrosion to start in these otherwise vulnerable areas. Owners of the cars today will know that not everything Jaguar did then had a long-term effect, witness the common problems experienced with bonnet and boot areas, but that is another story and we will deal with this later in this book. However, it still has to be considered that the XJ40 structure was a major move forward compared with anything Jaguar had produced before.

Jaguar made extensive use of zinc-coated steels in critical, underbody areas and cavities. Underneath, the bodywork was protected by an overall coat of sealant with an extra coat of anti-chip paint on the door sills. All box sections were wax-injected, using hot wax applied by a spinning lance for maximum penetration.

The majority of panel pressings were done for Jaguar by the Austin-Rover plant in Swindon. Quality control was to the forefront now with Jaguar and when received at Castle Bromwich from Swindon the parts were inspected and if more than 2 per cent of any batch was rejected, then the whole press run was returned to Swindon. Jaguar even had their own quality representative permanently based at Swindon.

Robots replaced many of the normal operations which led to higher efficiency and guarantee of sustained quality. All welding stations during the build process were linked to a Central Control Room where they were monitored to maintain standards.

The use of one-piece monosides made assembly

Structural integrity and safety was built into the XJ40 shell as shown here.

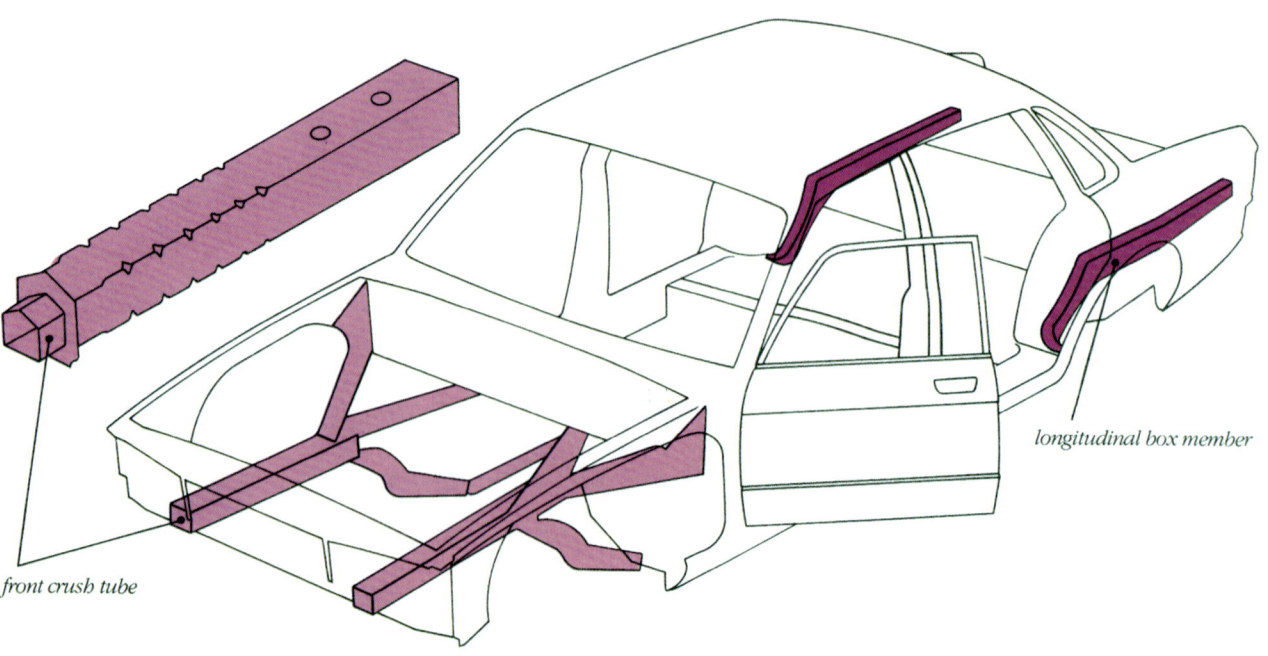

longitudinal box member

front crush tube

much easier and ensured quality control. The whole process was speeded up compared with previous Jaguar bodies. Ancilliary panels like bonnet, boot lid, doors, etc. were all brought to the assembly area by conveyor belts and, after completion, every body underwent intensive inspection under high-powered lighting, much as it is still done today.

Painting the shell

Jaguar had long been known for its poor paint finish and most customer complaints and warranty claims came from this area, so it was something of strategic importance if the XJ40 was not to be 'tarred with the same brush'.

New procedures were set up for the XJ40 starting with the conversion from a anodic electrocoat process to a more effective cathodic process. Primer was applied electrophoretically by totally immersing a negatively charged bodyshell into a tank of positively charged paint which had the effect of attracting the paint particles to the body. This provided for a more even and thorough covering of every part of the body.

Jaguar adopted the use of clear over-base paint technology, the procedure being completed in June 1986, just in time for the XJ40. This meant that the colour coats were applied first and then covered with two coats of lacquer to give a much smoother and durable finish. In the final painting high-speed spinning bells ensured a highly consistent haze of very fine paint particles were attracted evenly over the body. The bodies were extensively washed between paint stages with demineralised water to avoid staining. De-ionised compressed air was blown into the bodies as they passed through the paint booths, removing static electricity and inhibiting the attraction of dust and dirt. Inspection stages were also set up to ensure continued quality of all paintwork.

After painting and before transportation to the assembly plant at Browns Lane in Coventry, all XJ40 bodies were subjected to the injection of hot wax into enclosed box sections and structural areas.

At this stage we need to return to the aspect of corrosion because it was such an important issue, not just for Jaguar's reputation but also to meet ever-more stringent standards expected in the industry. For example, the Canadian anti-corrosion code at the time set the toughest standards in the world. Their test process involved a 12-week cycle simulating six years of the worst possible weather. This meant extensive exposure to sale and mud sprays, periods of storage at

> **DID YOU KNOW?**
>
> **XJ40 claims to fame**
> The longest gestation period of development for any Jaguar model.
> The adoption of new technology in design, production and assembly.
> The most electronically advanced motor car of its time.
> The biggest investment into a new car by Jaguar up to that time.
> The first all-new Jaguar model since 1948.
> The last car to have styling input from Sir William Lyons.

100 per cent humidity, and endurance trials over very poor quality roads. After all this the test cars were cut into pieces for major investigation and inspection of all panels, inside and out.

Reducing weight and noise levels

With the XJ40, Jaguar was able to significantly reduce the body's ability to transmit or amplify noises and vibrations by the use of flexible mountings for the front and rear suspension and the power unit. A greater understanding had been achieved about subtleties of design and the application of dynamic mounting systems.

Internally, the XJ40 was treated to a liberal coating of 12mm thick synthetic rubber foam as a noise barrier, which was not glued in position but was allowed to 'move' to absorb noise. This also contributed to a reduction in weight.

The total weight loss through the above, the use of less panels in the body, and by other methods, was between 150lb and 200lb. The bodyshell accounted for an 18lb saving over the previous model, on top of which were savings in the suspension and axles, and not least in the engine and gearbox.

Interior accommodation

Although there had been many attempts at 'improving' the interior of the car by moving away from traditional Jaguar features like wood veneer and leather, in the end, sense had prevailed and one of the company's strongest characteristics won through.

By the time of the last Series 3 interior changes, only eight separate pieces of wood veneer were being applied. For the XJ40, in Sovereign form, ten were used, some of a far more substantial nature to the former, and later this actually increased again. Walnut was used throughout.

A quarter of a million pounds was invested in this vibration rig to simulate the stresses of hard road use.

The issue of new technology and the need for weight saving was successfully addressed whilst maintaining that special Jaguar ambience. Allied to this, driver ergonomics had been considered, probably for the first time in a Jaguar saloon!

Initial thoughts of very high-tech multi-digital readouts for instruments had been abandoned in favour of a mix of analogue and digital presentation. A conventional electrically driven speedometer and rev counter were accommodated in a cowled binnacle in front of the driver, flanked on the left by vacuum fluorescent bar graph displays for the usual readouts of battery voltage, oil pressure, coolant temperature and fuel level. The logic behind these was to provide more accurate and stable readings and incorporate warning signals in the gauges should any reading fall below or go above the normal levels. To the right of the speedo/tachometer there was a VCM (vehicle condition monitor), in its day the ultimate in new technology for a car.

The VCM took the form of a microprocessor-driven unit capable of presenting a multitude of functional diagnoses and warnings to the driver. These were extensive, amounting to:

Brake failure (low pressure boost)
Coolant level
Seat belts unfastened
Doors/boot/open
Brake fluid level
Brake pad wear
Handbrake on
Bulb failure
Low washer fluid
Anti-lock braking malfunction
Fuelling failure (3.6-litre models only)

Plus audible warnings for:

Direction indicators
Hazard flashers
Drivers seat belt not fastened when ignition on
Gear selector not in 'Park' with ignition off (automatic transmissions only)

The system could determine problems with the car from minor issues like a blown bulb to major hazards

24 Jaguar XJ40

such as ABS failure – a total of 34 functions. All these messages were alerted to the driver through a 32 x 32 dot matrix screen and a further, smaller dot matrix display for messages, underneath which also doubled as a display for the on-board computer read-outs. Dependent on the importance of the message to be transmitted the colour of the display would change from amber to red.

The on-board computer was a major sophisticated advance over the previous system used on the Series 3 models. Functions were selected from a key pad on the instrument binnacle neatly placed and angled to the side of the steering column. The options included speed readings, fuel economies and distances covered with overall figures, averages and instant recordings, all of which could be converted from mph to kph, and litres to gallons.

Other readouts on the instrument pack included legends for the gear in use (automatics), direction indicators, headlamp main beam, use of trailer/caravan, etc. There was also a fluorescent digital display for the mileometer, which was supposedly tamper proof and had a preserved memory of two years in the event of the battery being disconnected.

The column stalks for indicators, wipers and allied uses were conventional although in the case of the former, electronics took over somewhat in that operation of the switch immediately pushed it back to the central position. A microprocessor identified when the steering wheel was returning to the straight position which would activate the cancel facility. To manually override the system the driver had to either hold the indicator stalk in position at which time it was released it would cancel or push it to the opposing position to cancel it on automatic – a nice idea in theory, but in practice one that was eventually to be replaced because of driver confusion!

Most of the switchgear was of an entirely new type, with positive action and less physical movement required. Design and position were adjusted according to the clinic assessments of the car and customer comments on other models. For instance, the electric window controls were moved from the usual Jaguar position on the centre console to the doors, following most other manufacturers at this time.

Equipment levels generally were much improved and the XJ40 took advantage of the latest offerings such as heated windscreen washer nozzles, heated door mirrors, the option of heated door locks and of course air conditioning. There were also novel functions like a 'panic' button on the dashboard allowing occupants to automatically lock all doors and, if necessary by keeping the button pressed, to automatically close all window and sun roof.

For standard models not equipped with air conditioning a microprocessor-controlled heater added sophistication to what was normally a very basic system of air blending with the elimination of mechanical control linkages and flap valves. Rotary

The compromise between the ultimate in high tech and the need for a sombre approach led to this instrument layout on the early XJ40s which incorporated the vehicle condition monitor on the right and graphic bar gauges on the left.

barrel valves operated by DC motors were controlled by feedback from potentiometers for quick operation. Temperature control was automatic, governed by temperature sensors inside and outside the cockpit which could be overridden for manual control if needed. Fan speeds were automatically variable to provide flexible response.

All the driver had to do was to set the mode to auto, select the temperature on the scaled rotary control to what he wanted the car to maintain, set the other rotary control to 'normal' and leave the system to run itself automatically, but there was full manual override if required. Face-level vents were also fully adjustable for volume and direction and a separate slider control allowed the driver to stratify control of the interior temperature allowing cooler air to face level and warmer to the feet. Side window demisting was also possible through ducts in the doors.

The new and sophisticated air-conditioning system, when fitted, not only offered more precise control over temperature and air flow, but also controlled humidity. Conventional systems at that time incorporated an evaporator which meant that the cooler the air, the drier it became. 'Teardrop' controls on the XJ40 system provided for humidity variations, as well as an 'economy' switch which turned off the compressor so that no dehumidifying occurred.

The new XJ40 system also incorporated solar heat compensation with temperature settings needing to change according to external weather conditions, bright sun, cloudy periods, etc. A sensor on the top of the dashboard allowed the system to react by directing the air-conditioning microprocessor accordingly.

This great attention to detail in the heating system also continued to the air-conditioning system with variable speed fans which were far more efficient and less noisy than on earlier models.

The audio systems fitted to the XJ40 models were built into the centre console area and all were push-button-operated and the aerial on the rear offside wing was controlled electrically.

With help from Loughborough University, Jaguar engineers perfected the seat design of the new car to provide for maximum comfort and driver/passenger location. Cold-cure polyurethane foam was used for the seat cushions and squabs. This provided consistent hardness and optimum support and was suspended from the metal seat frames by means of a rubber diaphragm. There were many other moves forward in technology and steps taken to reduce the weight of the XJ40's interior, as described in the next chapter.

Engine

The XJ40 was the first Jaguar saloon since the immediate post-war years not to be fitted with the famous XK straight-six twin-cam engine, an engine that had sustained the company for so many years. Just as Jaguar needed an entirely new technologically advanced car to replace the Series 3 XJ, so it also required a new, efficient power unit to accompany it. A sum of £5 million was invested in the former Daimler bus assembly shop at Radford. Automated processes improved productivity and considerable investment was made in the accuracy of the balancing stage for items like crankshafts.

The end result of several years of development was the AJ6 power unit (Advanced Jaguar 6-cylinder). Utilising aluminium alloy for the cylinder block and head castings, Jaguar proudly pronounced their new engines as the only all-alloy six-cylinder engines in volume production around the world. An investment of £5 million had been made in development initially resulting in a 3.6-litre straight-six engine which was launched in 1983, for the XJ-S sports coupé and new cabriolet models.

The 3.6-litre was a virtually 'square' engine with bore and stroke of 91mm x 92mm, a 9.6:1 compression ratio, twin-overhead camshafts, each with seven bearings, operated the valves via inverted bucket tappets housing the valve springs. Valves were inclined at 46.5° with inlets slightly larger than exhausts and a centrally positioned sparking plug in a pentroof combustion chamber.

The pentroof design was claimed by Jaguar to be very efficient and practical. The crossflow design allowed for a larger valve opening area and free flowing inlet tracts which assisted the flow of gases and provided for good engine breathing, with a larger volume of gas being drawn into the combustion chamber. The central position of the spark plug gave a short flame travel to the piston head for good burning. All this provided for a good power output with excellent performance.

The inclined valves in the head combined with a domed piston area achieved a compression ratio of 9.6:1, while a nitriding treatment given to the exhaust valves provided a high degree of resistance against corrosion and wear, not only necessary then for a high performance engine but also important later with the advent of unleaded fuel. Two-stage duplex chains provided the timing drive for the camshafts, hydraulic pump and other engine-driven ancillaries including the water pump, alternator and air-conditioning compressor belt which was driven in the normal way.

The heat-treated cylinder block was of a deep-skirted design for maximum strength, extending well below the crankshaft centre line before joining the sump. The cast-iron crankshaft (of slightly different design in both engines) ran in seven main bearings and was treated with a special hardening process, a two-hour bath in a hot mineral solution laying nitrogen and carbon on to the surface to optimise wear characteristics.

When announced in the XJ-S, the 3.6-litre engine was considered a little fussy and unrefined compared with other Jaguar engines. For the XJ40, installation improvements were made, for example to quieten the valve drive, cam profiles were modified, reducing the valve lift by 4 per cent, lighter bucket tappets were used, timing chain tensioners were changed, and by tightening balancing tolerances, improved engine balance had been achieved.

Alongside the 3.6-litre engine, although not launched until the XJ40, Jaguar had developed a smaller, 2.9-litre version specifically for the saloon. This was an engine that would never be used in any other application and only remained in production until 1991.

Although using the same cylinder block as the 3.6-litre engine (and the same bore), it was originally conceived that this smaller engine would be based around half of the 5.3-litre V12 engine block, in effect using the well-known May cylinder head and, of course, much of the same machining at the factory. Changes, however, had to be made to achieve the characteristics required for the new engine, but in the end this engine retained much of the V12 design.

The strategy behind the 2.9-litre engine was to enable Jaguar to market a cheaper alternative to the 3.6-litre-engined XJ40 and, at the same time, cater for the needs of some countries where vehicle taxation was based on engine size and performance.

The shorter stroke of 74.8mm achieved a displacement of 2,919cc and the single-overhead camshaft cylinder head featured high efficiency combustion chambers with a much higher compression ratio of 12.5:1, and modified inlet and exhaust systems. It is also worth noting that although smaller and perhaps less refined, the 2.9-litre engine developed 4bhp more than the equivalent XK engine.

The extensive use of aluminium in both engines resulted in a tremendous weight saving over the old XK

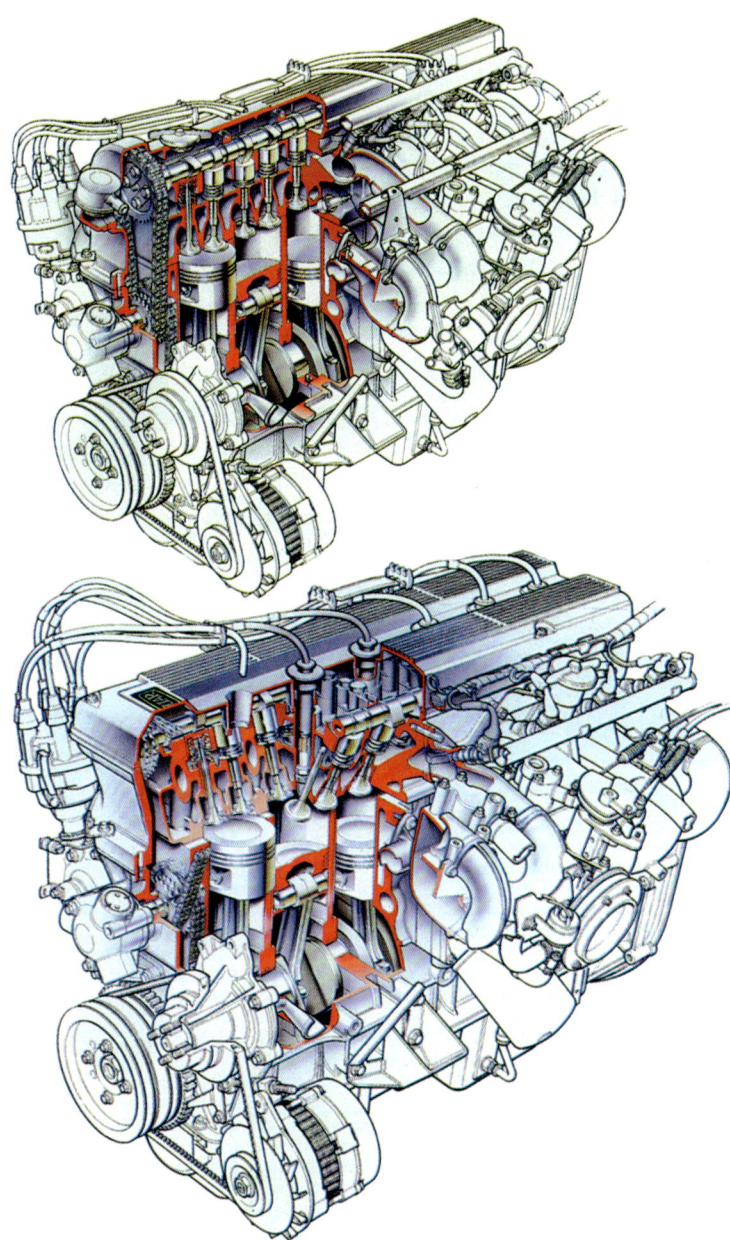

The two six-cylinder engines available for the XJ40. Top is the 2.9-litre unit and below, the 3.6-litre that had been in production since 1983 and installed in some versions of the XJ-S.

units. For example, the 2.9-litre unit was 25 per cent lighter than the old 3.4-litre engine and the 3.6-litre was more than 30 per cent lighter than the outgoing 4.2-litre model.

Engine management

A brand-new electronic ignition and fuel injection system, developed by Lucas for Jaguar, was employed on the new engines. Combined into a common digital engine management system and integrated with Lucas control units, this was highly sophisticated with a memory of four kilobytes.

The control of fuel injection was centred around a bypass hot-wire air flow meter which automatically took account of effects in the change of barometric pressure, such as when driving in mountainous regions. This was to prove far more efficient and controllable than the mechanical flap-controlled system used on the Series 3 XJ6 for example. Not only was it capable of injecting the exact amount of fuel into the system, but had other benefits including cutting off the fuel supply on the over-run, therefore saving fuel. The fuel supply, which only cut off when the engine was warm, reconnected when revs dropped to 900rpm, or when the throttle was opened again.

Idle speed control was maintained automaticaly compensating for any changes in load brought about by items such as the air conditioning or lights being turned on. Tickover therefore was controlled to a low, 650rpm. Due to the close monitoring of all engine operating conditions, a far more precise control over the fuel-air mixture was possible, particularly when the engine was warming up.

The Lucas electronic engine management system also incorporated a 'limp home' provision. This could detect up to eight different types of failure at which time the vehicle condition monitor alerted the driver by displaying the words 'Fuelling failure' followed by a number displayed, telling the service engineer later of the type of failure noted. This system allowed the driver to continue his journey to the nearest garage for repair.

For the smaller engine, Jaguar utilised the Bosch EZ-F electronic ignition system with a separate Bosch LH Jetronic fuel injection system. A less sophisticated limp home system was also employed.

Transmissions

Jaguar's image had changed over the years and for some time it had been considered unnecessary to offer a manual gearbox alternative in the big saloons. The refinement of automatic transmissions had improved to the point that the previous XJ Series saloons were only

Missed by some more sporty drivers Jaguar reintroduced a manual transmission option for their saloon car range. The Getrag five-speed box used a handy leather-covered gearstick like this.

An innovation from Jaguar was the J-gate transmission quadrant on automatic gearbox models which allowed the driver a method of control over intermediate gears.

available with either a Borg Warner or General Motors 'slush box'.

When the AJ6 engine was announced in 1983 however, Jaguar had equipped the engine with a five-speed Getrag manual transmission as an alternative in the XJ-S. The Getrag 265 unit had been well proven in the XJ-S and so it was continued for the XJ40 saloons, all models being dependent on customer order requirement. The prime difference between the installation in the XJ-S and the XJ40 was the use of a larger master cylinder to provide more disengagement travel.

For cars equipped with automatic transmission, Jaguar retained the ZF product, first seen in the XJ-S. In this case it was the 4HP 22 unit, a three-speed epicyclic gearbox, but with an extra fourth gear providing long-legged cruising ability at low revs. The box incorporated a lock-up clutch within the torque converter as an economy aid and the transmission had its own oil cooler integral with the radiator.

A brand-new and unique feature was the method of gear selection. Specifically designed by Jaguar it become known as the J-gate. Simplistic in design, the principle was to provide the ability to easily select intermediary gears manually when required.

With the conventional quadrant type of selector, it was possible to select the wrong gear inadvertently or at worst, move the selector into neutral, reverse or even park positions. With the Jaguar J-gate, normal automatic selection of P, N, R and D was applied via the right-hand side of the gate, but once in D, by moving the selector over to the left, a further gate enabled the driver to move between forward gears very easily. This feature has remained an aspect of all Jaguar automatic transmission-equipped models since.

Suspension and axles

Jaguar had established themselves at the forefront of ride and handling with the XJ Series saloons and to build on that success was a difficult task for the company with the XJ40.

All axle units, suspension, brake assemblies, etc. were produced at the former Daimler factory at Radford and again, the £10 million investment included computer-aided systems and other new technology to improve quality and efficiency for the new model.

Although nothing on the front suspension was carried over from the Series 3 model, the general principles remained unchanged. Double wishbones of unequal length and uprights in forged steel with pivoted angles to provide anti-dive characteristics, first seen on the Series 1 back in 1968, were still employed. The most significant difference to the old Jaguar design was that the pitch control arms now faced rearwards instead of forwards, anchoring into a stiffer part of the body structure. This gave better steer control of the subframe.

The all-new front subframe was fabricated from upper and lower pressings formed into a beam more simply constructed than the previous models to carry the two front engine mounts. The subframe was filled with foam to stop the transmission of noise, a good idea that would ultimately lead to problems with corrosion eventually, of which there is more in a later chapter.

The fulcrums and mounting points of the front suspension were machined after assembly, ensuring greater accuracy and eliminating the need for adjustment of camber or steering rack height.

The engine was slanted over 15° from the vertical to reduce engine bay height and the engine mounts were placed so that the line between them passed through the minimum inertia axis of the engine, thus minimising the movement of the engine. A third engine mount fitted directly to the body, this being of the spring mass type, incorporating coil springs.

For the rear suspension Jaguar moved away completely from the principles of the original independent rear suspension system as used by the company on models from 1961 and which had served them so well. Perhaps the major criticism with the previous system was the adoption of inboard-mounted disc brakes which were difficult to maintain and likely to collect heat and oil, and although finally this last matter was addressed from 1993 with the XJS, it was felt that a further updating of the entire rear system would be advantageous for the XJ40.

The new, patented suspension incorporated a unique pendulum arrangement which allowed fore and aft movement of the lower wishbone inner fulcrum, but this maintained a very high degree of lateral stiffness. The aim was to eliminate as much road noise as possible whilst maintaining accurate geometry control for the best handling characteristics.

A fixed-depth tubular drive shaft and hook joints were used as the top link of each suspension and the lower wishbone was fabricated from two pressings. Brake discs were now carried outboard and because of this, each wishbone would take brake torque as well as power and cornering reaction forces.

The complete drive-train layout of the XJ40 showing a 3.6-litre engine with automatic transmission, and the unique independent rear suspension layout.

Another new approach from the old indpendent rear suspension was the use of only one coil spring and damper per side with the damper containing the bump and rebound stops. The inner fulcrum of the lower wishbone was angled to give both anti-brake-dive and anti-acceleration squat characteristics.

The subframe itself was mounted on two rubber bushes at the front and a pair of angled links at the rear. The position of the spring damper meant the rear and static load was carried entirely by the front mountings while the rear links provided additional control for wind up under acceleration or braking.

A first for Jaguar was the adoption of a self-levelling device for the rear suspension. Standard on some models, but an extra cost option on others, an engine-driven pump shared the source of hydraulic power for the braking system and the self levelling. The system used struts instead of conventional dampers to provide the actual height correction. Each rear strut contained a gas accumulator which was pressurised hydraulically. Suspension height changes were gauged by an electro-mechanical sensor connected to the right-hand rear wishbone.

Thirty seconds after a load change the system's electronic control unit recognised that the alteration in height was long term and so allowed pressure to be fed to the strut to correct its setting. The system was never considered a major success and was later discontinued

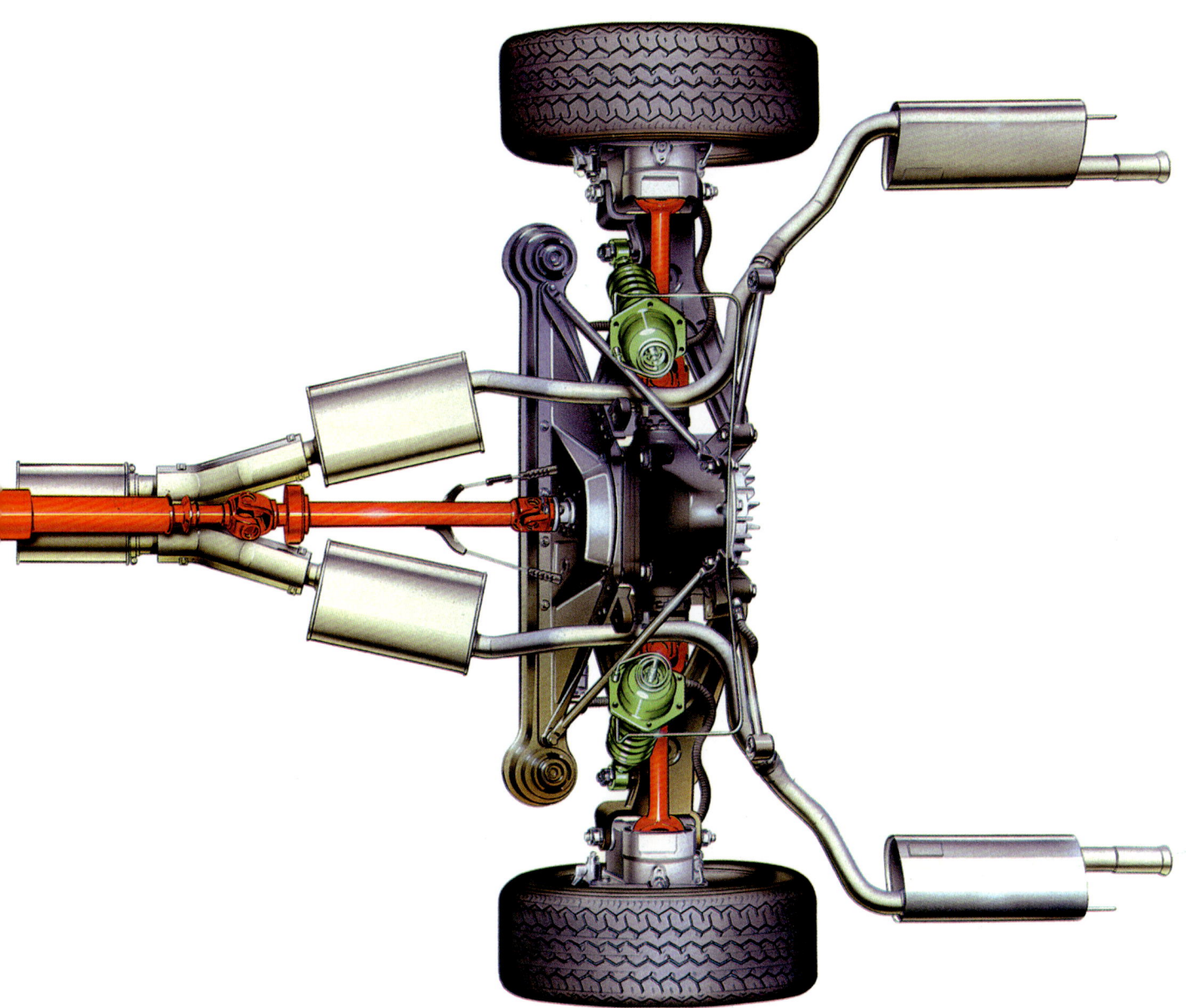

with many earlier cars later having the system decommissioned.

In line with Jaguar's intention to reduce servicing intervals and the cost of the new car, the front and rear suspensions were completely maintenance free on the XJ40 save for the need to grease the rear drive shaft joints at service times.

Steering and brakes

The steering followed conventional Jaguar practice with a hydraulically power-assisted rack and pinion. This was mounted on the front subframe with axial bushes pressed on to the outside of the rack tube. Precise steering response was achieved by gearing the steering to give 2.8 turns lock-to-lock which provided for a turning circle of just over 39ft. The power steering pump was driven directly via chain and skew gear off the timing chain.

Two major principles were changed with the braking system adopted for the XJ40. First, was the use of a brake power boost system instead of a conventional vacuum servo, and secondly, the fitment of a technically advanced anti-lock braking system (ABS).

The power boost hydraulic system took its power from the same engine-driven pump serving the self-levelling rear suspension (when fitted) although the former took priority. A pressure accumulator ensured that if the engine should stop, then sufficient pressure would be stored to provide between eight and 20 stops, significantly more than with a conventional vacuum servo system. The system worked when the brake pedal

New wheel and tyre technology from Dunlop, working with Jaguar, prompted a special brochure on the subject when the XJ40 was new.

was depressed at which time it boosted the driver's effort immediately, applying hydraulic pressure at up to 1,600psi.

The reason behind the use of this type of system lay not only in improved performance but also in the use of smaller under-bonnet components which took up less space, although later the system would be abandoned in favour of conventional servos.

Ventilated discs of 11.6in diameter were fitted at the front with 10.9in solid discs at the rear, each with an integral handbrake drum. Calipers were of the fist-type with the circuits split front/rear. The XJ40 was also equipped with a five-way brake malfunction warning system.

ABS was standard equipment on some models, using a special system developed for Jaguar by Bosch. It incorporated a sensor on each wheel to feed information back to an anti-lock processor. This processor controlled the braking system via three channels, one for each front wheel and one for the rear brakes, according to which wheel was most likely to lock.

The speed sensor was in the form of a magnetic probe positioned at a set distance from a 48-tooth rotor on each road wheel. As the toothed rotor turned it produced a pulsing of electromagnetic signals which gave the information on the rate of change in acceleration or deceleration. The processor then compared the rate of change with other wheels and so detected if a wheel was about to lock.

If an imminent lock was detected the processor first stopped any more brake pressure going to that wheel. With the desired effect of causing the wheel to accelerate and thus not lock, the processes then operated an electric motor pumping brake fluid back to the brake. This formed an on cycle which could occur up to eight times a second, depending on the state of the road surface.

Perhaps the biggest breakthrough for the Jaguar/Bosch system was that it incorporated a yaw control which allowed it to compensate for widely differing side-to-side braking requirements. The control unit also incorporated self-checking features with warnings to the driver via the vehicle condition monitor.

The ABS control unit had a self-checking feature which detected if the system was not working properly. This was wired up to the vehicle condition monitor to alert the driver – more on this in the maintenance chapter later.

Wheels and tyres

Another joint development project which, at the time, was unique to the XJ40, involved the tyres. Working with Dunlop and Michelin the TD tyre and matching wheel was conceived with a wheel rim design which reduced the likelihood of a punctured tyre coming off the wheel.

The metric-sized TD rims for the XJ40 had a special groove in which the TD tyre bead located. If a tyre went flat when running, its beads were restricted from escaping into the wheel well and exposing the flange. This also allowed the driver to drive carefully at slow speeds for a limited distance to safety. Inside the tyre a sealant gel was used which was capable of sealing small punctures, or at least, reducing the rate of lost air.

The new tyres were wider and squatter than used on the Series 3 models and the TD tyre size was unusual at

220/65 VR 390, and was specially developed for the Jaguar. The dimensions were apparently arrived at to provide a trapezoidal profile. This gave low vertical stiffness for optimum ride comfort but holding the tread area flat during cornering.

The principle concept was not only to allow better steering control in a blow-out and convenience, but also to lower running costs. As time went on, however, the use of metric-sized tyres was very limited and therefore they became expensive, so Jaguar eventually abandoned the project and returned to normal tyres and rims on XJ40s.

Advanced electronics

This aspect of the XJ40 model has been placed near the end of the chapter so as to give it greater emphasis, separate from other aspects of the new car. The XJ40 was heralded as a major advance in electronics when launched in 1986 and so it is fitting to devote space to identify the system's operation in some detail.

The major features of the car's electronics included a new type of wiring system, high reliability family of wiring connectors, a significant increase in the amount of on-board electronic microprocessor controls, and to support all this, a highly advanced diagnostic system.

On today's cars we take for granted the number of microprocessors and sophisticated systems they employ, but when the XJ40 was announced, it was far in advance of other cars in production. Apart from the

No less than seven microprocessors controlled the XJ40 which made it one of the most electrically advanced cars in its day.

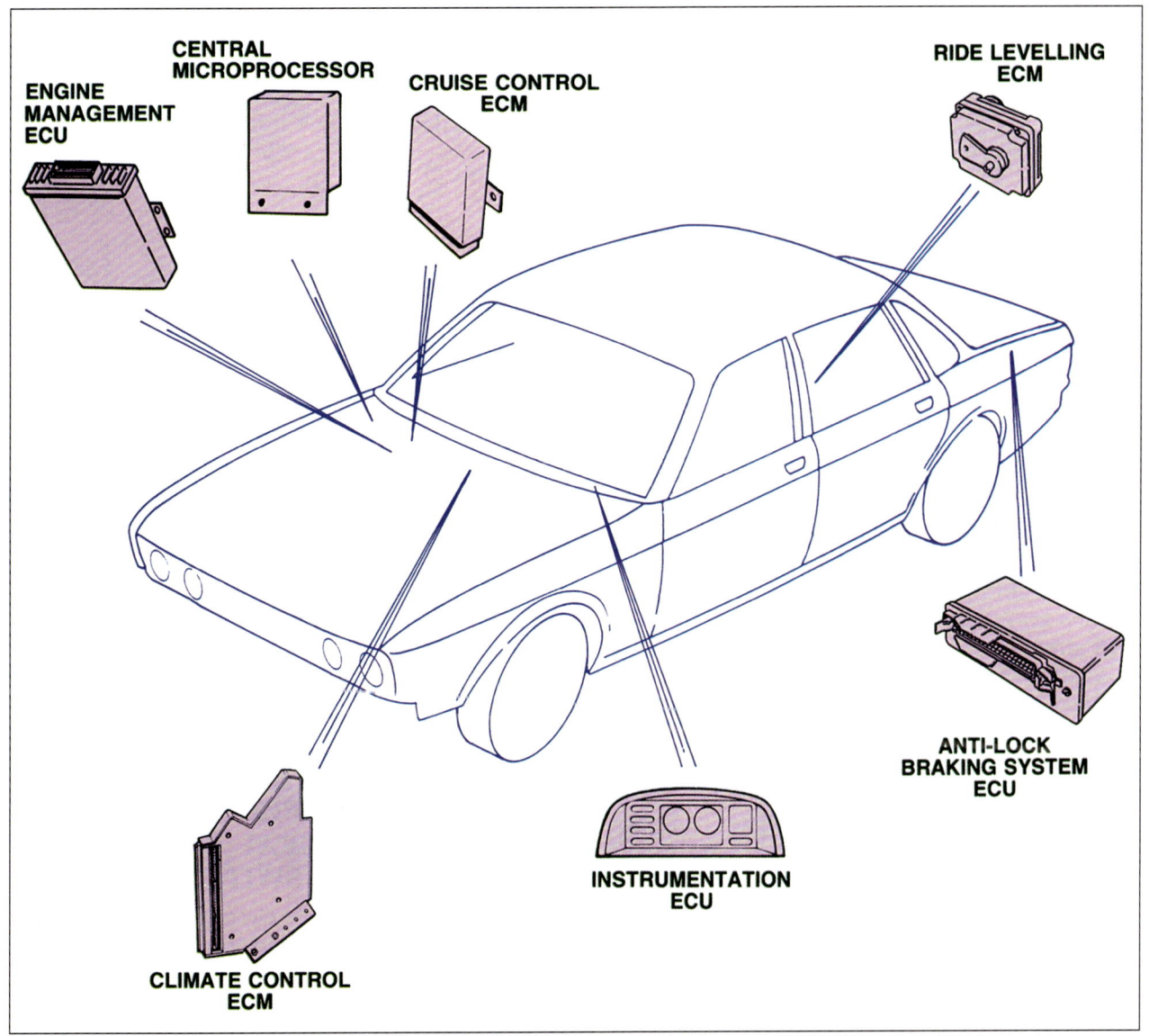

Technology to the fore 33

microprocessors controlling engine management systems (mentioned earlier) the XJ40 had no less than five other units looking after the instrument panel, air conditioning, anti-lock braking, cruise control (where fitted) and a central processor.

Jaguar adopted a low-current high-duty earth line switching system carrying a mere five volts, instead of the usual 12V. This not only saved weight throughout the electrical system of the car but also reduced electro-magnetic interference. It also made it possible to return all external earth connections to the ECUs to one cable in the harness anchored to a major earth point on the bulkhead, only 9in from the battery earth strap anchorage.

Ninety electronic relays were fitted to the XJ40 and switch-gear worked with the low power ECUs were of significantly better quality than before. The switches used noble metal 'clicker plates' with low working loads and bounce-free contacts. They were hermetically sealed, protecting them from condensation.

With over 1,700 pieces of electrical wire in an XJ40, Jaguar needed higher quality cabling to withstand all temperature changes around the world. To accompany this, new switch connections were required. Aircraft standard multi-pin connectors were therefore used so that it was virtually impossible to make a non-positive connection. Different grades, sizes and types of connector were used throughout the car, all colour-coded for ease of reference.

Of the different types of connector used, the ones to the exterior of the car were the most rugged. They were of the anti-backout type so that once connected they were held tightly in position with no allowance for movement. They also had a throw-apart design to ensure accurate assembly. If a connector was not mated positively with another it would literally throw itself apart by spring loading.

Despite the complexity of design access to everything was made as easy as possible. For example, the three fuse boxes in the car were easily accessible, two in the driver and passenger footwells and one in the centre console cubby box.

There was no doubt that electronically the XJ40 was a major leap forward from most other cars that had gone before.

Diagnostics

Many aspects of the diagnostic processes and systems fitted to the XJ40 have been mentioned above. Part of this major move in technology also involved the Jaguar franchised dealerships which also had to be equipped with the new JDS (Jaguar diagnostic system).

At the factory the JDC system allowed operatives to trace any electronic malfunction in the car. Similarly, dealers were equipped with this technology so that they could also trace any diagnostic problem quickly and efficiently, to the same standard as the factory back in Coventry.

A microcomputer and disk drive, it was linked to a visual display, a printer and keyboard. The computer had connection points for the various probes used (mainly current based), and could be connected to different diagnostic 'pods' with special computer programs for fault-finding.

Final assembly

Jaguar had invested significant sums in the improvement of the Browns Lane assembly facility in Coventry and the XJ40 was one of the first cars to take advantage of this. Just one of the changes to previous production methods was the lowering of the bodyshell on to the engine and transmission rather than the other way round. This saved time, was easier, safer and avoided any possible damage. This, along with the ability to use the pilot build facility (mentioned earlier) enabled Jaguar's operatives to gain significant expertise in the assembly of the new car before it was launched. All this led to the first production car rolling off the line in July 1986, on schedule.

XJ40 assembly order (early production)

Painted bodies arrive in Coventry body store from Castle Bromwich.
Completed axles, engines and allied mechanicals arrive from Radford.
Chosen body moves from store to start of assembly lines.
Underbody items are fitted to the body in a static raised position.
Pre-mount conveyor, underbonnet items and internal trim fitted.
Front and rear screens and side quarter windows fitted.
Console fitted, first electrical systems checks carried out.
Mount & Trim Line: body lowered on to power train.
Trim assembly and final fitting.
Major electrical checks (VETS – vehicle electrical testing system).
Air-conditioning gas charged, fluids filled.
Rolling road testing.
Five to eight-mile road test.
Final Line, audio fitment, external finishing trim.
JVS (Jaguar vehicle safety) checks.
Full electrical check with JDS (Jaguar diagnostic system).

Chapter **Three**

The launch of a new car with an old name – XJ6

For the new XJ40 Jaguar anticipated that the Mercedes S Class and the BMW 7 Series were the cars to meet head on. Jaguar still held around 50 per cent of the UK market for this type of prestige saloon, around 5,000 cars a year, but in other countries Jaguar was falling behind the competition and needed the new car to captivate these markets quickly.

Most significant of these export markets was the USA where it was estimated that in the mid-Eighties over 650,000 prestige cars a year were being sold, although much of this was dominated by the home-grown products from Lincoln (Ford) and Cadillac. Jaguar had traditionally sold over 55 per cent of its production to the States and the company estimated that 75 per cent of its potential customers lived there.

Marketing strategy

Jaguar's marketing department estimated that the XJ40 would not only hold on to the existing market share gained by the later Series 3 XJs, but would also encourage more people to trade up from existing US-manufactured large saloons. After all, there was still a significant panache in having a European prestige marque on the drive. They also hoped that the new car could capture sales from its German rivals on the basis of its improved quality, high tech and, not least, the name Jaguar.

Jaguar sales 1985 – pre XJ40
USA   21,843
UK   8,049
Europe   4,838
Rest of world*   3,005
*Dominated by sales into Australia and the Middle East

Looking at the UK market specifically, Jaguar anticipated a new growth area as the base entry level XJ40 might help them in the valued company car 'fleet' market. Although most executive luxury cars like the XJ6, BMW 7 and Mercedes S were owned and run by companies for their top flight executives, there was another even more lucrative market in middle-management and younger executives who might be eager to get their hands on a Jaguar, if the price was right. This then might help Jaguar gain conquest sales

EVOLUTION OF THE SPECIES

from the likes of the big Rovers or even the Ford Granada with other targeted areas being the Saab 9000, Audi 200, Volvo 760, Renault 25, Vauxhall Senator and even lower model Mercedes and BMWs.

Jaguar's logic here was that the 2.9-litre model would appeal to fleet managers because it was British, and backed by an established sales and servicing network, part of which they may already have been using for directors' cars if these were Jaguars. It would then appeal to the end user because of the prestige of driving a Jaguar.

The marketing strategy therefore revolved around the 2.9-litre XJ40 models to capture fleet business, middle and senior managers and those not wanting outright performance, plus sales in strategic markets where the tax system penalised cars with large capacity engines. The 3.6-litre cars, particularly the high-spec Sovereign models would cater for the existing traditional company director level, leaving the Daimler to suit the chief executive, and managing director.

Another ace up Jaguar's sleeve was that they would still have the old Series 3 design in V12 form (Jaguar and Daimler). This provided a fall-back to those elderly senior directors and chairmen who wanted to show their uniqueness in having a more traditional older style car to others in the company ranks.

It is interesting to consider that at this time little consideration was apparently given to the younger buyer, an area that Jaguar were remiss in catering for, and one that they would have to 'attack' later with the XJ40.

The dealer network

Many changes had beset Jaguar's retail dealer network over the years, not least the involvement with British Leyland, with many dealers turning over to multi-franchises handling everything in their showrooms from Austin Minis to Daimler limousines. That was all to change with the advent of XJ40 as the number of dealers would be reduced significantly in the years leading up to the launch.

What's in a name?

Logic should have dictated that the XJ40 was all new and as such was deserved of a brand-new name, but then again, the Series XJs had earned themselves such a good reputation over the years, and with the much improved build quality of the later models and the high demand still achieved for them in the mid-Eighties, it was felt that the new model should carry the same name to show a natural progression. It showed the buying public that a Jaguar was still a Jaguar and that the new model, although a major move forward in many ways, was still to be regarded as the next logical step in the XJ line.

Perhaps ironically, even to this day, the XJ insignia is still used on Jaguar's flagship saloons, only the number has changed to match the number of engine cylinders.

There was to be another name, however, to appear on the XJ40 and that was Vanden Plas. The VDP insiginia had been used by Jaguar since the BL days and the integration into the group of the old Vanden Plas Coachworks in London. The first use came in 1973 with the introduction of the up-market Daimler V12 Series 1 XJ saloon, then called Daimler Double Six Vanden Plas. The use of the name VDP continued through the XJ Series production up to 1982, when Jaguar lost the rights to use the name in the UK.

The name continued to live on in the USA where the top-of-the-range XJ Series model carried it, and that is where the XJ40 comes in. For the US market the basic 2.9 or 3.6-litre XJ6 XJ40 models were not sold, and for the top-of-the-range model, instead of Sovereign came just XJ6, and instead of Daimler, came the Vanden Plas (more on this later).

Model line-up

At the UK launch, the XJ40 model was available in a total range of five models:
Jaguar XJ6 2.9-litre saloon
Jaguar XJ6 3.6-litre saloon
Jaguar Sovereign 2.9-litre saloon
Jaguar Sovereign 3.6-litre saloon
Daimler 3.6-litre saloon

Cost of ownership

Most people knew, even in those days, that it was expensive to run a Jaguar, but from the initial concept the XJ40 had been designed to cut costs to the bare minimum.

For example, servicing intervals had been increased to 7,500 and 15,000 miles, not only longer than the competition, but also better than any previous Jaguar. Jaguar estimated that over 50,000 miles an XJ40 would incur only 13.95 hours of labour changes, given normal servicing involvement of course.

Furthermore all components in the XJ40 had been designed from the outset to be more easily accessed and repairable. For example, they quoted the fuel tank which, on a Series 3 saloon would have taken 3.3 hours to remove, only amounted to 1.8 hours on the XJ40. It was estimated that a Jaguar mechanic would take nine hours to change all four brake discs on the Series 3, reduced to a mere two on the XJ40.

Insurance group ratings were also improved because Jaguar had been working with Thatcham, the insurance industry's motor research centre, to ensure the simplest accident repair techniques in the new model.

The Jaguar diagnostic system also played its part in bringing down the cost of ownership because it would take a shorter period to identify and rectify any electrical faults on the new car.

All the hard work had been done by Jaguar in readiness. It was from then on down to the dealers and marketing, now it was time to announce the new car to the public and let the sales tell their own story.

Announcement by Sir John Egan to dealer staff upon the launch of XJ40

'You are about to be introduced to the most revolutionary car ever to come from the Jaguar stable. A car that outwardly enhances its predecessor's style and grace, disguising the technical revolution hidden beneath its shell. Now you, the Jaguar specialists are faced with a very great challenge and responsibility in getting to grips with the new technology in order that you may maintain the vehicle to your customer satisfaction.

'Many millions of pounds and years of development have gone into producing a car that is second to none, having already completed some 5½ million miles of road tests in climates and conditions as varied as the north of Canada to the deserts of Australia in proving its reliability.

The time has now arrived for you to take on the responsibility for the new XJ6 range, for as far as your customers are concerned the real expert is you and if you are to succeed in this, your product knowledge and after-sales expertise must be the best.'

J-Day – the XJ40 launch

In 1986, the XJ40 (we will continue to use this designation to avoid confusion with earlier and later XJ6s) made its debut, although not at this time to the public.

In March, the UK and overseas Jaguar dealer councils had their chance to see the new model at a special event. This was followed by a special viewing in April for Jaguar employees – a 'thank you' for the hard work and support given to the company over this time. Another show was held in August for the trade union officials, as a 'thank you' to them for their support.

On 28 August, engineering director, Jim Randle, conducted a major engineering presentation on the new car to the Institute of Mechanical Engineers in London. As if part of the initial razzamatazz for the car, an example of the XJ40 had to be specially rigged on a jig to travel sideways through the doorways of the lecture facility to go on display.

Although this was an all-new Jaguar, Jim Randle confirmed the heritage of the car. 'Style and elegance have always been of central importance to our product. The legacy of Sir William Lyons has been a series of beautiful cars whose style has impressed itself on the minds of the motoring public for over two generations.

'A marked change in our design philosophy would

The street motoring magazines were soon to publicise the new Jaguar model as this front cover of British *Motor* magazine showed in February 1985 when they 'caught' the car on test and cleverly worked out the style without the aid, in those days, of computer graphics!

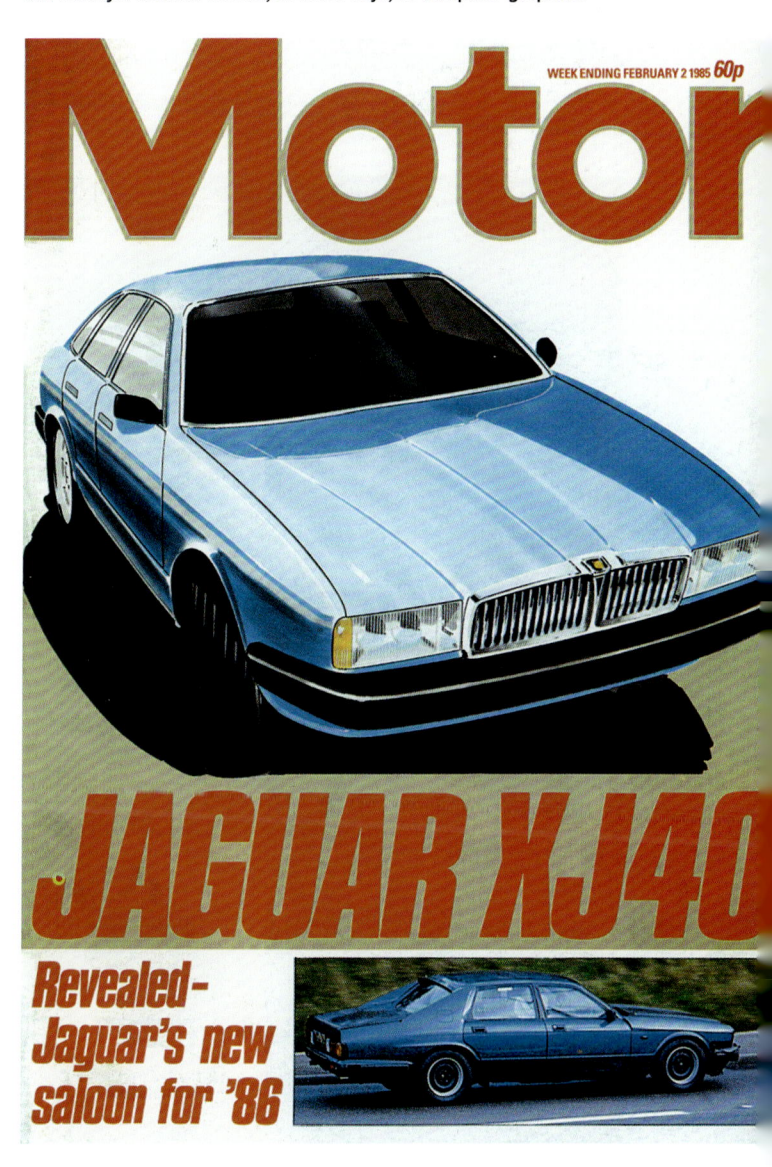

not be welcome by the traditional Jaguar customer and it was therefore decided that the market place demanded a more evolutionary style, the targets being to show a clear evolution of the Series 3 but to have a lower Cd than that car and better Cds than both the Series 3 and its competitors whilst maintaining our traditional stability levels.'

At the end of August and early in September, the trade launches took place at Browns Lane amidst dry ice and spectacle. First came the UK dealers, then the European dealers, then the fleet purchasers and even some Government officials and finally, the overseas dealers, not least the US contingent.

The pre-launch reveals didn't stop there. The show then moved to the National Exhibition Centre in Birmingham where over four days, in what Jaguar called their J-Days, all Jaguar employees, their families and friends plus employees from the dealers (28,000 in total) had the opportunity to view the new cars.

This was followed by the month-long official press launch of the car in the UK at the prestigious Dunkeld Castle in Scotland where Jaguar still wanted to emphasise the natural development and progression of its cars by having several examples of previous models on display, from a 1930's SS to a 420G.

Yet another move was made, this time to London for the 'City financial' launch on 1 October at the Hilton Hotel in Park Lane. On 7 October, by which time, XJ40s had arrived at the UK dealerships, it was their turn and they opened the doors to customers and prospective customers to see the car for the first time at a series of evening events. Some used their own showrooms, others hired special venues, and on average, 150 to 300 people attended each local launch. The announcement of the XJ40 also coincided with the Conservative Party's annual conference and Norman Tebbit MP joined in the celebrations at the local Bournemouth

Amongst the many launch shows that XJ40 was subjected to was this one at the Institute of Mechanical Engineers where, to get the car on display, a special cradle had to be erected to carry the car sideways through the doorways before Jim Randle's lecture and presentation.

One of the later development cars, still camouflaged which soon after the launch, was donated to the Coventry Motor Museum for display.

Jaguar dealer who later also provided courtesy cars for the conference.

Then, finally, the entourage moved back to the National Exhibition Centre in Birmingham for the public launch of the XJ40 in the UK, but something unusual happened just before that. For the first time ever, probably unique to the car industry, let alone Jaguar, the new car was announced to around 30 million people on the evening of 7 October 1986 – via UK television.

An in-depth film had been produced over several years of the XJ40 development with the film company working with Jaguar, covering aspects of development, testing and readiness for the final launch. This had involved camera crews accompanying the cars on testing and, at one stage, the early 'reveal' of the body styling in Canada just for the cameras – an incident which, back in 1983, did not find favour with Jaguar when so much was at stake. The film was called *The Making of the Forty* and was a major ploy to motivate the motoring public and the impetus it created paid off – suddenly the new Jaguar was on the tip of everyone's tongue

The motor show was no anticlimax, however. Although initially, Jaguar was positioned in a side hall with small commercial vehicles, after pressure was exerted, the stand was moved to a more appropriate central position. During the show there were apparently, three times as many firm enquiries about this car, compared with the previous show when the Series 3 was still selling so well.

After the UK launch came the rest of Europe with the German dealers having their parties on 14 November. The car appeared at the Paris Motor Show, then at the French dealers and the first XJ40 on the road in France competed in the Beaujolais Nouveau run that year which was held around the same time.

Launches continued in Holland, Italy, Dubai, then Australia and New Zealand, Japan and ultimately, North America and the rest of the world, all of course to vast acclaim for what some termed as 'Jaguar's best car yet'.

The Forty had arrived.

The launch of a new car with an old name

Chapter **Four**

2.9-litre and 3.6-litre models – 1986 to 1990

Launched in October 1986 the XJ40 was meant to be the all-new replacement for the aged Series 3 XJ6 saloons. The 4.2-litre model of that car continued to be produced and sold until April 1987, although not listed in the catalogue or price list, the very last example going to the Jaguar Daimler Heritage Trust and still owned by them today. Because there was no V12 engined variant of the XJ40 at this time, the Series 3 XJ12 and Daimler Double Six continued in production for a number of years, effectively expanding the model range of the company to three complete ranges: XJ40, XJ-S and Series 3 V12.

The prices and range of the new XJ40 models at launch were:

XJ6 2.9-litre five-speed manual saloon:	£16,495
XJ6 3.6-litre five-speed manual saloon.	£18,495
XJ6 2.9-litre Sovereign manual or auto saloon	£22,995
XJ6 3.6-litre Sovereign manual or auto saloon	£24,995
Daimler 3.6-litre manual or auto saloon	£28,495

(Prices based on UK sterling including car tax and VAT.)

The above is based on the models available in the UK at that time. In certain markets the 2.9-litre-engined cars were not sold and as you will read later, model names and designations were also amended depending on the market.

At the point of launch in the USA (1987), just two XJ40 models were available, the 3.6-litre XJ6 and 3.6-litre Vanden Plas.

The prices of other Jaguar models available at the time were:

XJ6 4.2-litre Series 3 Sovereign auto saloon	£24,000
XJ12 5.3-litre Series 3 Sovereign auto saloon	£25,995
Daimler Double Six auto saloon	£28,995
XJ-S 3.6-litre manual coupé	£20,995
XJ-SC 3.6-litre manual cabriolet	£22,995
XJ-S 5.3-litre auto coupé	£26,300
XJ-SC 5.3-litre auto cabriolet	£28,300

(Prices based on UK sterling including car tax and VAT.)

The five-speed manual gearbox was standard on all XJ40 models and a four-speed automatic transmission was an extra £650. Another significant aspect of the prices came with the entry-level 2.9-litre model, strategically priced at under £16,500, hopefully to hit new buyers and fleet purchasers, and with the smaller engine, was suited to tax-conscious markets.

Model line-up

Jaguar had long established a policy of producing several variants on the same model theme. With the last of the Series 3 XJs, external differences amounted to badging and wheels/tyres, the latter, of course, easily changed by special order.

In the case of the XJ40 Jaguar returned to a policy of differentiating the models by trim style so that it was easier to identify specific models. These changes are detailed below, along with other specification differences.

XJ6 models

You would have to go back to around 1983/4 to find a new Jaguar priced at anything like the figure quoted for the base 2.9-litre XJ40. Then, that would have been a smaller (3.4-litre) XK-engined model without leather upholstery and lacking other creature comforts, and so it was with the entry-level XJ40.

The smaller, 2.9-litre engine was not the greatest of performers, but it was still comparable to some of the detuned XK units, at 165bhp. This in itself brought down the cost of the car. A manual gearbox was standard, and as mentioned, those wanting the benefit of an automatic had to pay extra for the privilege. Anti-lock brakes also came as an extra at this time. You could also buy a 'base' model with the larger, 3.6-litre power unit for some £2,000 extra. Both these models were equipped similarly.

Internally, the XJ6 models featured the same style of

The XJ6, available in the UK with both 2.9-litre and 3.6-litre engines, was identified by its four-headlight treatment and matt black-painted window frames. The plastic rimbellishers to the wheels were originally a standard feature on Sovereign models as well.

In 2.9-litre form the XJ6 was never a very quick car, but equipped with a five-speed manual gearbox would pull well. In the early days, even fog lights were an extra cost option.

2.9-litre and 3.6-litre models – 1986 to 1990

At the rear, the UK XJ6 models featured open script badging with no mention of engine capacity.

This is the 2.9-litre engine installation with its single-overhead camshaft.

seating as other models but were trimmed in herringbone tweed cloth with Ambla for the seat sides and other soft trim areas. Lumbar support and map pockets were standard, but you had to pay extra for air conditioning, electrically operated seats and cruise

A standard XJ6 without leather upholstery is shown with the manual gearbox. Straight-grain woodwork and such luxuries as air conditioning and electric seating adjustment were extra cost options.

control. For most markets the radio/cassette player was the latest Clarion E920 stereo unit with electronic tune, three wave bands, LCD display, noise limiter, volume control and four speakers. There was also a sophisticated heating and ventilation system, on-board computer with the special vehicle condition monitor and, of course, the walnut veneer as expected in a Jaguar.

Externally, these models featured conventional steel wheels (although these were of new metric, TD size and design) with plastic wheel covers. Metallic paint had to be paid for as an extra and the window surrounds were finished in matt black paint, although with chromed gutters, screen surrounds and finisher to the D post (hiding an unsightly weld mark between the roof section and rear wing). A single coachline ran along the swage of the car's side, front to rear.

At the front the car came with four round headlamps with Halogen bulbs and a chromed radiator grille with growler badge atop the centre. Although very different to the old Series 3 style, there was no mistaking this was a Jaguar when one approached you.

The angular treatment at the rear was quite sparse with a simple chromed plinth containing the boot lock, the button to release the lock being placed underneath. The centrally mounted number plate had a chromed surround while the 'Jaguar' and 'XJ6' badges on the boot lid were of the open script type with no mention of the engine size. It is therefore a point of interest, that it was impossible to differentiate a 2.9-litre from a 3.6-litre XJ6 externally. These early models were not sold in the USA as they were considered below the equipment standard level expected in that market.

Sovereign models

The Sovereign name, originally used by the company on Daimler models from 1967 to 1983, had been turned over to identify the top-of-the-range Jaguar variants of the XJ Series saloons. The theme continued with the XJ40 adopting this insignia for most markets, although just as 'XJ6' for the States.

Essentially available at the time with either the 2.9-litre (not USA) or 3.6-litre engines, the Sovereign models were instantly identifiable from the front by the pair of rectangular headlamp units, and from the side by the fully chromed window surrounds. A twin coachline was applied instead of a single on the XJ6. At the rear, the Sovereign badge replaced the simple XJ6 insignia which matched the Jaguar badge on the other side, both being rectangular in brushed alloy-effect plastic and easy to clean. The very early Sovereigns also featured a charcoal-painted rear boot panel which was also used on Daimlers, but this was

In contrast to the XJ6, Sovereign models in the UK featured single, rectangular headlights and chromed window surrounds. The metric alloy wheels were, in the early days, an extra cost option.

Smart satin finished badges adorned the rear of Sovereign models, but again, no reference to engine size.

soon deleted from the Jaguar model.

Interestingly, the 20-spoke alloy wheels specially designed for the XJ40, were never originally a standard fit option on the Sovereign models, although they later become so. Metallic paint was a no-cost option on these cars.

Jaguar Racing F1 Merchandise Range

JEC DIRECT

Jaguar Racing 2002 Team Tee Shirt

£35.00   M/L/XL

Order Code JAG6201

Jaguar Racing 2002 Stripe Tee Shirt

£30.00   M/L/XL

Order Code JAG6202

Jaguar Racing 2002 Tour Tee Shirt

£20.00   M/L/XL

Order Code JAG6204

Jaguar Racing 2002 Helmet Tee Shirt

£20.00   M/L/XL

Order Code JAG6208

Jaguar Racing 2002 Spray Tee Shirt

£20.00   M/L/XL

Order Code JAG6209

Jaguar Racing Suede Peak Cap

£20.00   One size fits all

Order Code JAG5026

Jaguar Racing Team Cap

£18.00   One size fits all

Order Code JAG5667

Eddie Irvine Cap

£15.00   One size fits all

Order Code JAG5677

Pedro De La Rosa Cap

£15.00   One size fits all

Order Code JAG5687

JEC DIRECT   email: jec-direct@lineone.net

Page 2

Jaguar Racing Replica Racesuit Jacket
£270.00   M/L/XL
Order Code JAG3900

Jaguar Racing Cut & Sew Jacket
£135.00   M/L/XL
Order Code JAG3901

Jaguar Racing 2002 Classic Jacket
£100.00   M/L/XL
Order Code JAG3902

Jaguar Racing 2002 Full Zip Fleece
£75.00   M/L/XL
Order Code JAG5001

Jaguar Racing 2002 Hooded Sweat
£50.00   M/L/XL
Order Code JAG5601

Jaguar Racing 2002 Zip Neck Jumper
£65.00   M/L/XL
Order Code JAG7501

Jaguar Racing 2002 Team Pique Polo
£38.00   M/L/XL
Order Code JAG5007

Jaguar Racing 2002 Ladies Polo Shirt
£25.00   S/M/L
Order Code JAG5017

JAG 3900
JAG 3901
JAG 5001
JAG 3902
JAG 5601
JAG 7501
JAG 5007
JAG 5017

Tel: 01302 328336   Fax: 01302 328337

Jaguar Racing 2002 Classic Polo

£40.00   M/L/XL

Order Code JAG5101

Jaguar Racing 2002 Replica Team Shirt

£65.00   M/L/XL

Order Code JAG6101

Jaguar Racing 2002 Ladies Vest

£25.00   S/M/L

Order Code JAG0301

Jaguar Racing Girl V Neck MicroFleece

£30.00   S/M/L

Order Code JAG5018

Jaguar Racing Logo Mousemat

£8.00

Order Code JAG1101

Jaguar Racing Back Pack

£35.00

Order Code JAG3001

Jaguar Racing Drawstring Bag

£25.00

Order Code JAG3002

JEC DIRECT   email: jec-direct@lineone.net

Jaguar Racing Fan Pen
£1.50
Order Code JAG4035

Jaguar Racing Logo Flag
£8.00
Order Code JAG4039

Jaguar Racing Sport Drinking Bottle
£7.00
Order Code JAG4047

Jaguar Racing Woven Loop Keyring
£3.00
Order Code JAG4101

Jaguar Racing Spinner Keyring*
£10.00
Order Code JAG4102

Jaguar Racing Coffee Cup*
£8.00
Order Code JAG4701

Jaguar Racing 2002 Mug
£8.00
Order Code JAG4702

Jaguar Racing Executive Pen
£13.00
Order Code JAG4801

Jaguar Racing Logo Pin Badge
£2.50
Order Code JAG4901

* *Not Illustrated*

Tel: 01302 328336   Fax: 01302 328337

Jaguar Racing Sports Bag

£35.00

Order Code JAG5901

---

*Jaguar Racing Sunglasses**

£40.00

Order Code JAG6701

Jaguar Racing 2002 Golf Umbrella

£30.00

Order Code JAG7001

Jaguar Racing 2002 Compact Brolly

£18.00

Order Code JAG7002

---

*Jaguar Racing Lanyard**

£7.00

Order Code JAG8201

---

* Not Illustrated

JEC DIRECT   email: jec-direct@lineone.net

JEC DIRECT

Unit 1 Churchill Business Park
Churchill Road
DONCASTER
DN1 2TF

Tel: 01302 328336
Fax: 01302 328337
E Mail: jec-direct@lineone.net
Website: www.jec.org.uk

MAIL ORDER FORM

Please complete all boxes marked #

PREFIX: #	FORENAME: #	SURNAME: #	ORDER DATE:	MEMBERSHIP NO: #

ADDRESS: #

POST TOWN: #	POST COUNTY OR COUNTRY: #	POST CODE: #

DAYTIME TEL: #	EVENING TEL:	FAX/EMAIL:

Please allow 23 days for delivery. Payments are not processed until the order is despatched. **Cheques without a card number must clear in our account before goods will be despatched.** We will telephone you if any part of your order is out of stock and offer you the options of suitable alternatives, likely delivery date, deletion of 'out of stock' item(s) from your order or cancellation of your order.

Please keep a copy of this order for future reference. Photocopies are welcome and a new order form will be sent with your order

Page No	Order Number	Description	Size/Scale	Colour (if choice given)	Quantity Required	Cost Each (£)	Total Cost (£)
1							
2							
3							
4							
5							
6							
7							
8							
9							

	GOODS TOTAL
Postage & Packing is 10% of order value for UK (Min £1.00) and 20% for Overseas (Min £2.00). Minimum Credit Card Transaction is £5.00 A copy of our standard Terms & Conditions is available upon request	POST & PACKING (See Left)
	GOODS TOTAL

Please make cheques (UK Banks Only) payable to Jaguar Enthusiasts' Club Ltd

Expiry Date /	Card Type	Issue No (Switch)	DR Document No:	Desp Date:

Signed _____ Date _____

Membership enquiries to:

THE JAGUAR ENTHUSIASTS' CLUB LIMITED

The Old Library
113A, Gloucester Road North,
Filton, Bristol BS34 7PU
Tel: 0117 969 8186   Fax: 0117 979 1863
E-mail: graham.searle@btinternet.com
Website: www.jec.org.uk

The AJ6 3.6-litre engine installation in the XJ40.

This is the plusher interior of the Sovereign model with walnut veneer inlayed with boxwood, veneered instrument panel (not seen on the XJ6 models), and leather upholstery. As this is a slightly later model the audio equipment is of revised style.

Sovereign models were exceptionally well equipped. On the mechanical side the new ABS was standard, as was cruise control and automatic rear ride height suspension. Automatic transmission was the norm (at no extra cost) but an owner could specify the Getrag five-speed manual gearbox when ordering the car new.

Internally, Jaguar went to great lengths to ensure the new Sovereign models would live up to their previous reputation for the highest standards of trim. Not only did the new owner have everything that came with the 2.9s but they also had a sophisticated air conditioning system, headlamp wash and wipe, rear seat headrests, heated door mirrors, eight-way electrically adjustable front seats, Clarion E950 hi-fi quality stereo rado/cassette system with six speakers and, of course, leather upholstery. The walnut veneer incorporated boxwood inlays around the centre top panel, glove box lid and door cappings and wood veneer continued to the driver instrument display which was matt black on XJ6 models.

The Sovereign XJ40 models were the most highly specified cars to have come out of the Jaguar factory up to that time.

The Daimler

Daimler was the oldest surviving name in the British motor industry and Jaguar had purchased the company back in 1960, since when they had developed the

The prestige interior of the Daimler model with individualised rear seating in leather, centre console, revised door trims and veneered picnic tables.

From the side view the Daimler featured chromed swage line trims, and standard equipment alloy wheels.

All Daimlers, and some of the later equivalent US models, featured the fluted grille.

marque as a more prestigious variant of the Jaguar brand. Although the Daimler-badged model range had been reduced significantly, they still sold reasonably well to 'older money' and those who wanted something a little different from the sporting Jaguar image.

From 1986, apart from the Double Six (Series 3 design), only one XJ40 model would carry the Daimler mantle. Essentially a Sovereign variant only available with the 3.6-litre engine, the Daimler 3.6 was even more highly equipped than the Jaguar.

Externally, the Daimler retained the 'crinkle cut' fluted grille with centre mounted 'D' motif, so well known on the marque, accompanied by a similarly treated chromed rear boot plinth. A curved section chrome strip ran along the whole side of the car accompanied by a single coachline above it. The 20-spoke alloy wheels (with 'D' motif) were also standard equipment on this model. At the rear only the Daimler badge was featured, but the vertical section of the boot lid (containing the number plate mounting) was covered with a charcoal matt black finisher. Lastly, a different design of rear light unit was used on the Daimler, this being of the neutral density type, and much darker in appearance than on the other models.

Mechanically, the Daimlers were exactly the same as the 3.6-litre Sovereign model except for the use of a limited slip differential as standard equipment.

Internally, the Daimler was to be the ultimate in

2.9-litre and 3.6-litre models – 1986 to 1990

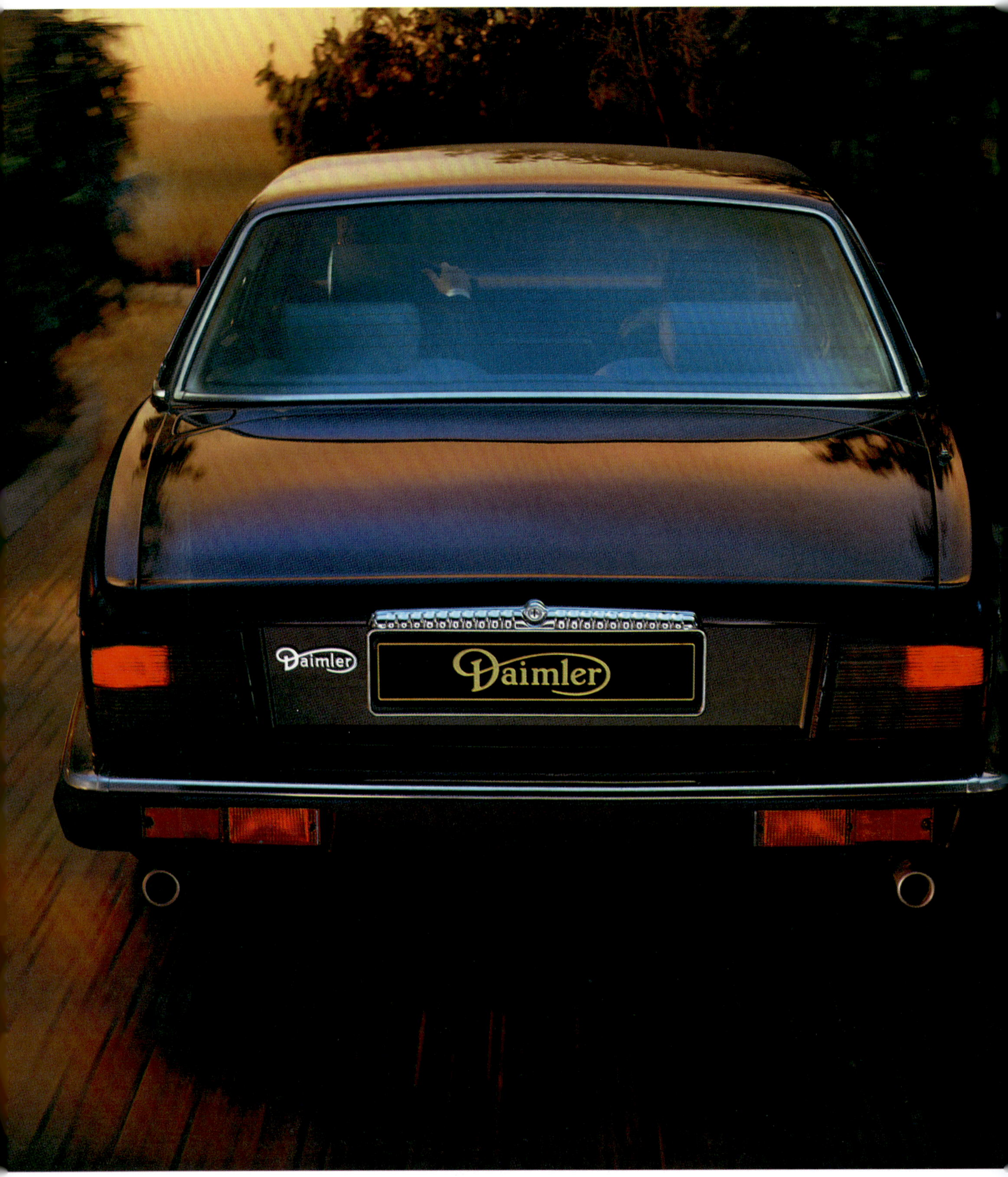
Daimler
Daimler

On earlier models the rear fluted trim was repeated with an open script Daimler name set on a matt black finisher panel.

luxury with best quality leather coverings to the seats, which in themselves were of a totally different design to the Jaguar's, and were individually heated for the front occupants. The rear seats were of the individual type with a prominent armrest and were fitted with headrests, similar in style to those fitted to all previous top-of-the-range Daimler models from 1973. In the rear of the front seats walnut-veneered picnic tables featured chromed integrated drinks coasters. An attractive rear centre console confirmed the model with a Daimler badge and wood-veneered oddments tray. All woodwork was made up from burr walnut of superb quality with additional fillets around the window buttons on the doors. The better quality veneer was not, however, boxwood inlayed at this time like the Jaguar Sovereign models.

The door trims were of an entirely different design to those on the Jaguar models, and again, were trimmed in the best quality leathers. The final touches of luxury came with the standard fitment of an electrically operated sunroof and nylon over-rugs – all for £3,500

DID YOU KNOW?

Unleaded fuel debate

By 1989, Jaguar was issuing details to its dealers about the use of unleaded fuel in the XJ40 models, to clarify the position.

These were: 2.9-litre engined cars from Vin No. 590114, which had a standard compression, meaning they could be run on leaded or unleaded fuel safely. Previous 2.9-litre engines were designed for leaded fuel only, while 3.6-litre engines were all suitable for unleaded fuel providing a minor modification was carried out at the Jaguar dealership.

more than the top-of-the-range Jaguar.

The Daimler 3.6 was even better equipped than the equivalent Double Six in the old bodyshell, but all models enjoyed a fully carpeted boot with full-size spare wheel and a comprehensive attaché cased tool kit of new design specifically for the XJ40.

In the US, because of different regulations, the side indicator repeater lights were eliminated and the holes in the wings covered with leaper badges. Note also the lack of coachlines on US cars.

2.9-litre and 3.6-litre models – 1986 to 1990

Market model differentiation

The specification and even the name of the various XJ40 models changed according to the market. To clarify this Sovereign models destined for countries like Germany were equipped as standard with 20-spoke alloy wheels, but in some European markets the 2.9-litre-engined cars were not sold, such as France and Germany where even the Daimler model didn't come equipped as standard with a radio/cassette player.

For the valued US market the line-up was also changed. You couldn't buy a 2.9-litre-engined model or a base model XJ6, although the Jaguar Sovereign model was badged merely XJ6 but with the standard four-headlamp arrangement. The US Sovereign model was effectively a Daimler badged as a Jaguar, externally and internally, although there was a slight difference in that the US Sovereign used boxwood inlays to the veneer whereas the Daimler didn't. Clear as mud isn't it?

The other change to US-destined cars was the elimination of the side indicator repeater lights in favour of leaper badges, which was necessary to meet their legislation.

US specification XJ40s from the base Sovereign model, nearest the camera, to the range-topper Majestic Vanden Plas.

XJ40 optional extras and prices at the time of launch in 1986

Optional equipment	XJ6	Sovereign	Daimler	£	£	£	£
Air conditioning	○	■	■	1003.35	83.61	163.04	1250.00
Alloy wheels	○	○	■	505.69	42.14	82.17	630.00
Anti-lock braking system	○	■	■	842.81	70.23	136.96	1050.00
Automatic transmission, four-speed	○	■	■	521.74	43.48	84.78	650.00
Cruise control	○	■	■	321.02	26.76	52.17	400.00
Headlamp power wash	○	■	■	216.72	18.06	35.22	270.00
Headrests, rear seats	○	■	■	72.24	6.02	11.74	90.00
Heated door lock barrels	○	○	○	40.13	3.35	6.52	50.00
Heated door mirrors	○	■	■	40.13	3.35	6.52	50.00
Limited slip differential	○	○	■	160.53	13.38	26.09	200.00
Ride levelling rear suspension	○	■	■	361.20	30.10	58.70	450.00
Seats, front, eight-way electrically adjustable	○	■	■	503.69	42.14	82.17	630.00
Seats, front, heated	○	○	■	208.70	17.39	33.91	260.00
Sunblinds, rear window	○	○	○	48.16	4.01	7.83	60.00
Sunroof, electric sliding steel	○	○	■	473.58	39.46	76.96	590.00
Audio equipment							
Electronic audio system with Dolby noise reduction and six speakers	○	■	■	136.46	11.37	22.17	170.00
Paint and trim							
Metallic paint	○	■	■	369.23	30.77	60.00	460.00
Herringbone tweed cloth seat facings	■	△	△	Available at no extra cost			
Leather trim	○	■	■	537.79	44.82	87.39	670.00
Magnolia leather upholstery	□	□	○	236.79	19.73	38.48	295.00
Passenger footwell rugs	□	○	■	72.24	6.02	11.74	90.00

Key
■ Standard
○ Optional at extra cost
△ Optional at no extra cost
□ Not available

2.9-litre and 3.6-litre models – 1986 to 1990

What the press said

The press had previously enjoyed knocking Jaguar for their poor build quality and longevity, but so many times they had had to congratulate the Coventry company on the success of its products. The problem with the XJ40 was that everyone, including the motoring media knew what a good car the Series 3 had turned out to be, a car that was still in demand and a car that had been finely honed over the years. So what did they make of the 'new kid on the block'?

Autosport in the UK was the first to publish a report, only a day after the public announcement of the car and perhaps we should blame their journalist Mike McCarthy, as he made it clear, even then, that the car should be known as the XJ40 to avoid confusion with the old XJ6.

Jaguar had to accommodate the different size and shape of rear number plates in the USA and this apparent XJ6 is really a Sovereign with satin-finished badging.

'There is only one word to sum up the new XJ40 (I suspect it is going to be called that by the public, no matter how hard Jaguar try and push the old names): brilliant. In almost every respect it is better than the Series 3 and that was a hard act to follow, but Jaguar has done it.'

He continued to wax lyrically about the new car with comments including:

'… Dynamically the XJ40 is the best saloon in the world … comfort levels are supreme, refinement better than the best, road-holding and handling to match the rest, and better than most.'

He did pick up on some issues however, which now make interesting reading:

'I wasn't too keen on the instrumentation or rather the computer and the electronics all over the place … Nor was I particularly taken with the interior trim, I like the wood but only in 30-year-old cars … the gnarled old wood is polished and caressed by workmen, until it gleams – just like Formica. In this respect, the new BMW 7 Series has it all over the Jaguar … the steering is still too light for my taste.'

His closing comments were to set the scene for many future reports:

'All in all, the new Jaguar is a superb motor car. With unsurpassed levels of refinement and noise suppression, superb road manners, incredible comfort and ride, it has catapulted Jaguar to the head of the queues. They've made it the same – only much, much better.'

Two days later the *Motor* came out with its own comments after driving the XJ40 in Scotland during the press launch. Their opening gambit was: 'Getting Better all the Time'.

The AJ6 engine has never been known for its ultimate smoothness, but their road tester Daniel Ward gave the engine the thumbs up:

'… The AJ6 engine has all the audible character of the E-type but with the volume turned down. Between 4,000rpm and 5,000rpm the Jaguar's power is at its most solid and dependable, yet it is well spread.'

He went on to comment that the AJ6 engine was much better in the XJ40 than the earlier units in the XJ-S. For the manual gearbox, however, he had less praise:

'The five-speed Getrag gearbox is like the Jimmy Young Show; with nothing else to judge it by, you could think it good in time, but in truth there are better ones around. This box has to handle 248lb ft of torque, and the gearchange lets you know it. Not because it is unduly heavy, it is not, but the lever prefers to be moved through its long movements with respect rather than speed. BMW and Mercedes have got things right.'

In the end his overall comments bore out what most of the press would say:

'Such breadth of ability is unexpected in a luxury car which trades as much on character and style as anything else.'

A week later, the might of the *Autocar* magazine came to bare on the XJ40. their enthusiasm for the car abounded with little real upsets except on boot space.

'Jaguar now has a truly worthy successor to the XJ6 Series 3, and more importantly, a world class luxury saloon car range with which to match the products of Munich and Stuttgart.'

It expressed a little concern at the traditional looks, which in fact were little different to the out-going model (a surprise to many these days), but they thought Jaguar had got it right, and the only problem might be keeping up with demand!

A few months later they acquired a 2.9-litre model for evaluation and said:

'The bottom line is that the 2.9-litre car is almost 1.5mpg less economical at 19.3mpg overall, showing that the engine needs to be worked much harder to maintain rapid progress. But the extra 20mph on top speed and 2.5 seconds off the 0 to 60mph time will set you back exactly £2,000 more. If you don't need that extra performance, then the XJ6 2.9 could well be the car for you.'

The American *Car & Driver* magazine's first comments on the new car were that it emphasised the important Britishness of the marque and that one of the world's better cars had been substantially improved.

The US *Road & Track* magazine didn't carry out a full road test until June 1987. Their sub-title read: 'Same space, more pace with more grace – the XJ6 has gone, long live the XJ6.'

'Ride and handling are more than what we hoped for. This is the best engineered part, as the steering has been sharpened and the ride more controlled ... The new XJ feels more nimble and more stable than the old one and, with the excellent Pirellis, almost impossible to push out of composure. Brakes are flawless ...'

Because of the importance of the new XJ40, and as a final confirmation of its successful launch, here are just a few one-liners from various magazines of the time:

'Jaguar has just announced what we and plenty of others say is the world's finest sedan.' *Car*

'World-class handling and ride and refinement, all in one chassis.' *Performance Car*

'Arguably the most comfortable car in the world.' *Motor*

'Its speed and ride will leave you breathless, its handling burns holes in your driving gloves.' *Popular Mechanics*

Competition comparison

So how did the new Jag compare with the old and the competition?

	XJ40 3.6	XJ6 4.2	BMW 735i	Merc 300E
0 to 60mph	7.4sec	10.1sec	6.9sec	8.4sec
Top speed	136mph	120mph	145mph	136mph
Average fuel economy	18.6mpg	17.4mpg	23.3mpg	22.7mpg

	XJ40 2.9	XJ6 3.4	BMW 730i	Merc 280
0 to 60mph	9.6sec	11.7sec	10.5sec	9.6sec
Top Speed	120mph	117mph	131mph	128mph
Average fuel economy	19.5mpg	18.4mpg	20.0mpg	21.6mpg

Model progression

During 1987, sales boomed and there was little need to make any changes other than minor modifications which assisted production. However, as is quite usual in the motor industry, there would be a need for some improvements, if only minor, for the next (1988) model year. So, in October 1987, for the forthcoming motor show, Jaguar announced some changes to the XJ40 models.

XJ40s had been equipped with a sound system as standard for most markets, varying in quality dependent on model. In all cases, although fitting neatly into the existing curved centre console area, they were still a separate unit, much like the equipment fitted to Series 3 and XJ-S models. For the 1988 model year a fully integrated Clarion 926 HP unit would be used which fitted flush with the curved console. With an enhanced performance of some 80 watts it was a standard fitment on Sovereign and Daimler models, but

The Clarion E920 audio system as first fitted to XJ6 models.

an extra cost option on XJ6 models. The new radio/cassette system had a much improved automatic tuning facility. To accompany this change all models had a revised cassette storage system in the centre console cubby box area.

Heated door mirrors, which had been standard on Sovereign and Daimler models, were now also to become a standard feature on XJ6 cars. Heated door locks had been an extra cost option on the Daimler model as had the rear window sun blind, both of which would be standardised for 1988 on that car only. Finally, the 20-spoke alloy wheels which were available for all cars at extra cost, except for the Daimler

The Clarion E950 audio system as fitted to Sovereign and Daimler models. Compare this with the later integrated style in the illustration of the Sovereign interior earlier in this chapter.

previously, were now standardised on the Sovereign models for most markets.

Along with these quite minor improvements Jaguar decided to increase the prices on all models by an average of 7 per cent from September of 1987. A not inconsiderable amount and one which they justified on the grounds of improved specification and high demand:

XJ6 2.9-litre saloon	£18,400
XJ6 3.6-litre saloon	£20,400
2.9-litre Sovereign saloon	£26,000
3.6-litre Sovereign saloon	£28,000
Daimler 3.6-litre saloon	£32,000

It was to be a momentous year for Jaguar in 1988. Their further success in car sales was in no small part down to the XJ40 with 10,000 units being sold in the UK alone that year (double the 1985 figure for the old Series 3 model), although the XJ-S was doing its bit as

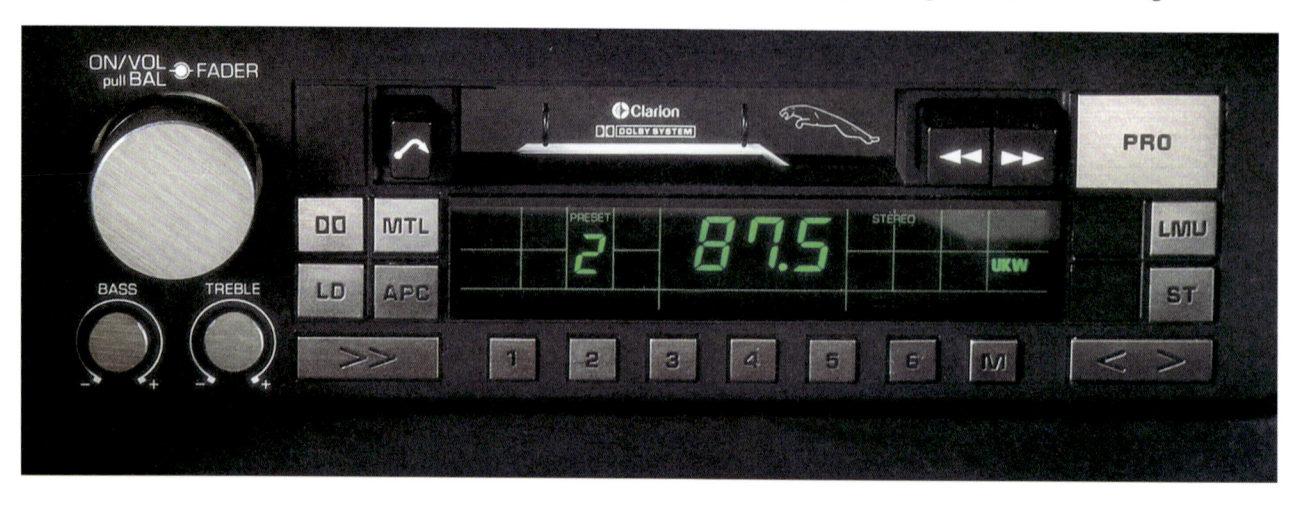

54 Jaguar XJ40

well, but for the motor show the everyday Jaguars were to be over-shadowed by the display of the fabulous XJ220 supercar.

The XJ40 saloon, however, was not to be outdone as an independent survey had been carried out amongst 1,000 UK company car fleet managers resulting in it being honoured with the 1988 Boardroom Car of the Year award.

Jaguar also announced more minor changes to the model range for 1989. The door mirrors (common to all XJ40 models) were to change style and shape slightly, a feature that would then continue to the end of production in 1994. A slightly revised style of bottom windscreen finisher was also fitted, most probably due to the necessities of manufacture and longevity. On the Daimler model the matt black rear finisher panel was discontinued.

All XJ40s from launch had used a central locking system similar to the Series 3 models but for the 1989 model year an infrared remote locking system was adopted, standardised on the Sovereign and Daimler cars, and an extra cost option on XJ6 models.

Rear E post reading lights found on the Daimler models were also to be fitted to Sovereign cars from 1989. This also became an option on XJ6 models but in truth was fitted to many cars during manufacture for which extra was charged.

For the first time the Daimler model in the UK now had boxwood inlays to the walnut veneered panels. This extending around the glove box, along the central air vent panel and on to the door cappings just like the Jaguar Sovereign although now, as originally, the centre section woodwork and allied console trim were of a different style on Daimler to Jaguar.

On all leather-equipped interiors Jaguar provided the facility for owners to select a contrasting colour piping to enhance the overall quality feel of the interior. This was only applicable to certain leather colour schemes, namely magnolia, doeskin and Savile Grey. Piping finish was either in red or blue.

A minor change to mechanical aspects for 1989 involved the cruise control system. Previously it was only operational in the 'D' position when physically in top gear. Now, for 1989, if the gear selector was on the left-hand side, cruise control could still be operated.

The 1989 model year also saw the introduction of a further (sixth) model in the XJ40 range, the XJR 3.6-litre saloon, a sports model aimed at a younger market, but more on this in a later chapter.

Some minor changes to US and Canadian

The earlier style of door mirror on the XJ40.

specification models for late 1988 and early 1989 model year included the standard fitment of an electric sunroof on the XJ6 (UK Sovereign).

By the end of 1988, Jaguar had achieved some amazing results. They had sold more cars in that year than any other year previously, a grand total of 51,939 units of which the XJ40 made up over 40,000. This momentous production figure would not be exceeded again until 1998, which proves the importance of the XJ40 during this period.

To further exemplify the success of Jaguar at this time they won Le Mans that year. Then, in 1989, there was another major change with the takeover of the company by the Ford Motor Company, a move that would have significant affects on the company to the ultimate good.

The later style of door mirror.

Chapter **Five**

Times of change – 1990 to 1991

A new 4.0-litre capacity version of the AJ6 power unit made its debut at the British Motor show in 1989. At the time, this was to be used exclusively for the XJ40 models, replacing the 3.6-litre engine.

The basic concept of the AJ6 engine remained unchanged with the all-aluminium, lightweight closed deck structure, four-valve pent roof combustion chambers and the duplex timing chain arrangement. But the fundamental objective of the new engine was to increase low-speed torque and enhance the feeling of effortless power and refinement, something the earlier engines did not have. Now, with changing circumstances around the world, unleaded petrol was becoming more of an issue, so the 4.0-litre engine would, from day one, be capable of taking this fuel without adaptation.

The capacity of the AJ6 engine was increased to 3,980cc which was achieved by increasing the stroke from 92mm to 102mm. In non-catalyst condition the peak torque was moved up to 250lb ft at 3,750rpm compared with 249lb ft at 4,000rpm in the 3.6. Maximum power for a non-catalyst version was therefore increased to 235bhp from 221bhp. (In catalyst form this was reduced to 223bhp.)

A new low-loss air cleaner system was used along with revised camshaft profiles, tappets, valve timing, improved idle smoothness and exhaust downpipes. Redesigned pistons and the selection of a crankshaft in forged steel instead of cast iron enhanced refinement.

To complement the engine change, Jaguar adopted a new engine management system with digital control of fuel and ignition. This new system, it was claimed, greatly increased computational power, allowing the design engineers to increase the control and diagnostic specification.

The benefits of this were several fold. First, improved engine starting, reduced to one second or less and secondly, improved idle control, tickover having long been a problem on the earlier cars, particularly XJ-Ss. It also helped engineers working on the car because the diagnostics system was also monitoring the engine and emissions control as well as electrical connections.

There was also a knock-on effect to the automatic transmission. Gear change quality was much improved because the system was able to communicate electronically with the transmission control unit.

Refinement was one aim of the new engine, but performance was another, as the figures below show. It was not significant, but enough to be noticed.

Performance comparisons of the two AJ6 engines

	3.6-litre	4.0-litre
Cubic capacity	3,590cc	3,980cc
Bore and stroke	91 x 92mm	91 x 102mm
BHP	221 @ 5,250rpm	235 @ 4,750rpm
Torque	248lb ft @ 4,000rpm	385lb ft @ 3,750rpm
Compression ratio	9.6 to 1	9.5 to 1
Maximum speed	134mph	141mph
0 to 30mph	3.0sec	3.3sec
0 to 50mph	6.3sec	6.3sec
0 to 100mph	24.6sec	21.4sec
Standing quarter mile	16.5sec	16.0sec
70mph to 90mph acceleration	7.9sec	6.6sec
Average fuel consumption	17.3mpg	18.5mpg

(Performance figures taken from contemporary road tests of same-specification cars under similar conditions.)

New transmission

A new automatic transmission came with the 4.0-litre engine, again from ZF, the 4HP 24E unit featuring electronic control that interfaced with the engine management system. It worked by retarding the ignition momentarily on upshifts, reducing the torque input as the gear change was made. This had the effect of smoothing out the gear changes and therefore the refinement of the whole car.

The new transmission featured two pre-programmed modes of operation – 'Sport' and 'Normal', commonplace these days but a relative first for Jaguar. The Sport mode allowed the transmission to become more sensitive to changes in throttle position so that it would change down more readily and at higher speeds. Using Sport gears were held longer and part-throttle changes down to first gear were possible. In the Normal mode of operation, which was designed for everyday driving use, changes were quicker but smoother with less reaction to throttle position.

Because of the increased torque of the 4.0-litre the Getrag manual gearbox also came in for some modification. The amended box was the Getrag 290 unit with a repositioned gear lever 15mm rearward to improve accessibility. Internally, a three-plane gate pattern made reverse gear easier to engage. An increased diameter clutch and two twin-mass flywheels were also fitted on 4.0-litre models.

Other mechanical changes

Little else changed on the new 4.0-litre model although the anti-lock braking system came in for some revision. Out went the original Girling/Bosch system to be replaced by a new Teves system, the only significant difference being standardisation with other Jaguar models and its compactness.

External alterations

Jaguar had always been known for its extensive use of chrome and the XJ40 had been no exception, that is apart from the rear of the car. The boot area had always been considered a little bland, particularly when compared with most previous saloon models. This matter was to be addressed from 1990 and would prove to be an easy identification point between the outgoing 3.6-litre model and the new 4.0-litre version.

A horizontal chrome trim was added to the leading edge of the boot lid just below the chromed plinth. This was accompanied by a similar chrome attached to the

The 4.0-litre version of the AJ6 power unit which, at the time, was unique to the XJ40 as the XJ-S continued to use the 3.6-litre engine.

existing black plastic panel along the top edge of the rear valance where the boot lid closed down to it, this applying to Sovereign and Daimler models only. The rear lights also came in for similar treatment with chromed surrounds, but only on the Sovereign and Daimler models, all of which enhanced the rearward appearance of the car and had the effect of widening the car optically. New headlamps were fitted to US-spec cars to meet revised legislation on adjustment.

A common fault, known to most XJ40 owners today, is the problem associated with the exterior door locks. They become difficult to operate eventually leading to a section of the casting cracking (see later chapter on maintenance for further information). Jaguar addressed this problem from the 1990 model year with the fitment of revised locks and, at the same time changed other locks, including ignition, boot and the glove box, to a matching style so that one key would operate all locks on the car.

Complaints had also been received about the boot catch being difficult to operate. Jaguar addressed this with a revised design which was smoother and required less force to operate.

Five new exterior colours were added to the list of XJ40 exterior finishes, three of which used new technology mica paint. With this new finish the

58 Jaguar XJ40

External differences were minor with the change to the 4.0-litre engine (Sovereign model on the left), and the 2.9-litre engined car, seen here in XJ6 form.

aluminium within it was replaced by reflecting mica silicate particles coated with titanium dioxide. This had the effect of providing a deep, almost 3D lustre to the finish.

Interior improvements

Although the XJ40 had achieved great acclaim worldwide, many still felt that the interior lacked something. As mentioned earlier, at one stage Jaguar looked at a major change in design to incorporate even

From the introduction of the 4.0-litre, brightwork appeared in profusion at the rear. Chromed surrounds to the lights and horizontal chromed strips to the plastic finishers above and below the number plate area looked so much better than the rather bland earlier cars. This combination applied to Sovereign and Daimler models in Europe and the higher specified US models.

Times of change – 1990 to 1991

The new instrument pack was welcomed by everyone and was generally considered to be more akin to Jaguar's image. It applied to all models, even the 2.9-litre cars.

more technological features in the new car, but the clinics carried out at the time indicated that traditional Jaguar buyers were turned off by such innovations. In the end, the interior was only marginally modernised with the use of bar gauges, digital read-outs and that vehicle condition monitor screen and read-out.

Even these features didn't find favour with many owners and in the end, after further market research worldwide, Jaguar bowed to the requirements for a more traditional approach to instrumentation.

A brand-new instrument pack containing analogue instruments was designed and fitted for all 1990 model year cars (including the new 4.0-litre model). A battery condition gauge and fuel gauge to the left of the very large rev counter and speedometer were flanked on the right by oil pressure and water temperature gauges. Taking all the binnacle space including that used for the VCM, the read-outs from this were replaced by conventional ISO symbol warning lights, arranged in two vertical strips, one at each end of the instrument pack with a further single horizontal bank underneath the main dials.

These warning lights were of the 'secret-till-lit' design and illuminated in sequence for a few seconds every time the ignition was switched on as a bulb-check facility.

In the centre of the panel there was a new six-character LCD display performing the roles of odometer, trip computer readout and diagnostic message centre for fault warnings. The trip computer design was also changed at this time with simplified functions selected by a dedicated button on a steering column stalk. The new instrument pack used a wood-veneered 'mask' panel for all models.

After customer complaints about the electronic direction indicator stalk which always returned to the neutral position and required it to be cancelled by pressing the stalk in the opposite direction, Jaguar reverted to a conventional mechanical latching stalk.

A new audible warning system was added on all models to warn drivers when the exterior lights were turned on. The graphics on the air conditioning control panel were also improved and a remote boot release catch was located in the glove-box. Illuminated sun visor mirrors were now also part of the standard specification on all cars.

The J-gate transmission surround also came in for change. Now with a switch to enable the driver to move between 'N' (Normal) and 'S' (Sport) modes for the gearbox, the surround was much improved aesthetically with leather trimming replacing preformed rubber. Cars with manual transmission were unaltered in this area.

Another move to satisfy complaints from owners came in the driver's door controls for the electric window lifts. The driver's window button now incorporated a toggle for ease of identification by feel.

To further insulate the interior of the car from mechanical noise Teroson sound-deadening materials were used. This special type of foam insulation was moulded to the contours of the body interior.

Along with a change in exterior colour schemes, new trim colours were available on all models for 1990 with grey and sage added for dashboard and door top schemes for Daimler and Sovereign models. Highly specified models also gained colour-coded seat belts at this time and there was the introduction of a grey headlining and upper trim colour to co-ordinate with Savile Grey, Isis Blue and charcoal interior trim colours. Champagne carpet was also introduced to replace the mink colour on cars with magnolia trim, the latter still an extra cost option.

Many of the above changes applied to the 2.9-litre models which, mechanically, continued unchanged at this time.

Prices for the 1990 model year cars in standard form were:

XJ6 2.9-litre saloon	£21,200
XJ6 4.0-litre saloon	£25,200
Sovereign 2.9-litre saloon	£28,000
Sovereign 4.0-litre saloon	£32,500
Daimler 4.0-litre saloon	£36,500

Performance comparisons of 4.0-litre with the competition

	BHP	Torque lb ft	Max mph	0 to 60 sec	Average mpg
XJ40 4.0					
XJ40 2.9 (man)	165	176	120	9.6	19.5
Mercedes 300 SE (man)	188	191	131	9.1	20.0
BMW 530i (man)	188	192	126	11.9	18.3
Rover 827 SI	177	168	137	7.6	22.9
Ford Scorpio (auto)	150	172	127	10.3	19.5

There were changes to the model range in the USA and Canadian markets also. For the new model year no less than four variants of the XJ40 were offered. First, the XJ6 was still equipped to Sovereign specification although the walnut veneer didn't feature any boxwood inlays. Externally, the car's appearance emulated the UK XJ6 with a four-headlamp arrangement and, new to the USA, matt black-painted window frames. Although the US model still retained the alloy wheels as standard, there was no single coachline along the side of the car.

The Sovereign offered full trim specification even down to the boxwood inlays on the veneer and chromed window frames, together with single headlamps, as in the UK.

The return of the Vanden Plas name in the States was mentioned earlier, and this continued virtually unchanged – a Daimler in all but name and fluted exterior trim at this time.

A Majestic moment

Lastly, a new limited edition model called the Vanden Plas Majestic entered the US market. The Majestic name had been acquired by Jaguar when they

Majestic in name and stature, the ultimate limited edition XJ40 for the US market with unique exterior paint finish, wheels, trim and security system.

purchased the Daimler Motor Company in 1960 and had first been used by Daimler in the 1950s for their 3.8-litre luxury saloon. Then there was the Majestic Major, with a 4.5-litre V8 engine, a model that Jaguar inherited and retained in production until 1967.

The Vanden Plas Majestic, only supplied in Regency Red (mica-metallic) paint, was effectively a UK market Daimler even down to the fluted grille and rear plinth, but was still badged as a Jaguar. On top of the 'normal' Daimler specification were added highly polished diamond-turned lattice wheels with each spoke faceted in red. The brakes were fitted with protective shields to prevent brake dust from damaging the highly polished surface of the wheels.

Internally, the Vanden Plas Majestic was trimmed in the best Autolux leather in magnolia finish with matching magnolia leather gearknob, handbrake surround and steering wheel. The leather seats were

For the US Majestic model Autolux leather was used, even on the steering wheel and gearknob.

The passive restraint seat belt system employed on US models at this time incorporated manual lap belts with a diagonal shoulder belt which automatically came into operation around the occupant when the door was closed.

trimmed in contrasting Mulberry Red piping with matching red wool carpets and Racemark-red sheepskin over-rugs. All the mirror-finish burr walnut veneer was boxwood inlayed.

Another feature unique to this model was the fitment of an integrated security system with one-touch operation allowing windows to be closed as well as doors locked. Finally, gold inlay plastic badges adorned the boot lid carrying the emblems Vanden Plas on one side and Majestic on the other. All this luxury cost the lucky US buyer an extra $5,000!

Also in the US, all but the XJ6 had a standard fitment electric sunroof and another first for Jaguar was the fitment of a front seat passive restraint system. This required a great deal of detail engineering and incorporated the automatic adjustment of the front seat belts running on a rail system above the door frames. The principle was that the self-anchoring seat belts rested at the base of the A post allowing the driver and passenger to get in the car. Upon closing the doors, the belts would automatically slide along a rail in the roof and lock the occupants in position.

Allied factors during 1990

It was at the beginning of this year that Jaguar publicly announced its proposals for a new research and development facility at Whitley in Coventry. This was too late for the early XJ40s but it would eventually make a marked difference to later models and new ranges.

Jaguar had announced the proposal to sell the business to the Ford Motor Company and when this finally happened, in July, William Hayden CBE, a Ford man, was appointed chief executive of the company. Coinciding with this Sir John Egan retired from his involvement with Jaguar after a remarkable ten years during which time he had brought the company and the cars back from the brink. His commitment to the XJ40 showed now in the sales figures and the improved credibility of the marque generally. Jaguar will long owe a debt of gratitude to Sir John Egan and his legacy for us is the XJ40.

Sales continued to boom with Jaguar announcing record sales in Europe and Japan. On top of this the 4.0-litre XJ40 was voted Best Luxury Car by *Fleet News*. Confirming Jaguar's commitment to the future they finally announced that production would go ahead for the XJ220 supercar.

If that wasn't enough in 1990, Jaguar achieved another win at Le Mans – all was very well indeed for Jaguar.

The 3.2 engine installation in the XJ40, the only model to ever receive this engine.

Enter the 3.2-litre

Yet another major move forward in the XJ40 range took place at the end of 1990 for the 1991 model year. During the launch and production of the 4.0-litre model, the 2.9-litre had remained pretty much unchanged save for the cosmetic and a few mechanical items addressed earlier in this chapter, and not least, the change in instrumentation layout. Now, at last, it was the turn of this model for major revision.

The 2.9-litre engine had never been known for its outright performance. It was a ploy by Jaguar to achieve sales in a different marketing area with a lower price, lower performance car and this had only been relatively successful. Of all XJ40s sold up to this time only 31 per cent were equipped with this smaller engine.

Jaguar finally introduced a new engine to replace the 2.9. This was based on the existing 4.0-litre engine, so unlike the 2.9, it used a twin-overhead camshaft cylinder head.

The capacity of 3,293cc came from a stroke reduced from 102mm to 83mm while retaining the original bore measurement. Power output was nicely increased to 200bhp thanks to the four-valve head and an extremely efficient catalyst exhaust system, in fact this was the first time that a Jaguar engine was only available in catalyst form, identifying future requirements on all cars.

The 3.2-litre engine was a vast improvement over the 2.9-litre with performance enhanced to a level comparable to the 3.6-litre engine with a top speed estimated at 131mph and a 0 to 60mph acceleration time of 9.5 seconds with automatic transmission and, of course, the catalyst fitted.

Jaguar anticipated that with the improvement in the smaller engined XJ40, the new car would ultimately account for 40 per cent of all sales in the UK, a figure not too far wrong over the whole production period.

External differences were minimal with just the '3.2' badging appearing on the boot lid.

3.2-litre comparisons with the competition

	BHP	Torque lb ft	Max mph	0 to 60 sec	Average mpg
XJ40 3.2-litre (auto)	200	220	131	9.5	19.6
Mercedes 300 SE (auto)	188	191	131	8.9	20.5
BMW 530i	188	192	126	11.9	17.8
Rover Sterling (auto)	177	168	134	8.7	19.2

All model changes for 1991

Jaguar took the opportunity to make other modifications to the XJ40 models at the time of the 3.2-litre launch. For example, out went the TD metric wheels and in came conventional 7in x 15in steel

A new rimbellisher for steel-wheeled cars introduced with the 3.2, to fit the non-metric wheels and which was available for other models if alloys were not requested.

Another minor change to the exterior at this time was the fitment on non-US cars, of a square side indicator repeater on the front wings.

wheels using 225/65 VR15-sized tyres, although a buyer could still have the TD type by special order, but few did.

The Daimler 4.0-litre gained an entirely new alloy wheel of 15in diameter, called Roulette, again of 20-spoke design and with flush-fitting caps over the wheel nuts.

For the new models the fitting of a fingertip lip to the fuel filler cover eliminated the need previously to 'push' the lid in order to open it – an arrangement that often failed! Another change enabled the driver to open all the door locks by triggering his own door handle.

To clarify the issue of catalytic converters on the XJ40 at this time, all 3.2-litre models came equipped with a low-loss system irrespective of market. For the 4.0-litre cars they could be supplied equipped or not with converters. In all cases, when a catalytic converter was fitted, the fuel filler had a narrow neck and carried a label reading 'Premium Unleaded Fuel Only'.

Sports Handling Pack

Also new for the 1990 model year was a Sports Handling Pack developed by Jaguar engineers to enhance the road-holding performance of the XJ40 saloons. It was not at this point fitted as standard, but was an extra-cost option comprising:

Stiffer front and rear road springs.
Larger diameter front anti-roll bar.
Revised damper settings throughout.
More direct power steering.
Lowered ride height.
Limited slip differential.
8in x 16in forged lattice alloy wheels*.
Pirelli P600 225/55 ZR16 tyres*.
Two-tone sports coachline (not on the Daimler model).
* 17in wheel and tyre combinations also available as a separate entity if required.
The Sports Handling Pack cost £2,900 on XJ6 models, £2,100 on Sovereigns and £1,600 on Daimlers.

The package, which had to be fitted from new by the factory, provided drivers with a more sporty and taut feel to the car, a reduction in float and pitch, and more precise steering.

There were no more changes to the XJ40 range through this period, in fact attention was given over to the XJ-S which was relaunched mid-year taking some of its styling cues from the saloon cars at the rear, with build techniques and interior instrumentation.

What the press said

Autocar and Motor magazine in the UK was one of the first to test the new 4.0-litre in September 1989 and its comments show a perfect example of hindsight!

'Whilst applauding Jaguar's response to criticism, we feel this Jaguar XJ6 is the car which should have appeared at the launch in 1986. There is still room for improvement, the switchgear is rather cheap and fiddly, the exterior, while graceful, is looking dated and back seat room and comfort are mediocre ... Not a new generation of Jaguars, but it is the best XJ6 yet.'

What Car? magazine compared the Daimler 4.0-litre with the then current BMW 735i and came up with the following results:

'The BMW's leather and walnut tend to look something of an after thought ... The 735i engine does tend to get a little noisy when worked very hard and there is not much to criticise in the handling or ride. The Daimler could only be British, you enter the world of fine leather and walnut and thankfully, the awful electronic instruments have been replaced by proper dials which are far more in keeping with the name ... The new engine with improved automatic transmission gives the sort of performance one would expect.'

Writing about the 3.2-litre XJ6, *Autocar and Motor* said:

'Judged as a replacement for the 2.9, the 3.2 is a knockout success. It blows its predecessor away in every conceivable respect and, at

The Sports Handling Pack gave the car a more 'chunky' look with the lattice-style alloy wheels.

Times of change – 1990 to 1991

last, gives Jaguar the means to bite a man-sized chunk from the lucrative low-end of the luxury car market.'

Performance Car also tested a 3.2, but with the sports pack suspension, and their findings were:

'The new 3.2-litre motor frequently couldn't keep up with the pace of the chassis. It's not a bad engine by any stretch of the imagination but when the chassis was demanding more it was hard pushed to deliver. Surprisingly (given its deep-breathing capacity) it thrived on revs in typical multi-valve fashion ... The Sports Handling Pack is spot on. All that Jaguar needs to do is supply a thicker-rimmed steering wheel and a pair of sports front seats.'

Forty into the future

At a conference of the European Car Industry in Turin to publicise progress on research and development under the name *Prometheus* (Programme for European Traffic with Highest Efficiency and Unprecedented Safety), Jaguar took the limelight with three prototype examples of 'cars of the future', based on the XJ40.

The first featured a vision enhancement system enabling the occupants to see more clearly in adverse weather conditions. Jointly developed by Jaguar and Pilkington Glass, this Sovereign model was fitted with a GEC Far-infra-red camera located beneath the header rail on the inside of the windscreen. Good quality pictures were displayed on a small CRT display inside the car, for engineering evaluation. A head-up display was also developed for this application, the device enabling occupants to see more clearly in adverse weather conditions such as fog and at night.

The second car featured a computerised vision system developed in conjunction with Lucas which provided an early warning system for drivers. The camera converted the road scene ahead into a computerised map identifying road edges, white lines and objects ahead of the vehicle. By recognising road lanes, the trajectory of the driven vehicle and surrounding vehicles, potential difficulties could be identified early and the driver could be warned so that corrective action was taken.

The third XJ40 was fitted with a radar system which measured the distance and closing velocity of the car in front. With this technology the car could, if required, maintain a safe distance from the car in front by automatic operation of brakes and throttle.

Although as yet the first two ideas have not come through to production, the third is seen today on the likes of the current Jaguar XKR sports car and is known as ACC (automatic cruise control). The XJ40 lead the field in this development.

Jim Randle with the vision-enhanced development XJ40, seen outside the then relatively new Whitley research and development facility.

Chapter **Six**

Mid-life crisis

Just before we move on to the 1992 model year it is worth mentioning one important factor in the world's luxury car market that would have an effect on Jaguar's thinking – the Lexus LS400.

So strongly was this 'threat' considered that Jaguar even devoted space in their annual *Know Your Jaguar,* a guide book produced for dealer salesmen covering the selling points, specifications, etc. of its models. In the 1991 edition three pages were given over to this competitor. The opening comments were:

'The Lexus is significant not only because it is a well-engineered and sophisticated motor car, but also because it heralds the arrival of the Japanese in the luxury market, traditionally the domain of Jaguar, Mercedes-Benz and BMW in the UK … The arrival of Lexus must not be understated, or indeed overstated, but we must be aware of its potential.'

The strengths of the new threat were summarised as:

Success in the United States.
Body and paint build quality.
Refinement, smoothness and quietness.
Low drag coefficient.
High speed performance and ride.
Flexible driving positions.
Excellent specifications.
Comprehensive warranty.
Good dealer network.
Perceived value for money.
First year free membership of Club Toyota and RAC.

Although Jaguar had less to worry about in some of these areas, the quality aspect, warranty and value-for-money aspects did. For the moment, the XJ40 alone had to address these issues.

The 1992 for 1993 model year

Initially, 1992 saw the range of Jaguar XJ40 models unchanged for the UK and Europe.

XJ6 3.2-litre saloon
XJ6 4.0-litre saloon
Sovereign 3.2-litre saloon
Sovereign 4.0-litre saloon
Daimler 4.0-litre saloon
XJR 4.0-litre saloon

There were yet more changes for the US market, however. First off, that special limited edition Vanden Plas Majestic covered in the last chapter was continued and revised. Now painted in Black Cherry mica-metallic paint, it also sported a chromed strip down the centre of the bonnet and the Roulette alloy wheels first seen on the UK Daimlers. The exterior also now displayed rubber and chrome rubbing strips along the bottom swage line, an item that would become an extra available for all XJ40s, even in the UK.

Internally, the Majestic colour scheme changed to cream with coffee piping and matching carpets, over-rugs, steering wheel and gearknob.

The 'ordinary' Vanden Plas model continued, now sporting the fluted Daimler grille as standard and the Roulette alloy wheels. XJ6 and Sovereign models remained unchanged.

Perhaps the most important news for Jaguar and the XJ40 came at the beginning of 1992 when former Ford man Nick Scheele was appointed as vice chairman of the company under Bill Hayden (also a Ford man who had replaced Sir John Egan). Nick would go on to become chairman and subsequently a major force in the on-going success of the company.

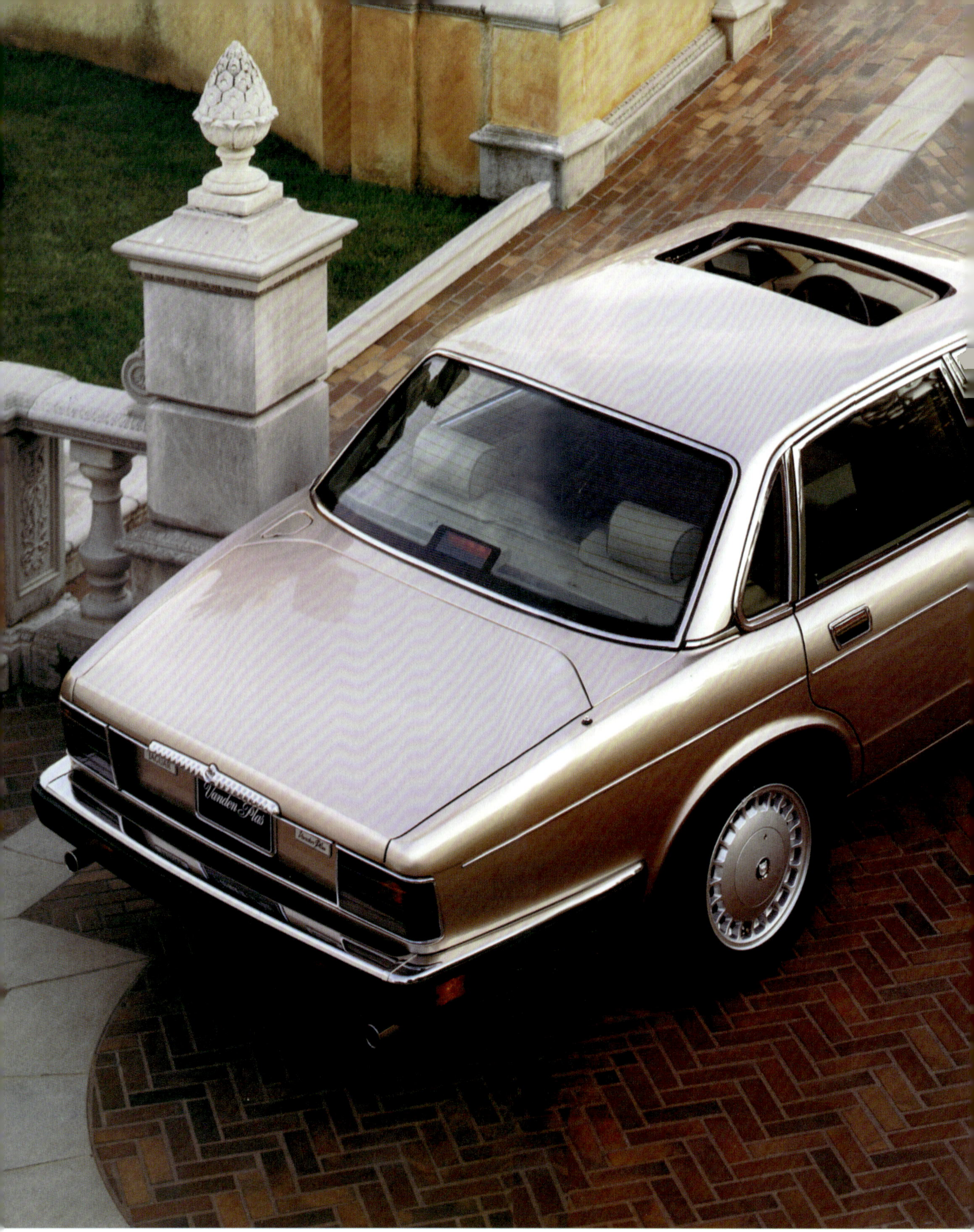
Vanden Plas

The reincarnation yet again of the US Vanden Plas model, now sporting the Roulette alloy wheels, was a Daimler in all but name.

Mid year Jaguar made a strategic announcement that they were to look closely at and commit to offering ever better value for money in their products, and with this confirmed the extension of warranties on new cars to three years, perhaps to match the threat posed by Lexus who already offered this incentive.

Jaguar announced lots of other changes to the XJ40 models for the 1992 model year. Externally, a new front under-spoiler appeared which was of much better design with a restyled air intake. Foglights became a standard fitment on the Daimler model, and an extra cost option on the Sovereign and XJ6 models. Colour schemes changed for 1993 with Black Cherry being replaced by Morocco Red.

The handling was improved by the use of Pirelli P4000 225/65 ZR15 tyres on all models as standard equipment, Jaguar claiming these also enhanced refinement and comfort. Although the wheels remained unchanged yet another new style of rimbellisher appeared for those cars fitted with steel wheels.

Mechanically, both AJ6 engines now incorporated revised camshafts and associated components to reduce noise levels. Engine refinement and efficiency were also improved by the fitting of twin electric cooling fans on all models. The power steering piston diameter was increased to provide more assistance and reduce steering effort at parking speeds.

Gearshift refinement on the automatic transmission was also improved by a recalibration of the ZF gearbox and on the 4.0-litre model only, a first-gear inhibit mode was introduced which engaged first for one to two seconds before changing to second. This aided traction in snow, mud and other slippery road conditions, which was not thought necessary on the 3.2-litre engine cars because of the lower torque level.

Jaguar also introduced a gearshift interlock system on all automatic equipped cars which provided additional security against driver error. This meant you couldn't engage any gear from the 'park' position without applying the footbrake. In a similar vein it was no longer possible to remove the ignition key from its lock if the gearshift lever was not in 'park' although there was a facility for this feature to be over-ridden in the case of an electrical failure.

To cope with increased electrical load the battery and alternator capacities were increased with the resiting of the battery in the boot with remote terminals in the

Mid-life crisis **69**

From the 1992 model year yet another rimbellisher appeared on steel-wheeled cars and the new valance incorporated standard fitment fog lamps, as seen on this 3.2-litre model.

engine bay, achieved by moving the boot venting system. A carpet-trimmed boot lid liner was now fitted on all cars. To compensate for the loss of space in the boot (although the battery was neatly covered and upholstered) the boot width was slightly increased which apparently made it easier to carry a set of golf clubs!

Catalytic converters were now standard on all models and a new environmental evaporative emission control system was introduced to eliminate fuel vapour loss to the atmosphere.

There were more changes inside, with the adoption of higher density foam and shaping to the seats, resulting in an increase in the side roll height of the cushions. The electric seat adjustment controls were revised although still fitted on the centre console sides. Full electric seat adjustment came as standard on Sovereign and Daimler models including electrically adjustable head restraints and electric lumbar support. They also had a two-position memory control to allow the driver's seat, headrest and door mirrors to be predetermined for two drivers by the touch of a button.

The base XJ6 model was now equipped with electric height control as standard. All the head restraints were redesigned with manual height and tilt adjustment. On the Daimler model a two-position memory feature also applied to the front passenger seat. All electric seat features could be specified at extra cost on XJ6 models.

Originally, most of the XJ40 range had been fitted with reading lights in the rear section of the front seat headrests. For this model year these were moved to the seat backs instead.

The door trims were also redesigned, and not unlike the previous Daimler model, they provided better storage accommodation and on the Sovereign and Daimler models were finished and stitched in leather. A new switchpack was also fitted to the doors, on a wood-veneered plinth. On the driver's door the new switch design included a resited entry and exit switch which, when operated, moved the seat back for easier entry and exit from the car. The pack also contained a single joystick for the exterior mirror adjustment which also allowed the passenger door mirror to be dipped to provide the driver with a better view when reversing near to the kerb. A further enhancement at the time, now considered a must, was the one-touch down facility for the driver's window. Finally, new graphics on the switch pack and full illumination eliminated criticisms often levied at the earlier XJ40 models.

Air bags

An issue of major consideration to Jaguar and other manufacturers was safety and Jaguar was one of the first to fit driver's air bags in its cars, the XJ40 being the first model to receive one for the 1993 model year. Much of the backroom work had been carried out with the aid of Ford who, internationally, were the first to fit air bags to any car.

To accommodate the air bag in the XJ40 a new style of four-spoke steering wheel had to be adopted.

Visibility for the auxiliary lower switch pack (fog lights/hazards/computer) was not as good and the horn buttons had to be incorporated in the top two spokes of the wheel. The new wheel did however come with a five-position height adjustment, a better method than previously. The wheel also had an improved feel with a slightly thinner rim and this was subsequently adopted for the XJS as well.

The air bag, fitted in the centre section of the steering wheel, could be inflated and then deflated in less than half a second by a control unit activated from sensors located in the centre of the air bag unit. It was fitted on XJ40 models initially as standard equipment in the UK, European, US and Japanese markets, but followed later for all other countries.

With the horn removed to the steering wheel spokes, the push facility on the left-hand column stalk changed to allow the driver to scroll through the on-board computer read-outs. The right-hand stalk now controlled a program wash-wipe and wiper speed-sensitive intermittent function.

Also on safety issues the seat belts came in for revision. The front belts were fitted with web lock devices to prevent excessive tightening of the belts after the inertia reels had locked. At the rear, seat belt buckle storage was built in to the seat backs and all the buckles were changed in design to meet new legislation.

The air conditioning control panel was completely redesigned to a more logical fashion. Temperature graduations in centigrade and large, positive action switchers were fitted. A recirculation feature was also added to circulate air within the car avoiding the intake of fumes from outside the vehicle. A new 'maximum' A/C function was also incorporated replacing the former humidity controls and provided maximum cooling for rapid pull-down of temperature on very hot days when the car had been parked in bright sun. Along with Jaguar's commitment to the environment and safety all cars were now fitted with non-ozone depleting HFC 134A gas instead of CFC 12.

Another new option available for all models at extra cost was a heated front windscreen with the fine elements running through the glass sandwich. Activated from a switch on the air conditioning panel the facility would automatically switch off after about seven minutes of use and was also activated automatically if Defrost was selected.

Vehicle security had also been addressed by Jaguar with the 1993 model year XJ40s. A new factory-fitted,

The new-style XJ40 boot incorporated the battery, the repositioned spare wheel and a tool kit.

fully integrated security system on all models was now standard equipment although the Daimler benefited from an ultrasonic space intrusion sensor facility as well (first seen on the limited-edition US Majestic model), an extra cost option on the other models.

Comparison with the original XJ40 boot area, where the tool box was stored top left. Look carefully and the depth of the side saddles has also changed to make a very slight improvement in boot space, in the later cars.

Mid-life crisis

The front interior of the revised XJ40 with the air bag steering wheel and the revised door trims with better pockets.

The revised switch pack on the driver's door with veneer and another revision in the style of switch.

Remotely controlled by RF by using a hand-held transmitter, the system would central lock and unlock the car, activate a headlamp illumination feature and switch on and off the security system. The system sensed the perimeter of the car, i.e. the opening of doors, bonnet or boot. Visual deterrents included a flashing red indicator on the dashboard when armed, and warning labels on the side windows. It also activated visual and audible alarm signals, involving direction indicators and a dedicated alarm siren.

Extra features could also be programmed by the Jaguar dealer including inclination and shock sensing and a remote release for the boot catch. A valet mode was also provided which allowed the operation of all the enabled convenience features via the transmitter, but inhibited the arming of the security function.

Finally, the 'panic' button on the centre console was revised to unlock all the doors as well as locking them and closing the windows and sunroof.

In an effort to further upgrade the fixtures and fittings of the XJ40, Jaguar provided an all-new sound system. Of hi-fi capability with four enlarged (6in) door speakers and no less than four tweeters to handle high frequencies, two positioned on the rear parcel shelf and two on the front dashboard roll, this meant the deletion of the two speakers normally mounted on the heelboard under the rear seat. A CD

72   Jaguar XJ40

auto-changer was now also available from Jaguar as an extra cost option, fitted when new or afterwards. The CD changer was mounted in the boot above the spare wheel where it wouldn't be damaged by luggage and the controls were integrated into the auto system panel on the centre console of the dashboard.

Although the trim style remained the same on the non-leather-equipped models, the previous tweed-style material was replaced by a new fabric, available in four colours. Sheepskin over-rugs were by then standard on the Daimler and optional on the other cars. The rear parcel shelf also came in for change, not only to fit the tweeter speakers but also to improve the fit and finish of the rear seat belt anchorages.

Sixteen-inch lattice-style wheels, which had been available with the Sports Handling Pack, were to become a running option for the 1993 model year and would be fitted with Dunlop SP2000 225/55 ZR16 tyres.

All this represented a comprehensive set of upgrades to the XJ40 range in an attempt to keep abreast of the competition, and which would hold off any other changes until the introduction of yet another new model to the range in 1993.

Prices had inevitably moved upwards again by the end of 1992, and for the UK market were:

New material was used for the non-leather seating and the rear seat lighting was moved to the seat back from the headrest.

A more logical and improved air conditioning control panel layout and better quality audio system were another feature of the revised XJ40s.

Mid-life crisis 73

XJ6 3.2-litre saloon	£26,800
XJ6 4.0-litre saloon	£29,800
Sovereign 3.2-litre saloon	£34,800
Sovereign 4.0-litre saloon	£38,300
Daimler 4.0-litre saloon	£44,300

Expanding the market

Towards the end of 1992, Jaguar's boss, Nick Scheele had spent some time in the Far East promoting Jaguar with an eye to expanding distribution in that region. There were also moves to extend the Jaguar arm further into Eastern Europe, South America and even China, a market he felt particularly important to Jaguar's expansion plans.

The first chance the Chinese buyers had of seeing the XJ40 was at the Guangdong Motor Show in a province adjacent to Hong Kong, at the beginning of 1993. XJ40s were now selling in a total of 44 countries around the world with new importers appointed in the Czech and Slovak republics, Hungary and Slovenia.

Early 1993

By the end of 1992 and early 1993, most of the above changes in the models had filtered through to the very important US market where yet more deviation in model style had occurred.

All US cars were still fitted with the 4.0-litre engine only and the entry model XJ6 was, as before, built to Sovereign spec although now, the electric sunroof was an extra cost option, there were no coachlines along the side, or boxwood inlays to the interior veneer. The single rectangular headlights appeared now on this model and after a move from black-painted window frame to chrome and then back to black, they were for 1993 chrome again! The alloy wheels were a later development of the original 20-spoke style, now incorporating no less than 36 spokes.

The Vanden Plas model was not changed cosmetically and retained the Daimler fluted grille and rear plinth, but the limited-edition Majestic had been dropped from the range. Greater things were yet to come from Jaguar with the introduction of another new model based on the XJ40.

Into 1993 and yet more changes for the US market. While the XJ6 (Sovereign in the UK) featured most of the UK changes it was still without a coachline and note the later-style wheels which would eventually find their way on to UK-sold Daimler Double Sixes.

Chapter **Seven**

The revitalisation years – 1993 to 1994

As pointed out earlier, the XJ40 bodyshell was originally, never intended to take the V12 engine. But in the end, particularly with Jaguar's revival and the expansion of production V12 engined luxury cars from Mercedes and BMW, there was a need for such a model.

The V12 is dead, long live the V12

We have already covered the issue of why the XJ40 was not initially released with the famed V12 engine and it took the company until February 1993 to redesign the car and engine with a total investment of some £35 million to achieve this goal.

Nevertheless, the 'old' Series 3 in V12 form had still been selling well and in fact only in December 1992 had the last Daimler version rolled off the line, leaving a slight void of a couple of months before the new model was launched.

Two variants of the V12-engined car were announced. The Jaguar, under the usual XJ12 designation and the Double Six for the slightly more upmarket Daimler model. Both used the XJ40 bodyshell design with subtle external trim differences, but with major modifications carried out to the front framework and inner panels. Indeed, some of these changes had been quietly taking place during 1992 with all six-cylinder XJ40s being built with this new shell so that Jaguar in future would only have to produce one bodyshell for all XJ40 cars.

> **DID YOU KNOW?**
> **Yet another award**
> *What Car?* magazine voted the XJ40 the Best Luxury Car for 1992 against stiff competition from the likes of Mercedes and Lexus. It won the award again in 1993!

A tremendous amount of detail work had to be put into the bodyshell design which resulted in a total of 140 new or modified panels in the shell (over 44 per cent of the total number of panels that make up the body in white). No less than 60 of these changes were directly attributable to the front of the car to accommodate the V12 power unit while the rest were made for the fitment of the driver's side air bag mentioned in the previous chapter which affected all models.

One of the other changes to the XJ40 bodyshell was the E post finisher and rear quarterlight trim on all future cars. This E post finisher would no longer be chrome, but finished to body colour.

To support the physically larger engine a new, unique front subframe had been designed for these models. This was entirely different to the six-cylinder cars, not only because of its mounting points but also in the form of its construction. We have commented already and will re-emphasise in a later chapter, the problems associated with the XJ40 front subframe in that they rust out rather badly. This was not to be a problem feature of the V12 subframe as its construction was of the open form so that water and damp couldn't accumulate.

To handle the extra weight of the V12 engine, the front springs were uprated and the rear ones also stiffened with revised dampers and a thicker (26.9mm) anti-roll bar on the Jaguar model. For the Daimler they also benefited from stiffer springs to support the weight, but less so than the Jaguar and with a thinner anti-roll bar, all to provide a softer and more cushioned ride.

The V12 models followed suit with the six-cylinder cars in having a ZF rack and pinion steering system. Forged lattice alloy wheels of 8in x 16in diameter were fitted with Dunlop SP2000 225/53 ZR16 tyres, and were ideally suited to the slightly stiffer and sporty suspension of the XJ12 which also became an extra cost option on other XJ40 models.

In contrast, the Daimler Double Six was not a car designed for the sporting motorist so it was offered as standard with the softer ride suspension package. Cast alloy wheels, 7in x 15in, were fitted to this model, with Pirelli P4000 tyres.

The new V12 engine

The heart of the new models was, of course, the well-known V12 power unit, the capacity of which had been enlarged to 5,995cc, achieved by increasing the stroke from 70mm to 78.5mm, the bore remaining unchanged at 90mm. This longer stroke gave an increase in power and particularly a gain in mid-range torque.

A revised, cylinder head with new 'flat top' pistons, reduced compression ratio, new cylinder liners, inlet valves and camshaft profile, added valve train refinement, while a new forged-steel crankshaft and new hydraulic engine mounts, were all part of the new V12 package for the XJ40. The one downside to all these changes was a slight increase in weight of 1kg over the 5.3-litre engine.

There were many other changes to enhance the V12 further. A new low-loss catalyst system was fitted, with a twin-in-tank fuel pump system, a beefy starter motor, improved alternator and a Lucas Marelli engine

The 6.0-litre version of the Jaguar V12 engine, as installed in the XJ40.

> **DID YOU KNOW?**
>
> **Rent-a-Jag**
> Jaguar received their biggest ever order from a single customer for saloons during the XJ40 period. A total of 500 XJ6s were supplied in 1992/3 to the Budget Rent-a-Car Group in the USA, a total value of $25 million (£17 million). This was followed by another 110 cars for the UK and European operations in 1994, comprising XJ6, 3.2, Gold and S models.

management system, all playing their part in enhancing the engine. The air conditioning also came in for revision with a new, compact compressor fitted to the engine which also had the knock-on effect of improving serviceability, not least in the changing of the front spark plugs.

Even the under-bonnet appearance of the daunting V12 engine had been tidied up with a cosmetic cover to the top of the engine. It did look better but underneath the cover it was the same old V12 with its complex array of leads and cables!

The V12 had lost a lot of its 'urge' over the years with many changes, some due to emissions legislation. The new, 6.0-litre variant for the XJ40 (also to find its way into the XJS) was to put a lot of that punch back. Improved standing start performance with better mid-range response and a slight improvement in fuel economy, all paid tribute to an engine which stemmed from 1971 and was still competitive in 1993.

A new transmission

The 6.0-litre engine was mated to an entirely new automatic transmission, the larger General Motors GM.4L80E although it used the same gear train as its predecessor.

For the new gearbox GM had fitted an additional set of gears to provide a fourth, overdrive ratio along with a new low inertia torque converter with a lock-up clutch for added economy and improved take-off from rest. The box had both 'Sport' and 'Normal' modes with a winter or first gear inhibit mode combined with the latter. This meant that in Normal the car would always start in second gear unless the throttle was opened fully.

The transmission intelligently interacted with the Marelli engine management system to trigger a reduction in engine torque during shifts which

Fat wheels and tyres, a gold grille badge, black vanes and the more aggressive look of four conventional round headlights identified the XJ12 from six-cylinder models.

enhanced the refinement of the gear changes.

The V12-engined cars were tested extensively, both in the UK at the MIRA circuit and on the Nardo circuit in Southern Italy.

Both Jaguar and Daimler models were equipped with a limited slip differential as standard with a change of axle ratio from 2.88:1 to 3.58:1 allowing for quicker downshift response and improved mid-range performance.

Only the badges and the new style of wheels differentiated the Double Six from the six-cylinder Daimler models. The E post finisher separating the roof from the rear wing is now body colour on all cars.

The similarities and differences between the XJ12 and Double Six models. Here, the Daimler features the usual seat trim but a higher standard of specification included a CD player and leather trim to the handbrake handle and gear lever surround.

The revitalisation years – 1993 to 1994

In comparison, the XJ12 still had black vinyl-covered handbrake and gear lever surround and the usual Sovereign style seating.

This is the later style of Daimler seating as also used on the Double Six with stiffer bolsters. The button at the base corner of the seat is for lumber support control.

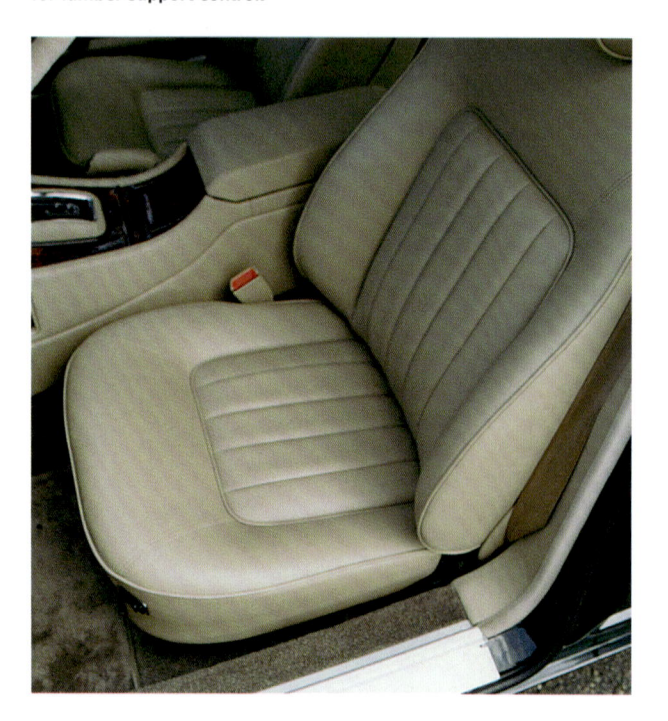

Although all Daimlers came as standard with the individualised rear seating arrangement, it was possible (for an extra £250) to order your Daimler with a conventional bench-type rear seat.

The impressive sight of the V12 engine installation in the XJ40. Some cleaning up of the appearance had taken place by this time.

Performance comparisons of Jaguar XJ12 models

	Series 3 XJ12	XJ40 XJ12	Daimler Double Six 6.0
BHP	260	318	318
@ rpm	5,250	5,400	5,400
Maximum torque	279lb ft	342lb ft	342lb ft
@ rpm	2,750	3,750	3,750
0 to 60mph	8.9sec	6.8sec	6.9sec
0 to 100mph	23.3sec	16.5sec	16.9sec
Maximum speed	139mph	155mph	155mph
Average fuel mpg	17.9	18.4	18.4

If there was just one disappointing feature of the V12s it came with the noise level. More so than on the Series 3 models; much of this was down to the induction system.

Cosmetic changes

Lots of subtle changes were made to the interior and exterior to differentiate the V12s from the six-cylinder cars. In this instance we will treat the Jaguar XJ12 separately from the Daimler Double Six.

The XJ12 was in essence a sporting model with stiffer suspension and ride, fatter wheels and tyres and was further emphasised by the use of the four-headlamp treatment, even though the equipment levels of the car were to Sovereign specification.

Sporting emphasis was given to the car with the black-painted radiator grille vanes and the Sports Handling Pack (with the lattice wheels and tyres) gave the car a slightly lower stance than normal. A gold growler badge adorned the grille top and the alloy wheel centres, and of course, an XJ12 badge appeared on the boot lid.

Internally, the V12 was no different from the six-cylinder Sovereign models except for a revised instrument pack with amended legends and the V12 legend prominent in the veneer of the glove box lid.

For the Daimler Double Six differences between it and the Six were even more subtle. In fact, externally there were no differences except for the gold 'D' on the grille, the Double Six badge at the rear and the 38-spoke alloys. Internally, all was as before except for the use as standard equipment of Autolux leather, a matching leather gearknob, surround and handbrake grip and a CD player, also fitted as standard, as was the revised rev counter legend and the V12 legend on the dashboard.

Perhaps surprisingly, Jaguar at the time anticipated that around 75 per cent of all V12 sales would come

A still taken from Jaguar's TV advert of 1992/93.

from the Daimler model although this did not turn out to be the case.

Jaguar XJ12 production comparisons

XJ12 Series 1	1972 to 1973	4,113
XJ12 Series 2	1973 to 1979	22,606
XJ12 Series 3	1979 to 1991	25,491
XJ12 (XJ40)	1993 to 1994	2,814
Daimler Double Six Series 1	1972 to 1973	885
Daimler Double Six Series 2	1973 to 1979	4,334
Daimler Double Six Series 3	1979 to 1992	10,039
Daimler Double Six (XJ40)	1993 to 1994	985

XJ40 price comparisons

Jaguar XJ12	£46,600
Daimler Double Six	£51,700
Jaguar Sovereign 4.0-litre	£37,800
Daimler 4.0-litre	£44,200

Right from the start the XJ12 was aimed at a different market from the existing XJ40 models, a class act against the onslaught of BMW and Mercedes who by now had dominated this end of the market. In the USA, where the V12 would also be sold, there had not been an XJ12 since the late Series 3 XJ days so Jaguar were expecting good things now. Targets, however, had been set reasonably at a modest 3,000 cars sold worldwide in the first year, compared with 6,000 Series 3 V12s sold in 1991 (Jaguar and Daimler).

TV promotion

Initially introduced on 7 December 1992, Jaguar was in the spotlight with a return to television advertising in the UK after a break of something like 12 years. They spent £2 million to develop the ad as part of an aggressive new promotional campaign for all models, but specifically for the XJ40, not the least of which to benefit would be the 'new' V12 models.

'What are dreams for if not to come true' was the slogan behind the advert which was also backed up by a major campaign of media advertising elsewhere. The TV ad strategically shown just before the ITV *News at Ten* programme with a shortened version during the commercial break, featured a young boy with a love of Jaguar's epitomised by a 1960s Mark 2 and dreaming of owning one 'one day', with the XJ40 turning up driven by him as a man later in life.

A measure of Jaguar's success with the XJ40 (and XJS) was its continued climb in the US customer satisfaction stakes. From a position of 25th in 1991, to 10th in 1992 and then up to 9th position for 1993.

Later in 1993, the Department of Transport in the UK issued a *Buying a Car, Choose Safety* booklet and in their statistical ranking tables of cars, the XJ40 came out tops in the executive/luxury sector against the BMW 5 Series and Mercedes W123.

What Car? review

In February 1993, the British *What Car?* magazine carried out a major analysis of the Jaguar XJ40 model range and their conclusions make interesting reading:

'Jaguars are better made and equipped than ever before. The cheaper models, particularly the XJ6s also offer a lot of performance and equipment compared with their rivals. With their three-year warranties, security systems and safety air bags – not to mention their slowly firming second-hand values – they offer private motorists good value.

'But can they cut it against the Germans? We say they can. A Jaguar is not a uniformly modern product like a BMW 5 Series, but if correctly specified it gives away little in dynamics or refinement.

Above all, it has a uniquely attractive character and history. We believe buyers can now afford to be swayed by that, knowing that there is no significant downside.'

They identified no less than 14 competitive rivals to the manual transmission 3.2, five of them hatchbacks with offerings from BMW, Mercedes, Alfa Romeo, Audi, Honda, Rover, Saab, Vauxhall, Volvo, Citroën, Ford and even Renault in this price bracket. Although they didn't come up with a definitive answer as to the best car, they did say:

'The '93 Jaguar model range is the best ever and we reckon you can buy one of these cars without compromising your expectations of build quality, ride refinement and performance in this class. But before you put your hand on your wallet, pause, and take a look at your options. You've got the best of the European car makers clamouring for your attention, offering you some of the world's finest cars. You can afford to be choosy.'

Jaguar had achieved their aims in producing the best Jaguars yet but competition was hotting up from all directions.

A new threshold model

It was to be a momentous time for the XJ40 in 1993, not only because of the V12 but also because another new model was to find its way into the showrooms. The Jaguar marque had long been associated with the company chairman image or more vividly, the 'old man's car'. Already the likes of BMW were taking younger drivers away from Jaguar and the image of the XJ40 and its range content, emulated the older car driver.

That was to change from April 1993 when, at the Fleet Motor Show held at Silverstone, a new, more youthful variant of the XJ40 was announced – the 3.2-litre S model (standing for Sport). The principle being to offer a model at a very attractive retail price which had tauter handling and control with a more youthful exterior and interior finish. By offering a good standard of equipment with a limited range of colour schemes, this new model, Jaguar hoped, would captivate a younger generation and ultimately, longer term, Jaguar customers.

Daimler Double Six, the most expensive UK XJ40 variant.

The new model was instantly recognisable from the outside by a number of subtle but positive changes. Colour-keying was the most effective change, the radiator grille vanes, headlamp surrounds, door mirrors and front valance were all matched to the exterior paintwork of the body. The growler on the grille was painted silver to further differentiate this model from the others. The four headlamp treatment also provided more of a sporty look to the front just as it did to the XJ12.

From the side the 3.2 S was akin to the XJ6 except that it featured twin coachlines and the '3.2 S' motif to the lower swage line as well as the conventional single gold coachline just below the door handles. The car was fitted with new, 7in x 16in five-spoke cast alloy wheels with lower profile Pirelli P4000 225/60 ZR 16 tyres. The wheels could either be finished in eggshell or silver, dependent on the customer's choice of body colour. The wheel centres featured the growler image in silver on a red background.

At the rear there was either red or grey neutral density light units, dependent on body colour, and the car featured a plastic in-fill panel on the boot lid bringing the panel out flush with the rear light units to which the number plate was attached. Painted to body colour this panel also contained the '3.2 S' badge.

The 3.2 S model was only available in the following exterior paint colours:

Flamenco Red
British Racing Green
Kingfisher Blue
Silver Frost
Diamond Blue
Black

The interior was adapted to create a more youthful image although it was essentially of the same design as the other models. The layout was the same, but the walnut veneer of the traditional models was replaced with rosewood-stained maple with matching gearlever knob. The dashboard top roll and door tops were colour-keyed to the seat trim along with the handbrake grip and the gearchange surround.

Seat facings were unique to the S with horizontal centre flutes in embossed leather with a mulberry colour seat stitching. This contrast stitching was also carried on to the carpets and centre console area as well. Cloth trimming in the same style was available at no extra cost.

Interior colour schemes were limited to:

Magnolia
Doeskin
Savile Grey

The 3.2 S (and later 4.0 S) models were aimed at a younger market. A limited range of colour schemes with colour coding, new wheels and badging helped a little in creating a more youthful image for the XJ40.

Changes for the interior of the S models amounted to a different style of seat finish, rosewood woodwork and little touches like the matching gearknob.

These were combined with barley, doeskin or mid grey facia and ruby or grey carpeting.

The sporting nature of the car's image was emphasised for the driver by a special Sports Handling Pack with uprated dampers and anti-roll bar stiffening up the suspension somewhat, helped by the low-profile tyres.

Automatic transmission was standard although the Getrag five-speed manual gearbox was available to special order at no extra cost. Other standard equipment features included leather upholstery, front fog lamps and metallic paint, all for £28,450. This model was only available on the UK market.

The UK range and prices changed again and in mid-1993 after the launch of the 3.2 S, it consisted of the following in price-ranked order:

XJ6 3.2-litre saloon	£26,200
XJ6 3.2 S saloon	£28,450
XJ6 4.0-litre saloon	£28,950
Sovereign 3.2-litre saloon	£34,550
Majestic 3.2-litre lwb saloon	£34,700
Majestic 4.0-litre lwb saloon	£37,450
Sovereign 4.0-litre saloon	£37,800
XJR 4.0-litre saloon	£42,000
Majestic 3.2-litre Sov lwb saloon	£43,050
Daimler 4.0-litre saloon	£44,200
Majestic 4.0-litre Sov lwb saloon	£46,300
XJ12 saloon	£46,600
Daimler Double Six saloon	£51,700
Daimler Majestic 4.0-litre lwb saloon	£52,700

The inclusion of Majestic models should not be confused with those of the special edition US market car mentioned earlier. These were special, longer wheelbase models produced to order by the factory, details of which are given in a later chapter.

1994 model year

Jaguar announced that all models for the 1994 model years would carry a brand-new feature, a front passenger air bag. They became one of the first companies to offer this facility as standard equipment

In colours like the new Flamenco Red, the XJ6 S was very appealing, as Jaguar's sales brochure shows.

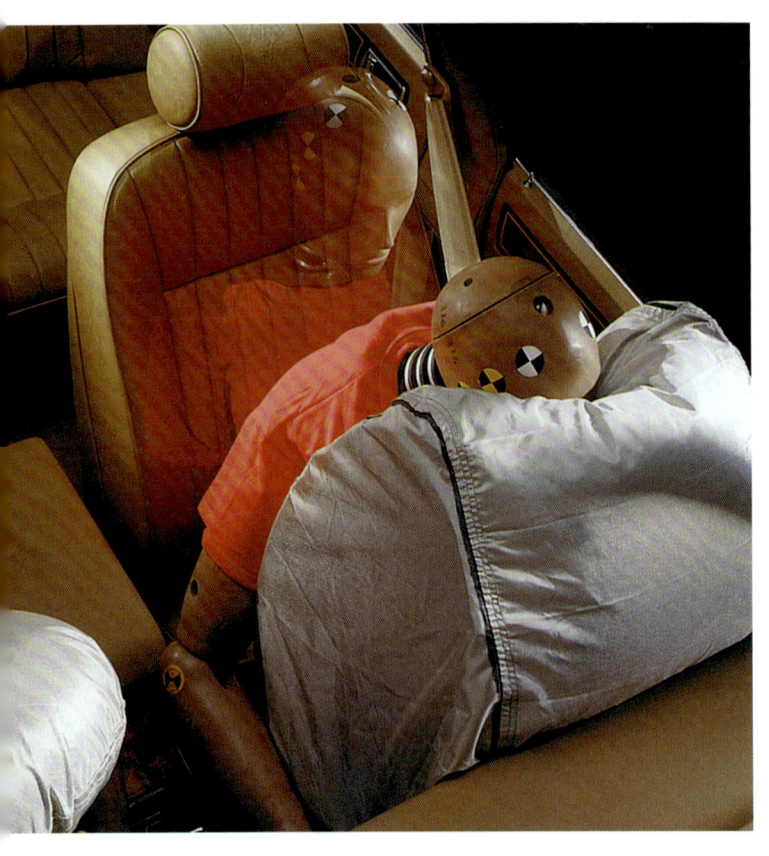

The provision of a passenger air bag on the XJ40 moved the car forward again in technology terms even if, at the time, it caused a great deal of work for Jaguar to instigate effectively.

(along with Ford) and rode on the back of their successful launch of the driver's air bag earlier.

A significant amount of redevelopment had to take place yet again to accommodate this feature and the major change made to the XJ40 cars aesthetically was the deletion of the glove box arrangement, the air bag and mechanism taking priority in this space with a sealed wood fillet carrying the legend 'SRS' (supplementary restraint system).

Some at Jaguar were concerned at the loss of this feature as the XJ40 had never been well known for its minor stowage facilities, but it was felt the safety aspect would be a major promotional feature for the car.

Hot on the heels of the new 3.2 S model, Jaguar announced a 4.0 S version with the same stiffened suspension and colour-keyed trim. The price of the 4.0-litre-engined model was nearly £5,000 dearer but it was otherwise exactly the same car as the smaller engined version.

To compensate for yet another new model, something had to go and from the range went the base 4.0-litre XJ6 and the smaller engined Sovereign model, although the 3.2-litre XJ6 remained, now priced at £27,350. It was considered important to have this inexpensive entry model still on the stocks.

For the remaining models it was a case of ringing the changes and enhancing the specification for 1994, to further complicate the range at this time! Starting with all the 4.0-litre models they gained 16in alloy wheels of a new Kiwi style with brushed finish as standard equipment with Pirelli P4000 225/60 ZR16 tyres on the Sovereign (but optional on the 3.2-litre models). Dunlop SP2000 225/55 ZR16 were from then on fitted to the XJ12 and on the 3.2 S both Daimler models had 7in rims with Pirelli P4000 225/60/ZR16 tyres.

All cars now had a space-saver spare wheel as standard equipment of size 3.5in x 18in with 115/85 R18 tyres, although you could still specify a full-size wheel and tyre at extra cost, which in reality, most cars ended up with.

The Sports Handling Pack was now available for most models, including the Daimler Double Six. This comprised a larger diameter front anti-roll bar, uprated front and rear springs and dampers, although retaining 7in wheels. In contrast, perhaps due to complaints about a harsh ride, the XJ12, became available to special order at no extra cost with the 'comfort' softer suspension package, and 7in wheel rims.

Cosmetic changes started to appear on some models such as the black-painted window frames on XJ12 models replacing chrome and black centre and rear door posts on this and the 3.2-litre XJ6. The base 3.2 model now also had grey-painted radiator grille vanes.

Both the S models carried their own unique badging and colour co-ordinated flush boot panel.

The earlier chrome additions to the rear end styling (which started with the 4.0-litre Sovereign) altered from model to model and car to car. Sovereigns, for example, temporarily 'lost' the chrome strip above and below the numberplate, on some cars one or the other appeared and on others they both came back. This may well have been down to a supply problem at the time more than any deliberate policy.

Jaguar XJ12 models also gained new-style 20-spoke alloy wheels and both the Daimler models had the same seven-vaned alloys as standard equipment. A new exterior paint colour of Rose Bronze metallic replaced the Meteor Red colour.

A few of these very late XJ40 models also had another revised flush-mounted side indicator repeater light on the front wing, not dissimilar to the later X-300 style.

Internally, there were also trim changes with revised steering wheel stalks that had the same operation as before but were better shaped and their position was raised by about 15mm for ease of use. Improved security came with flush-fitting locking buttons on all the doors.

An electrochromic automatically dimming rear view mirror was now available as standard equipment on all models except the XJ6 3.2, 3.2 S and 4.0 S. For convenience, a cup holder could now be incorporated in the centre console glove box lid which could be ordered, although not when a fitted mobile phone was specified.

A new, ruched style of seat with curved base and squab was available as a cost option with Autolux leather on Daimler models only, and the upper interior trim areas were now colour keyed to the facia which had already been made standard on the Double Six

The very late XJ40 models also had another revised flush-mounted side indicator repeater light on the front wing, not dissimilar to the later X-300 style.

model. Lastly, XJ12 models had their own, unique door sill treadplate design.

On the convenience side two-position check straps were fitted to all doors which allowed them to be

The revised look of the very late Sovereign models, with their distinctive alloy wheels.

The revitalisation years – 1993 to 1994

Very late model Daimlers had the cost option of this new style of seating which also included cup holders in the front centre console armrest, and there was a 'tilt' sunroof available if required.

The later style of six-cylinder engine with oil filler cap moved to the camshaft cover.

retained in a partly open position when parked close to other vehicles. The door sealing was improved to cut down wind noise.

Minor mechanical changes also took place. On AJ6-engined models a new style of camshaft cover incorporated the oil filler cap, an integral crankcase breather system for improved breather performance, and 13-bolt fixing for better sealing. Also, a new, one-piece cast inlet manifold was used with integral ram pipes, water heater breather restrictor and one thin layer gasket.

For the V12 engines revised hydraulic engine mounts were used to improve refinement while a cam action throttle cable pulley was introduced for improved throttle progression and pedal feel.

Three electrical plug sockets were fitted from the 1994 model year. One was in the boot, another under the facia and the third in the engine bay. This allowed the easier fitment of Jaguar approved accessories. A radio telephone harness was also now available from the factory when required as an extra cost option.

More changes for the US market saw the XJ6 4.0-litre appear with black-vaned radiator grille, the Vanden Plas 4.0-litre (still sporting the Daimler flutes) and new to the USA, the XJ12, in all but name and flutes, a Daimler Double Six.

Prices of XJ40 models for the revised range in the UK for 1994 were:

XJ6 3.2-litre saloon	£27,350
XJ6 3.2 S saloon	£28,950
XJ6 4.0 S saloon	£33,700
Sovereign 4.0-litre saloon	£39,800
Daimler 4.0-litre saloon	£46,700
XJR 4.0-litre saloon	£43,800
XJ12 saloon	£48,800
Daimler Double Six saloon	£54,000

The special, long-wheelbase Majestic models (detailed in the next chapter) were not listed but warranted a mention in various brochures as they were still available at this time to special order.

A new production line

During the traditional August summer holiday factory shutdown, the Jaguar Browns Lane assembly plant underwent an £8.5 million refit involving completely stripping out the old assembly lines in favour of a new, overhead conveyor system, all in just three weeks.

The new single-track (as opposed to twin-track)

system provided more space at the side of the track to work, providing greater efficiency and safety along with other economies. A 25 per cent increase in build numbers could be accommodated.

The principle of the new assembly system involved the painted bodies arriving as normal, but at which time the doors were removed to another allied assembly area while the bodies were mounted on overhead cradles, part of a continuous 1km long conveyor. A total of 197 body cradles carried the cars along the line during normal assembly and midway the bodies joined the complete power train in one operation this being raised to meet the body. At the end of normal assembly the doors which had been independently assembled with their trim, electrics and fittings, rejoined the bodies. With this new method of assembly all 1994 model year XJ40s were fitted with a revised, demountable door hinge system.

Examples of the 1994 US-spec XJ40s; on the left is the XJ6 and to the right the XJ12. There was still also a 4.0-litre Vanden Plas (Daimler!).

The official handover of one of the XJ40s by Nick Scheele to Peter Giamakva, vice president of Budget Rent-a-Car.

The revitalisation years — 1993 to 1994

A new assembly line late on in XJ40 production necessitated some changes to the bodyshell, all of which were really meant for a forthcoming brand-new model.

Owner running costs down

With improved efficiencies and quality control, Jaguar was also able to offer 1994 customers an extended 10,000-mile or 12-month service interval on all models. This had the potential to reduce owner operating costs by up to 22 per cent during an average 60,000-mile, three-year ownership, during which the car was still under full factory warranty.

Another 2,500 miles to travel between services was one enhancement, but another was that there was actually less to do when the car did need servicing. On a new car, the traditional 1,000-mile service was also eliminated.

Although sales were still doing very well abroad, with increases of 43 per cent shown over the previous year in the US, 100 per cent increase in Singapore, 40 per cent in New Zealand and 55 per cent in Sweden, plus the opening of a new subsidiary, Jaguar China, with 40 cars sold in that year, back in the UK the net increase, despite new models, was only 11 per cent. News of an impending, entirely new model (coded X-300) abounded even though it wouldn't be launched until the motor show of 1994, but this must have had an effect on XJ40 sales.

In view of this, Jaguar decided to strike back and took the decision to offer new car customers buying a car between October and December 1993 two years or 40,000 miles free maintenance, the only things payable being consumables such as fluids, tyres, etc. By the start of 1994, the company expanded this offer to all cars sold during that year as well.

Jaguar was by now, claiming the most comprehensive warranty and service package available from anyone in the world, which on XJ40s at this time, meant:

60,000 miles/three years mechanical and electrical warranty.
10,000-mile service intervals.
RAC 24-hour rescue service with home start, vehicle recovery, loan car, hotel accommodation, etc. included.
Full mondial European emergency assistance.
Three-year unlimited mileage paint and surface warranty.
Six-year unlimited mileage corrosion (perforation) warranty.
40,000 miles or twice yearly free servicing on cars purchased between 20 October and 31 December 1993.
The aspect of reduced running costs echoing Jaguar's longevity and quality was also addressed in the USA where the Lexus had made such an impact. Announced in 1993 was the Royal Charter Care Scheme. This provided for a comprehensive four-year, 50,000-mile warranty with other benefits including RAC membership in the UK.
As a further incentive in early 1994, Jaguar announced the Privilege Contract Purchase Scheme, available only through the franchised dealerships. This combined low monthly payments and guaranteed residual values with the three-year warranty and two-year free scheduled servicing plan. Using the entry level XJ6 3.2-litre saloon as an example, and provided you didn't exceed 10,000 miles a year, you would pay just £238 per month, the only other things to pay for being insurance, road tax, tyres and other normal forecourt costs.
At the end of the scheme the customer had three options:
1. Buy the vehicle at a guaranteed value.
2. Hand the car back and walk away with no further liability.
3. If the car was worth more than the guaranteed residual value, the customer received a cheque for the difference to use as a full or partial deposit on another Jaguar.

A variant of this scheme is still used today by Jaguar dealers.

XJ40 goes Gold

Yet another XJ40 model entered the arena early in 1994, the XJ6 Gold as it was known. Jaguar were looking to boost their entry level range and were keen to promote the fact that with the new Gold model they had no less than three options in the under-£30,000 price bracket. Aimed at the 'limited edition' market the Gold represented excellent value for money as an integrated package for just £28,950, or only £2,000 dearer than the standard XJ6, but offering a much higher specification.

That higher specification was based on the 3.2-litre-engined car but featured leather trim, burr walnut veneer, automatic transmission and alloy wheels, all in the price.

A unique flute seat styling to the leather-faced seats was adopted with gearshift surround and handbrake grip to match the interior colour. Facia and door cappings were also colour keyed to the rest of the interior. Mechanically, the Gold, only available with the 3.2-litre engine, was a standard XJ6.

Externally, the Gold was identified by its 16in Kiwi alloy wheels, gold on black wheel centres and bootlid

The very last variant of the XJ40 was the Gold which was marketed at a strategically low price to encourage sales.

badging, gold radiator grille badge and twin gold coachlines running along the side of the car. All Gold models were painted in a range limited to seven colours including a new micatallic Sapphire Blue finish.

The cost price of £28,950 was pitched strategically to undercut the then current BMW 730i and Mercedes E280 by around £2,000.

The total range had been slightly reduced by this time and amounted to the following, in price-ranked order:

XJ6 3.2-litre saloon	£26,950
XJ6 Gold saloon	£28,950
XJ6 3.2 S saloon	£29,950
XJ6 4.0 S saloon	£34,950
Sovereign 4.0-litre saloon	£41,400
Daimler 4.0-litre saloon	£48,600
XJR 4.0-litre saloon	£45,600
XJ12 saloon	£49,950
Daimler Double Six saloon	£56,200

The revitalisation years – 1993 to 1994

The Gold models incorporated features seen on other models, but with different seat pleating yet again.

Jaguar's position in the market place was good although they were still having problems encouraging the younger, more affluent drivers to get into their cars. If we take the Gold or the XJ6 3.2-litre model as an example, in the region of £27,000 to £29,000 what else could you buy in 1994?

Citroën XM V6	£27,390
Rover 800 Sterling	£27,994
BMW 525i SEX	£28,120
Alfa Romeo 164 Cloverleaf	£28,400
Saab 9000 CDE Turbo	£28,795
Peugeot 605	£28,865
Mercedes-Benz 280E	£28,950
Ford Granada Scorpio 2.9	£28,900

Compare the performance, equipment levels and prestige and this list soon shortens and shows that Jaguar's thoughts of marketing at the time were not too far short of the requirement. It just needed another body style to meet the demands of some younger buyers although the company still struggled in this area until the launch of models like the S-type and X-type.

Later press comments

The XJ40 had received some excellent press over the years and the cars were still being tested at the end of 1993 and into 1994. By this time things had moved on, newer cars from the competition had been launched and it would appear that the media's reaction to the Forty at this stage was dulling.

Car magazine, for instance, had a 3.2-litre XJ40 on long-term assessment, covering a total of 37,000 miles in less than two years. Although very happy with the car right from the start they noticed the engine to be rough when pushed hard when compared with the opposition. From 7,000 miles on problems started to occur such as the gearshift which needed pushing into 'P' to allow the engine to start, something that was never fixed completely.

After the 15,000-mile service, the very same day a lambda exhaust sensor failed causing the engine to stall. At 18,000 miles the rear self-levelling system failed when a valve stuck. This had gone wrong again by the 22,500-mile service. Just after this the steering became 'stodgey', resulting in the pump being changed and the interior trim started to suffer, the carpet on the centre console was peeling and the plastic trim panel below the glovebox (covering some of the electronics) had come loose.

In only another couple of hundred miles the

indicators and hazard lights stopped working and the brake warning light and buzzer came on, which turned out to be a faulty microprocessor. Despite replacement, the same happened a couple of days later, but soon extinguished itself although this problem appeared again momentarily throughout the life of the car.

By 27,000 miles the steering was playing up again, the ride height had stopped working again and the heating system didn't. Before the expensive, 30,000-mile service, one of the rear door locks had failed and the aerial was sticking. Apart from several bulb failures along the way, the car remained healthy and reliable for the rest of the 23 months.

Good comments were that it was a special driving experience and all those who drove the car considered to wax lyrical over it. The downside however was lack of room, both for the driver and in the boot, and the maintenance costs over the period. During the 23 months it had cost £1,452 in servicing, £337 in tyres, and had depreciated in value by £15,590.

Probably one of the last road tests for the XJ40 came in February 1994 when *Autocar and Motor* compared the 4.0-litre S model with the Mercedes S280. Overall, their comments covered the poor accommodation in the Jag compared with the Merc, and the better build quality of the latter, but their final sentence read: 'The Jag, with its tautness and power, is the logical choice for press-on drivers.'

The end of the line

Although there had been an exceptionally busy period of model development and revision since 1993, with the S models, the V12s and then the Gold as late as March 1994, the end was in sight for the XJ40. By mid year trial production had already started of the model's successor, coded X-300, and final assembly of the XJ40 was planned for June. The installation of the new production line at Browns Lane earlier, of which the XJ40 had taken advantage, was really done to produce the new model. If the XJ40 line could be shut down during the summer break, all would be made ready to build the brand-new XJ, with stock available for the important UK motor show in October.

So it was that in June the very last XJ40, a Solent Blue 4.0-litre Sovereign with all the extras they could muster, was prepared and officially handed over to the Jaguar Daimler Heritage Trust, a car they keep today as a tribute to the XJ40 and the revival of Jaguar.

The model name was, as we know, to carry on – the XJ6 (XJ40) was dead; enter the XJ6 (X-300).

The very last XJ40 left the line and was presented to the Jaguar Daimler Heritage Trust by Nick Scheele on the right (chairman and chief executive of Jaguar at the time), and Richard Hudson (manufacturing director at Browns Lane).

Nick Scheele, chairman and chief executive of Jaguar Cars during the later years of the XJ40, a man appointed by Ford, but who had Jaguar in his heart.

The revitalisation years – 1993 to 1994   93

Chapter **Eight**

Variations on a theme

The XJ40 became Jaguar's most prolific and popular model up to that time. It was inevitable that there would be variants produced by Jaguar and outside companies to enhance its popularity and build interest. Perhaps in this respect, the XJ40 is almost unique as only the XJ-S appeared to attract more attention in this area.

The following cars give an indication of the depth of work carried out on the XJ40 in-house by Jaguar, and by outside specialist companies.

PS models

The UK market for police-specified vehicles had been important to Jaguar for many years. Right from the start of the XJ40 story a Police Specification prototype model had been built, shown around and had then become available for demonstration to many forces across the UK. Jaguar even arranged three special demonstration days for the UK forces at the Gaydon Technology Test Track in Warwickshire. Within months orders were placed and we began to see the familiar sight of the XJ6 'jam sandwich' on our roads and motorways.

A number of cars were specially prepared for police use, all carrying the PS insignia, equipped with Police radio, Vascar radar system, special lighting, luminous side flashes, etc. Many cars were subsequently issued to the Police, among them some literally going out as standard equipment models, others substantially modified.

Some of the common modifications included the

A typical red and white XJ40 as used by UK police forces; this one is seen on the M6 motorway in the Midlands.

94　Jaguar XJ40

Here is a different approach to Police livery, on this 1990 car. This particular example also sported a manual transmission, plastic upholstery and rubber matting instead of carpets.

fitting of rubber matting, replacing carpets and black vinyl panels to the doors and other trim areas. This was not only cheaper but more durable considering the extensive use to which the cars were subjected. Dashboards were adapted with or without veneer to accommodate the specialist equipment demanded of a modern police force, there was cloth seating and, in some cases, uprated suspension and steering.

The theme of Police Specification cars continued with the later 4.0-litre models, some even being supplied in XJR state of tune and others provided in standard colours for official use by chief constables and the like. It was also not uncommon to find that cars initially supplied for chauffeur use (such as chief constables) would later be downgraded to traffic use.

Although several forces took up the option to buy

Some police cars, like this ex-demonstrator, found a new lease of life as a fire tender, in this case for the Donington circuit in Leicestershire, and was later fitted with an XJR body kit and wheels.

Variations on a theme **95**

XJ40 models, in real terms Jaguar had lost a lot of ground to other manufacturers, not least because of the excessive cost of purchase and running compared with the smaller BMWs, Volvos, etc. The XJ40 was also hampered by its limited boot space which, in some cases, resulted in even spare wheels not being carried!

Janspeed

Janspeed, well-established engine specialists from Salisbury in Wiltshire, introduced a Janspeed version of the XJ40 at the 1987 British motor show (the Motor Fair) with a view to production starting in 1988.

Janspeed took a standard XJ6, stripped the engine down and rebuilt it employing high grade, low compression Jaguar pistons. The standard ignition and injection equipment was replaced by fully mapped Zytek digital systems featuring sequential injection.

The engines were then turbo-charged with two Roto-Master RM60 watercooled turbo-chargers, regulated by Rajay modular wastegates pre-set at 7psi and mounted on specially made stainless steel exhaust manifolds. The compressed air, cooled by two purpose-designed, high capacity air-to-air intercoolers, fed the standard induction plenum chamber. The cooling system was modified substantially. The original exhaust system, however, was retained from the turbine downpipes backwards and in consequence the modified car suffered very little apparent noise penalty. Janspeed claimed that normal service frequency and work was all that was required with their modified cars.

In turbo-charged form the engines produced 293bhp at 5,000rpm. Performance resulted in a significant leap forward compared with the standard 3.6-litre production car. A 0 to 60mph time of under six seconds was claimed (which compared favourable with say a Ferrari Testarossa) and a maximum speed of 150mph, comparable to the old E-type. They also claimed fuel consumption was not hampered, in fact, at an average of 23.5mpg in their tests it must be considered remarkable.

It appears that only about five or six of these cars were produced, at least one of which was a Daimler model. Interior and exterior changes were carried out to personal taste but it appears that mostly they were pretty standard, save for the fitting of a special Janspeed leather-covered steering wheel of smaller dimension. All the cars featured Janpseed badging on the steering wheel, dashboard, B/C exterior posts and boot lid. At least three of the cars were painted black and one was fitted with wider, lattice wheels and tyres as wel as a body-coloured exterior trim.

One of the specialist turbo conversions carried out by Janspeed on the XJ40 earlier in the model's life.

The price of the conversion to an existing car was about £6,500 plus VAT in 1988. One other car (an XJ-S) was apparently converted, but the demand was not there at the time.

XJR 3.6-litre Sports saloon

JaguarSport was a joint organisation set up by Jaguar Cars Limited and TWR (Tom Walkinshaw Racing) with the principles of producing modified versions of existing production cars and developing new ideas, all of which would enhance Jaguar's position in the market place, particularly for the younger driver, as Jaguar had unfortunately developed an image of traditional club comfort instead of sporty, trendy motoring.

TWR had produced some cars themselves under the name JaguarSport earlier, in particular XJ-S Coupés and a few XJ40s. Basically to similar specification as the later factory-sponsored JaguarSport models, they were finished in two-tone paintwork. It was after this that the organisation was to become more involved with mainstream production cars, working with Jaguar.

For the National Motor Show in Birmingham, England in 1988, the joint company announced its first project, the XJR 3.6-litre Sports saloon. The car was always intended for UK sales only, probably due to legislation in other countries such as the USA, and sales were initially handled by only 20 Jaguar dealerships, although this was later expanded.

The basis behind the model was to offer a more sporting alternative that would look sufficiently different, and perform and handle better, but at the same time, would not affect normal factory warranties and service requirements.

A typical Janspeed installation showing the revised manifolding required.

Bodily, the car looked more modified than it actually was. Front and rear bumpers were changed for a new design, colour keyed to the rest of the exterior paintwork. Colour-keyed glass-fibre sculptured oversills were fitted along with a neat boot spoiler, also in glass-fibre; all this to create a more aerodynamic and sporty package. Door mirrors were also colour keyed and although initially the car was to be based on the Sovereign, chromed window framed-model, later

This is the early XJR model, based on the 3.6-litre-engined car. In practice, most of the models produced had matt black-painted window surrounds.

Variations on a theme 97

The one-off XJ40 Coupé, devised by Jaguar's Special Vehicle Operations Department.

models turned out with matt black finish like the XJ6 saloons. Similarly, the four-headlamp treatment of the XJ6 was adopted as it was felt to be more in keeping with the sporty look of the car, but incorporated a power wash system as standard. To finish the vertical radiator grille, slats were painted matt black.

To complement the sporty aspects of the style and to meet the demands of better handling, a new style JaguarSport Speedline 16in diameter alloy wheel was fitted shod with Pirelli P600 225/55/ZR speed-rated tyres.

The suspension system was uprated to enhance the handling characteristics and featured special dampers and an uprated anti-roll bar. In addition, the power-assisted steering was modified with harder bushes to provide greater feel and responsiveness for the driving enthusiast, and the cars were equipped with a limited slip differential. There were no plans at this stage to upgrade other aspects of the mechanics, including the engine, some of which would come later, by special request from owners.

The interior was also given the JaguarSport treatment with revised-style leather seating in a choice of two colours with contrast colour piping and the 'Sport' motif embossed on the headrest centre panels. Leather was now carried over to the door pockets and armrests with a special JaguarSport colour-keyed four-spoke Momo steering wheel fitted to match the interior colour scheme. The door casings were of the Daimler style and trimmed in the same leather. The only additional cost extras you could buy for the car were an electric sliding sunroof and heated front seats.

The new XJR came in a limited range of four exterior paint finishes: Solent Blue, Arctic Blue, Alpine Green and Tungsten Grey, with either magnolia or doeskin upholstery.

XJR 4.0-litre saloon

It was only natural that once Jaguar had introduced the 4.0-litre engine in the XJ40, that JaguarSport would follow with the XJR version, which was still only available in the UK market at a cost of £39,450.

JaguarSport had worked closely with the Browns Lane engineers to enhance the 4.0-litre engine further, so for the first time, the XJR had a power advantage over the standard saloons. Top end breathing was improved with a special inlet manifold, also with high lift camshafts and

Variations on a theme **99**

a remapped engine management system and the compression ratio was increased to 9.75:1, all of which raised the power output from 235bhp to 251bhp at 5,250rpm, more than a 7 per cent increase.

The top speed of the XJR was increased to 150mph with a 0 to 60mph time of 6.7 seconds in manual gearbox form, reduced to 7.7 seconds with automatic transmission, and a 146mph top speed.

The suspension system was also upgraded specifically for the XJR model, very much as the 3.6-litre XJR was before. Uprated dampers, anti-roll bar and modified power steering were featured for better feel, and the car also had 16in Speedline wheels and sports interior fitments.

For the 1991 model year, some major cosmetic changes were made to the XJR 4.0-litre. Starting at the front a new style 'egg crate' black radiator grille was fitted, but still with a chromed surround, and discreet JaguarSport badging at the rear. A new front spoiler was designed incorporating the then latest style of projection fog lamps, along with cooling ducts. New-style halogen headlights were also fitted to this model, now of the rectangular style.

Along the side the flared sills were from then on fully integrated into the body and to accompany this, a full-length body moulding appeared on the bottom swage line. In body colour, these bore the XJR insignia. A new style of 16in alloy wheel with exposed wheel nuts was introduced specifically for this model, a design that would later appear on the next-generation Supercharged X-300.

At the rear, a glass-fibre in-fill panel to the centre of the boot incorporated the numberplate surround, and neutral density lighting was used, as on the Daimler model. A GRP wrap-around panel also blended in with the bumper, and gone was the boot spoiler from the previous model.

The car now looked much cleaner than the older car and, with the performance enhancements made, it was an even more sportier model. For the interior Jaguar traditionalism showed through to some extent with the very best leathers, sap-figured walnut veneer and inlays as used in the Daimlers.

Initially, the 3.6-litre and 4.0-litre XJR models were produced as standard production vehicles at Browns Lane with relevant trim items left unfitted. Then the cars were shipped over to the TWR factory in Oxfordshire where they were finished off before delivery to the dealerships. Later in production, assembly was completed totally in-house at Jaguar and the cars distributed in the normal way.

JaguarSport 'kits' were also made available during this time which permitted owners of existing 'standard' saloons to have them cosmetically converted to look

Here is the later 4.0-litre XJR, this one produced towards the end of the model's life. It is easily differentiated from the earlier models by the sculpted sills, revised wheels and new frontal treatment.

like XJRs. Uprated steering and suspension kits were also available, prices of which were:

XJ40 body kit (pre 1990 models)
Front and rear apron, sills and spoiler £1,297
XJ40 body kit (post 1990 models)
Front apron, brake ducts and undertrays, modified towing eye, front fog lamps, upper and lower grille, sills, rear quarter panels, boot and bumper in-fill panels, gas struts and badges. £1,762
XJ40 body kit (post 1990 models)
As above plus side mouldings and badges £1,900
XJ40 boot in-fill panel only £200
XJ40 rear boot spoiler £295
XJ40 colour-coded door mirrors £128
XJ40 dechroming to black finish including door handles £1,650
XJ40 steering package £248
XJ40 suspension package £439
XJ40 Momo leather steering wheel £225
XJ40 leather gearknob £19
XJ40 Speedline alloy wheels (five with tyres) £1,333
XJ40 JaguarSport wheels (five with tyres) £1,515

JaguarSport at one time even offered organised driving courses on the models in three styles, touring, advanced and high performance.

The interiors of the XJR models had special treatment, such as the colour co-ordinated leather steering wheel.

The JaguarSport cars were only moderately successful in sales and it is interesting to note that later developments of the concept resulted in the launch of the XJR Supercharged model in the later X-300

Most JaguarSport models used standard mechanics as far as the engine was concerned, except for revised badging and manifolding.

Variations on a theme **101**

bodyshell, which has been infinitely more saleable. It may also be of interest to note that at one time Jaguar had an XJR (XJ40) model equipped with the supercharged engine on test.

Lynx

Lynx Engineering at St Leonards-on-Sea in East Sussex were the first to offer styling body kits for the XJ40 outside of the JaguarSport models. The four-piece body kits made from glass-fibre comprised front and rear under-bumper spoilers and side skirts to the sills. At the time you could buy them as a kit or ready fitted for £1,150, and £1,750 plus VAT respectively.

Later developments with the XJ-S Performer might have led to enhanced XJ40s being made available, but these were never followed up.

The Humberstone estates

The only time Jaguar had ever become involved officially with an estate car prior to the XJ40 was in the 1960s with the Mark 2 Countryman. Built externally the car was used extensively by Jaguar themselves until sold off, but it was never contemplated seriously as a production model.

When the XJ40 arrived, with its angular styling, it was perhaps ideally suited to conversion to an estate car and Jaguar had one idea up its sleeve, as mentioned later in this chapter. However, before that, one forward-thinking Jaguar dealership, Ernest Hatfield's of Sheffield, South Yorkshire, was intrigued with the concept, or at least its chairman, Mr David Williams was.

He had already instigated the manufacture of an XJ Series 3 estate which he used, and with the introduction of the XJ40, thought there was another opportunity here. Using two ex-demonstrator XJ6 3.6-litre models, he commissioned the Bristol-based coachbuilding firm of Humberstones to design and build the cars for him in 1989.

The conversions took some considerable time and many components were specially manufactured just for these cars. Everything forward of the rear doors is pure XJ40 but rearward the car had to be totally rebuilt.

The rear wings, although still XJ40 were significantly modified to remove the natural curvature inwards which meant widening the rear of the car by about 4in extending the rear valance and bumper bar accordingly. The rear side windows and tailgate glass were specially made up, laminated and even the trim surrounds had to be hand-crafted to match the original XJ40 style. The tailgate was of glass-fibre, hinged from the top. The rear roof section (in steel) followed the standard XJ40 line which resulted in a low line which restricted access and hindered the rear view from the driver's mirror, but looked aesthetically pleasing. The completely new roof section was grafted in and smoothed out with filler before painting, the chromed Mercedes roof rails

Lynx produced body kits for the XJ40 and also engine, suspension mods, but it appears few took up the option.

From the rear the combination of XJ40 styling and an estate made an attractive proposition that worked well. The tailgate is glass-fibre.

Rear accommodation in the Humberstone estate was excellent although the roof height was a little too low.

adding a finishing touch to the design.

Internally, the rear seating of the XJ40 was literally cut and reupholstered to provide for a ⅓rd, ⅔rd split arrangement. The cars were also completely reupholstered in the best Autolux leather, even down to the dashboard top roll and steering wheel and then contrast piped to good effect. Wilton carpet throughout including the loading area, the finished interior being very plush and well executed.

To accommodate the estate car section of the interior, major changes had to be made to the existing XJ40 design. To start with an entirely new fuel tank had to be fabricated under the loading area floor with space left for the spare wheel to be accommodated and, of course, all the electronics from the standard car had to be rearranged to fit. New metalwork, even down to the rear valance, had to be made up specially which must have been particularly costly at the time.

The two cars produced for the Hatfield family prompted at least one other to be produced, which is

One of the very specialised Humberstone estate cars produced on the XJ40. This 1990 model has the later additions of directional rimbellishers and side rubbing strips.

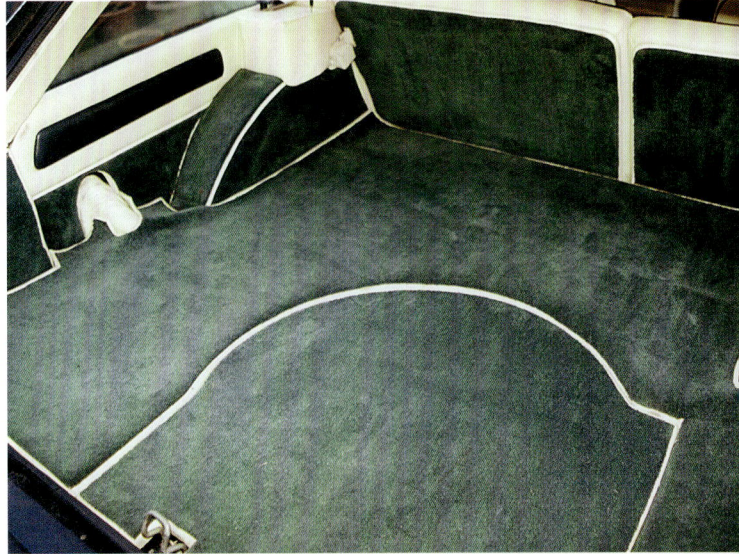

Variations on a theme

believed to reside abroad. The other two still exist, one at least in enthusiastic hands as it has recently been completely restored, such is the uniqueness yet practical nature the present owner has found with the car.

Chasseur

Trying to deal with the XJ40 variants in calendar order, as they became available, is not easy as they overlap to some extent which now brings us to the Chasseur. The Chasseur models came on line in May 1989 although they had been undergoing development three years earlier, literally immediately after the launch of the model.

Charles Whittaker, one of the men behind Chasseur (and still well known today in Jaguar modification circles) had a desire to emulate the Germans in creating the ultimate sporting saloon, building on Jaguar's success with their latest model. This meant development work on the engine, suspension and even the bodywork to enhance the performance, aerodynamics and feel of the car.

The result was the Stealth, supplied as a complete package fitted to a new or used 3.6-litre or 4.0-litre XJ40, but which could also be purchased in 'phases' to customer requirements.

Phase One took care of the bodywork, some interior trim and upgraded suspension. A full body kit of front and rear valance, side skirts and badges, all painted along with the bumpers to body colour was supplied. Fondmetal one-piece alloy wheels had Chasseur centre caps and were shod with Goodrich Comp T/A 245/50 ZR 16 tyres or Borbet 8.5J x 17 wheels with Yokohama AVS 235/45 ZR17 tyres. The suspension was lowered by the fitting of shorter length, uprated springs with manually adjustable shock absorbers, and the power steering rack was rebushed to improve location, along with a modified valve reducing the servo assistance delivered.

Phase Two involved the Turbo Technics Company of Northampton. A specialist company who had already carried out some work turbo-charging the AJ6 engine, they produced a pair of water-cooled Garrett T25 turbos, set to develop maximum boost at 0.60 bar (9psi), sufficient to increase power output of the 4.0-litre for example, from 235bhp to 340bhp (310bhlp on the 3.6-litre engine), and with a massive 405lb ft of torque.

The turbos were mounted on a new exhaust manifold, cast in high nickel content iron and separated to give total pulse separation. They were coupled to a special Piper, large-bore stainless steel exhaust system with the ability to fit catalytic converters. The inlet manifold was also equipped with

The Chasseur was another turbo-charged version of the XJ40 usually accompanied by the special body kit, Chasseur in-fill panel and badges to the boot lid, revised front spoiler, and wider wheels and tyres.

A Chasseur Evolution like this early example, featured a close-ratio gearbox and bespoke treatment to the trim.

A touch of class with this Chasseur model fitted with additional head restraints and treated to a total retrim with contrast piped upholstery.

six extra fuel injectors to meet the increased demand under power. The compression ratio was lowered to 8.1 to 1 with the fuelling requirements met by a Turbo Technics digital control unit with a purpose-built air filter box.

Other items could also be added to the car, including limited slip differential, smaller, thicker-rimmed steering wheel, extra woodwork, reupholstered seats, etc. The basic conversion of body, suspension, steering and engine set you back something in the region of £11,000 at the time.

Chasseur performance comparisons

	0 to 60 mph (secs)	0 to 100 mph (secs)	Max mph	50 to 70mph (held gear) (secs)
XJ40 3.6-litre	8.8	24.6	140	4.8
Chasseur 3.6-litre	6.3	16.5	150	3.3
XJ40 4.0-litre	8.3	21.4	141	4.2
Chasseur 4.0-litre	5.9	15.8	160	3.2

The turbo-charged engine of the Chasseur was a formidable performer.

Variations on a theme

Quite a number of cars were converted, including at least one Daimler and a Majestic long wheelbase version. The company later closed down although most of the cars are still around and running well, providing an awesome performance boost over even the V12 versions.

Lister

Around the same time Lister, then under the WP Automotive name, who had already been producing a successful Lister-XJ-S, set to work on the 3.6-litre XJ40, and announced their own 4.0-litre-engined version before Jaguar introduced theirs.

By fitting a longer throw steel crankshaft, this increased the stroke to 102mm, the connecting rods were shortened and fitted with special big end bolts, although the pistons themselves were standard. A highly polished cylinder head and an increased compression ratio to 10.2:1, with reprogrammed fuel injection gave a net result of 264bhp. They also claimed an improved acceleration figure of 7.8 seconds from 0 to 60mph and mid-range torque up into Series 3 V12 standards.

The engine conversion cost in the region of £6,000 and then you added stiffened suspension components, wider tyres on split-rimmed alloy wheels, etc. to boost the price further.

A four-door cabriolet of the XJ40 makes a good choice for open-air motoring in comfort, or for the odd wedding!

It was from this concept that Lister later developed a V12 model, the culmination of which was the ultimate XJ40, discussed at the end of this chapter.

Cabriolet's International

In the early 1990s, a company called Cabriolet's International in Blackpool, Lancashire were producing custom body styling and paint jobs on various cars, not least Jaguars and Rolls-Royces. They also came up with the idea of modifying the XJ40 (and other models) to effectively four-door convertibles.

For £3,000 they would 're-engineer' the car by cutting off the roof, supporting the structure underneath with cross bracing, and create a cabriolet style. The beauty of the idea was to retain all four doors and interior accommodation, even down to the full window frames and electric windows, but have a fully retracting (full-length) hood section. Ideal for summer cruising or weddings!

It is not known how many of these cars were produced, and unfortunately, the company no longer survives but other companies later emulated their ideas, but again, they are not produced today.

Insignia

Jaguar took what was, for them, an unusual direction in launching a bespoke finishing service for their cars in 1992. Called Insignia, this followed the revisions to the XJ40 range announced in the mid-year.

Developed by Jaguar's own Special Vehicle

An example of the extensive modifications that could be made to the XJ40 Insignia model: special seating, Autolux leather, two-tone colourings, and stained woodwork.

Operations Department, buyers could choose a range of options to personalise their cars when purchased new from Jaguar. For example, there was a choice of ten special exterior paint colours together with interiors trimmed in a unique range of matching semi-aniline hides, some of which included specially designed seats. These could be complemented by a choice of natural or tinted wood veneers selected to enhance the paint and trim finish, added to which came deep pile carpeting. Even specially designed road wheels and trims could be specified.

The cars were hand-finished by the SVO, staffed at the time by some of the most experienced craftsman at Jaguar, usually associated with special projects, including everything from police vehicles to governmental cars, and the Daimler DS420 limousine to one-offs.

The options were very extensive, and were based on the following:

Interior – replacing all trim completely with semi-aniline leather finish, many in two-tone colours and new-style seating. Matching Wilton carpeting to interior and boot, bird's eye maple woodwork stained to complement the interior, Daimler-style picnic tables and other wood trim.

Jaguar Sovereign/V12	£5,450
Daimler 4.0-litre	£3,950
Daimler Double Six	£3,450

Wheels – polished flush fitting wheel trims painted to body finish. Only available with 15in steel wheels and cars equipped with ride height control.

All models	£250

Variations on a theme

Special woodwork only – bird's eye maple woodwork veneer stained to complement the interior of the car.

All models   £250

Exterior paintwork – choice of ten specialist colour schemes.

Metallic   £2,000
Pearl   £2,300

Majestic by name and size

In October 1992, at the motor show, Jaguar announced another XJ40 production variant primarily for the UK market which was to carry the name Majestic, but not to be confused with the US special edition model, discussed in a previous chapter.

By effectively cutting and shutting the floorpan of the existing XJ40 bodyshell, it was possible to incorporate a 125mm increase in the wheelbase (around 5in), all of which was managed behind the B/C door pillar, so providing better accommodation for rear seat passengers.

If one was cynical it could be said that this merely followed previous Jaguar practice when they increased the wheelbase of the Series 1, followed by doing the same to the Series 2 XJs back in the Seventies.

With the XJ40 however, Jaguar had gone a stage further because the roof line was continued back at a slightly higher level to provide better headroom in the rear compartment. The extra length necessitated the fabrication of new rear door frames and skins, window frames and glass, and even a new rear quarter window and rear screen.

All this extra work was carried out by a company called Project Aerospace in Coventry. Taking complete, normal body-in-white shells from Jaguar's Castle Bromwich site, the bodyshell was cut with additional metal and support added to the floorpan, the new roof panel was fitted, returning the completed bodyshell to Castle Bromwich where it went through the normal paint process. Then, the body moved to Browns Lane and Jaguar's Special Vehicle Operations Department for trimming and final work.

The expensive Majestic models could either be built in Jaguar or Daimler form, 3.2-litre, 4.0-litre or later 6.0-litre engine size, and it was intended they would meet the needs of owners who wanted something with extra space, even perhaps being built up to the fairly new Insignia style (see above). In reality, the cars were too expensive and time-consuming to build, so only about 50 were produced in total.

An example of the improved rear legroom in a Majestic model, here also shown with trim mods carried out by Chasseur.

The Majestic's extra length was softened by the raised height of the roof, the ultimate gain being in rear compartment accommodation.

Estately carriage

After Humberstone had developed their version of the XJ40 estate car, Jaguar themselves also set to work to design and produce such a car with the help

The very well executed Jaguar XJ40 estate, created for Jaguar themselves.

The well-designed interior included a split rear bench seat arrangement making the XJ40 the ideal dual-purpose vehicle.

of the SVO and an outside coachbuilder. Using a production 4.0-litre Sovereign model in 1992 the concept was evolved.

To keep costs down and to retain as much of the XJ40 style as possible, everything forward of the B/C posts was pure saloon. However, they also did a lot of research into the estate car market at the time taking ideas from the likes of Volvo and Mercedes who were really the only luxury manufacturers in this sector then. Hence the carrying capacity had to be good as did headroom and, of course, the important retention of passenger comfort.

The XJ40 body style leant itself well to estate car conversion. Only the roof panel had to be raised very slightly and extended backwards. With this the rear door window frame was made taller. The car's natural swage line was followed and with entirely new rear wings, good-sized side windows could be accommodated.

At the rear, a special tailgate was constructed with better than average glass area and, although the rear lighting was retained, the valance had to be raised to meet the need for a flat loading floor.

Under the skin, major changes to the XJ40 shell had to be made including the movement of the petrol rank, remaking of D posts, under-pan areas and the adaptation of the rear seating arrangement to fold down. Great attention had been paid to rearward visibility and a flat deck along with adequate height, and this had been achieved exceptionally well, particularly so compared with the earlier Humberstone 'private' conversion.

Stylistically, the car was excellent with a well-proportioned rear end, the long low look at the side and virtually no difference to the saloon at the front save for a very slight increase in the roof panel height. Perhaps the greatest problem was that to the general public it didn't look like a Jaguar and to many at Jaguar they felt at the time that this was not a market they wanted to explore. Hence only one example was made, registered for the road and still regularly used today by the Jaguar Daimler Heritage Trust.

Arden

Arden, the German coachbuilder had already produced a range of different body kits for the old Series 3 XJs and the XJ-S models. They also turned their attention to the XJ40 in producing a spoiler package, colour coded to the car with matt black finishing to other aspects. You could also choose from wider alloy wheels, which could also be colour-coded, suspension lowering kits, revised shock absorbers, and sports exhaust systems.

They also produced some modified interior packages

An unusual interpretation of the XJ40 in the form of the German Arden model. The external body transformations could be specified in addition to the mechanical changes.

110 Jaguar XJ40

which included revised woodwork and, if you really had the money, you could order a cocktail cabinet in the rear.

XJ40 Coupé

Many Jaguar enthusiasts still regard the Jaguar XJ Series 2 Coupé as one of the most attractive saloons the company has ever produced, although in many ways it was not successful primarily through build and quality problems. Jaguar's Special Vehicle Operations Department in Coventry came up with the proposal to convert an XJ40 to a shortened wheelbase, two-door variant – another Coupé.

Built in late 1993 around a conventional XJ12 taken from the production line, the Coupé was conceived and built as a one-off. It could be said that this was never intended as a serious production project for the XJ40 as, by that time, the closing stages of development had taken place on its replacement (X-300) which would start manufacture in 1994. No, this was an exercise which, if it had been successful, might have led to a two-door X-300 at a later date.

The XJ12 was stripped of all trim, the propshaft removed and the body jigged so that it could be cut to take 18in out of the middle section. Welded back together with the rear wings extended forwards and the front doors expanded by welding in sections of another pair of doors (not too dissimilar to what Jaguar had done in production with the old Series 2 Coupé), and the basic structure was formed. A new propshaft was made up, the exhaust shortened and many other minor changes to mechanics were made necessary to ensure the vehicle was not only a running prototype but that it could eventually be taxed and put on the road.

Externally, the car was modernised to give it a sporty look with extensive colour co-ordination of trim (including the bumpers), five-spoke alloy wheels and a

The XJ40 Coupé interior was magnificent with XJS-style seating, contrast trim and hand-stitched leather dash rolls.

An interesting short wheelbase concept for the XJ40 was a coupé model, a one-off prototype that never progressed further.

Variations on a theme **111**

Similar treatment was continued to the back seat of the Coupé with Daimler style fitments.

boot lid in-fill panel as later to be seen on the S models. Internally, the Coupé enjoyed the height of luxury with magnolia upholstery piped in red with red stitching, carried over to similarly leather trimmed dashboard and door trims. The front seats came from

Not so long in the tooth, the Wilcox Eagle limousine took to the lengthened floorpan and raised roof well.

Jaguar even prepared a special badge for the Coupé model.

the latest variant of XJ-S and the rear ones were styled like the Daimler 4.0-litre, but with pleating similar to the XJ40 S models. The SVO even had a new boot badge made for the car.

The XJ40 Coupé wasn't actually registered for road use until 1995 and it was first seen by the public at a Jaguar 60-year celebration at the National Exhibition Centre in Birmingham. The car is currently in the hands of the Jaguar Daimler Heritage Trust.

112 Jaguar XJ40

The long stretch

Although Jaguar attempted, with little success, to produce a stretched version of the XJ40, it wasn't until 1994 that a specialist company in this field threw down the gauntlet and produced a viable car suitable for the carriage trade, ambassadorial and other uses.

Wilcox Limousines from Chalfont St Peter in Buckinghamshire were, and still are, very well known for their purchase, sales and production of specialist carriage trade vehicles. Having cut their teeth on the usual Rolls-Royces, Fords and Vauxhalls, they inevitably grew to deal in and maintain the Daimler DS420 limousines produced in-house at Jaguar, and utilising many parts from existing production saloons.

Now Wilcox, via their coachbuilding arm, Eagle Specialist Vehicles in Lancashire, came up with an effective stretch design based on the XJ40 model. The start of this was a ten-car order for stretched XJ40 limousines from Berryhurts, London's premier chauffeur drive company. So successful was the model that they continued to build XJ40 limousines (and hearses) until the X-300 took its place and, today, produce cars based on the XJ8.

The production of the stretched XJ40 took the form of cutting the body in half after being suitably jigged for support, welding in new metal and support members, to increase the wheelbase to 4,070mm (160in) or a full 47in longer than the standard saloon. The roof line was suitably raised to provide more than adequate headroom and an extra set of doors was added.

With an extra set of seats, inside the accommodation could cater for up to eight people in the utmost comfort. The basic accommodation included the usual leather and veneer fittings, centre division, separate heating and air conditioning systems for the rear, but almost any combination could and was supplied, according to specific demands, such as conference seating, on-board TV, cocktail cabinet, etc.

Mechanically, the cars were suitably uprated to meet the demands placed on them in service, and to satisfy the extra weight requirements. For example, XJ12 braking systems were fitted, as was rear ride height levelling for the suspension with modified springs for longer travel, and in some cases, items such as uprated alternators to drive the extra equipment installed.

Prices for the Eagle XJ40 started at £55,000 plus VAT for the conversion, and £57,000 for the hearse, on top of the cost of the original vehicle.

Four or six-door options were available along with an extensive choice of interior fitments. This car is fitted with the Insignia style of wheel trim.

Variations on a theme

The ultimate Forty

The thought of spending over £125,000 on a motor car is daunting for any of us, but for one man it represented the ultimate in personal transport and must be the most expensive XJ40 ever produced.

In 1993, after the launch of the V12-engined model, Mr David Hall from Newcastle upon Tyne, who is best known for being the boss of the highly successful Newcastle United football team, instigated the manufacture of a rather special Lister-XJ40.

It all started with an order placed with his local Jaguar dealer for a black V12 XJ40, but upon delivery, the car was immediately shipped down to Lister Cars in Leatherhead, Surrey for the modifications to be carried out. Lister had a celebrated history of involvement with Jaguar and were at the time producing superbly modified versions of the XJS models. This XJ40 was to be their first, and the modifications were to be extensive, to say the least.

Engine

The standard Jaguar engine was removed from the car and completely stripped. A new EN40 B steel crankshaft with lip seal rear main was fitted with revised steel conrods and Cosworth forged pistons to increase the compression ratio to 11.2:1. The cylinder head was polished and gas flowed. Larger, 1.800 inlet valves and 1.500 exhaust valves were fitted to the head with lightened steel followers, special springs, reprofiled camshafts and patent Lister twin-throttle body.

The whole induction system was modified, the fuel injection system reprogrammed and twin turbo chargers fitted and the engine bench tested before being refitted to the car.

The end result was a 7.0-litre power unit with 94mm bore and 84mm stroke. At 6,000rpm the engine produced a fearful 604bhp and 425lb ft of torque. Moreover, at the quite modest revs of 4,000, the unit pumped out an incredible 612lb ft of torque. The engine conversion alone cost £28,350, and that was only the start.

Gearbox

To meet the demands of this uprated performance a six-speed manual transmission was fitted, adapted from a BMW 840i. Accompanied by modifications to the propshaft, there was a revised rear axle ratio and then electronic traction control; the package was starting to come together. The cost of these changes was £7,540.

Brakes and suspension

To improve the handling the rack and pinion steering was remodelled to remove 40 per cent of all the power assistance – another £679. Then, the front and rear springs were changed for new, specially designed ones to provide a slightly firmer ride along with replacement dampers – price £1,455.

For brakes Lister chose the fitment of Brembo ventilated racing discs 14in at the front and 12in at the

Probably the wildest XJ40 ever produced, this 7.0-litre Lister muscle car even carries Newcastle United football colours.

Even the body kit is a little extreme with colour-coded bumpers and an S in-fill panel.

The interior of the Lister V12 includes a total retrim and a very sporty six-speed gearbox to handle.

rear with massive four-pot calipers – just a touch over £7,645 in price.

To put as much tread on the road as possible the wheels were changed for 18in alloys of Lister design fitted with 245 x 50 Michelin Pilot XX tyres at the front and 265 x 50 at the rear – the complete set, a mere £5,888.

Finally, to help the engine breath a new tubular exhaust manifold was made up along with revised stainless steel silencers and pipe sets: price £2,450. The bottom line of all this meant an unrecordable top speed, and a timed 0 to 30mph time on the Millbrook proving ground of a mere two seconds.

Trim

Not only was the car made to perform but it had to look the part as well. Internally, much of the upholstery was retrimmed in the finest Connolly hide dyed cream and piped in black with black carpets, piped cream. Specially designed Lister front seats were made up to provide sufficient support for the G force of this awesome motor car. The cost: another £3,950.

Then there was the outside. Still finished in black from the factory, a specially designed body kit incorporating full sill skirts curved to meet the wheelarches was fitted. At the rear an off-the-shelf Jaguar XJ40 S boot in-fill panel was painted and fitted. A neat boot spoiler, rear skirts and at the front, a skirt/spoiler incorporating the fog lamps and JaguarSport radiator grille was included.

A few more, not so subtle changes, included the fitting of blackened windows and the finishing touch, a subtle repaint with graduated silver to the bottom of the body – guess what – Newcastle United colours! The cost of this work added another £6,035 to the overall bill.

Lastly, to add to the comfort, a Kenwood sound system with CD player was added at a cost of £4,785, and just in case you wanted to use that power on the open road, there was a radar detector at £612.

The all-in-price of £69,389 for the conversion, plus the £55,000 for the original purchase of the standard

The 7.0 litres and 604bhp must make this the fastest XJ40 ever.

The Rapport Forté, a totally different approach to Jaguar!

V12 car, makes an impressive figure, although this is not as impressive as the car itself. One man's interpretation of his ideal motor car, regardless of cost, and comparable perhaps to a Bentley Turbo R, or a Maserati Quattroporte.

The most unusual

From perhaps the ultimate XJ40 to what must have been the most unusual, and as far as the author knows, the only time when someone has totally rebodied the car in an attempt to launch a production model.

Rapport International Group operated from plush premises in Mayfair, London although their working base was in Surrey. The concept of the new car was to be based around the then XJ-S but this later turned into something loosely based on the XJ40, hence the name Rapport Forté.

This was to have been the ultimate grand touring sports machine, equipped with the V12 engine, capable of speeds up to 140mph. The bodywork was of steel construction on to which was grafted alloy panels. A four-seater, it incorporated a forward hinged bonnet structure, an impressive metal folding roof and monoroof with separate blind. Other novel features included an electronically raised airfoil, West of England cloth upholstery and the total reworking of the interior and exterior trim, from anything vaguely associated with Jaguar.

The exterior design was somewhat of a cross between a Fiat X1/9, Triumph TR7 or Lancia Stratos, dependent on how wide open your eyes were! An incredibly expensive project which, as far as is known, only resulted in one car being produced. Later options were considered including a five-speed manual gearbox, turbo-charged engines and even a fastback, three-door coupé and an estate car.

Other styles

There are probably other variations on the XJ40 theme that the author has not identified. Certainly, some XJ40s have now been stripped for their mechanics for use in replica cars and of course, we should not forget that several examples of the XJ40 were reserved for other uses.

Not only did Wilcox produce hearses from their Eagle Coachworks, but Jaguar at one time even produced an in-house version!

And finally, we must make mention of the rather high-profile versions of the XJ40 supplied to the UK Government and for some special uses overseas. The UK's Prime Minister, for many years, used a bullet-proof Majestic long-wheelbase model, the much-loved Princess Diana also had her own Daimler, chauffeur-driven for state occasions, many governmental officials and ministers had the use of Jaguar pool cars during the life of the model, and even the boss of the Bank of England had a Daimler. All of which goes to show that the XJ40 found attention in many areas outside of the normal production vehicles.

A one-off Jaguar hearse on the XJ40 floorpan, bodywork and mechanics, not to be confused with the Eagle Coachworks version.

Ex officio XJ40, this one was used by Lady Sarah Ferguson and was specially prepared by Jaguar with revised electrics to carry Police Special Branch radio equipment, etc.

Variations on a theme **117**

Chapter **Nine**

Choosing and buying an XJ40

If you already own one of these cars and are considering upgrading, or are purchasing one for the first time, then you need to determine two elements. The first is the price you want to pay and secondly, the model to go for. The price you can afford will somewhat control the other aspect, but it is not the intention of this book to help you set a budget, although one thing we can do is to give you one simple piece of advice. Regardless of the amount of money you want to spend on a car: buy the *best* you can for the money you have

Whether a late or an early model, buy the best car you can afford, regardless of age, colour, etc.

available. Disregard elements like colour scheme, mileage, number of owners and, to some extent, model type. The better the car you buy, regardless of model, the better your experience will be, the more enjoyable the car will be to own and the less you will have to pay out in the future. To qualify this a stage further, if you have no or little knowledge of these cars, although we try to give you as much background and help as possible here, there is no substitute for getting someone else, who *is* very knowledgeable on these cars, to look over your intended purchase *before* you buy. We also recommend you join a club such as the Jaguar Enthusiasts' Club and learn all you can about the cars.

Which model?

The range of XJ40 models is extensive – 15 in the UK alone – and that doesn't include the specialist conversions. The most prolific in manufacture were the 3.6-litre and 4.0-litre Sovereigns with over 50,000 made of each engine size. This provides plenty of choice even today and is good because they are well equipped. The more standard models were and still are least popular, but it is not unusual to find a XJ6 with lots of additional equipment specified by the owner from new so don't rule out one of these until you check its specification *and* the condition. Remember, it is always best to buy a 'good' but poorly specified car, rather than an ordinary, well-equipped model.

Looking at engine size, the 2.9-litre models are the least desirable. They are under-powered, not as economical and are becoming difficult to maintain. In some cases, car dismantlers are just scrapping 2.9-litre engines when the cars come in because there is so little interest in them, and many cars have already been converted to the larger engines anyway. Only 20,000 2.9s were produced in total, most of them to XJ6 spec rather than Sovereign, so equipment levels will be worse as well. However, a really nice 2.9 model with a low mileage and a reasonable standard of equipment can still be an enjoyable car – again, it is all down to condition.

The 3.2-litre cars are a much better bet. The engine performs well, they are more economical and smoother than even the bigger engines and will enjoy a longer life. Here there are masses to choose from although only 3,500 Sovereigns were produced with this engine. A big advantage, however, is that there was also the S and Gold models, much later cars that will inevitably be in better condition and have more appeal because of their limited production run and better equipment levels. The downside to these models is that there are fewer around, say 4,500 made, compared with over 13,000 standard models.

Back to the 3.6-litre and 4.0-litre, the former are known for their 'unburstability' and both only suffer from minor ailments such as cylinder head gaskets or perhaps burnt out valves if not well maintained. These engines are capable of very high mileages and actually enjoy hard use. Although 3.6-litre-equipped cars will be cheaper, because they are older, it is likely that areas such as the bodywork or electrics won't be in such a good condition. With something like 86,000 4.0-litre models and 53,000 3.6-litre cars produced, there is still plenty of choice

There are lots of cars to choose from, and consider joining the Jaguar Enthusiasts' Club to gain help and knowledge on these models.

around. Also remember, there is the S model with the bigger engine.

Then there are the V12-engined models where only a total of around 3,800 were made for all markets. With so much concern over environmental issues, and fears of increased taxes by engine size or horse power, the V12s have lost a lot of ground and can be purchased for little money. The V12 is a very different animal to the six-cylinder XJ40s – smoother and more refined, they are without doubt the jewel in the crown – if you don't mind the extra running and maintenance costs (more on this in the next chapter).

So, with over 200,000 cars to choose from, there is something for everyone. Price issues are dictated by condition and equipment levels, manual transmission cars were never that popular in their day but enthusiastic owners these days seem to prefer them, so there is not a lot of differential in price at present. As the cars get older you are less likely to find one with full Jaguar service history and because of the relatively complex nature of some of the electrics on these models, fewer DIY owners are 'having a go'. Many specialist independent Jaguar garages have been set up to look after these cars, some good, some not so good,

One of the advantages with the XJ40 is that models altered very little throughout its production life. On the right is an early 2.9-litre XJ6, and on the left, a very late 3.2-litre. Spot the difference!

There is no substitute for getting a car on a ramp with a professional to help you establish exactly how good or bad it is.

so plenty of care should be taken when buying one.

Again, it cannot be emphasised too much the need to thoroughly check a car over bodily and mechanically and to use the facilities of local expert knowledge, particularly from organisations like the Jaguar Enthusiasts' Club which has a strong membership of XJ40 owners and experts.

Once you have determined your budget and arrived at the model you most desire, then the search can start in earnest and the following can provide some useful tips on what to look for.

First it should be stressed that these are complex vehicles and any cursory inspection will not reveal all the problems as many are not immediately obvious. The availability of a full service history record is good but even this is not conclusive and if such a record is there it would be advisable to see specific and recent invoices to show the amount and type of work that had been carried out.

It should go without saying that the impending purchase of such a car should be made with great care and again we strongly recommend a very thorough inspection, perhaps seeing the car on a four-post ramp and viewed by a professional who knows these cars. Even if this costs you money, it will probably save you much more in the long term

120 Jaguar XJ40

A brief guide on what to look for

Bodywork

Historically, the Achilles heel of Jaguars has been the bodywork, deteriorating quickly because of a cocktail of poor design and build quality, and the ravages of the weather. Although the XJ40 is not a shining prince in this area, it has survived significantly better than most previous Jaguar models, although it cannot be compared favourably with today's cars. The moral therefore is that things have improved over the years, but the XJ40 still requires a lot of attention to identify and rectify problems, before they become terminal.

As a general principle, more problems with corrosion affect the earlier cars, not just because they are now older but because the attention to detail wasn't quite as good as with subsequent cars, although by now, most cars are showing some signs of deterioration. We will work along the bodywork as follows:

Bonnet

The forward-hinged one-piece bonnet is well known for corrosion and stress cracks. The latter is caused by a stiffening of the hinges which should be cleaned and greased regularly to avoid this. Much more common and applying virtually to all the pre-1990 models is corrosion along the leading edge of the bonnet caused by ingress of damp and dirt from the road thrown up from the front of the car. The first signs of this are usually in the form of bubbles underneath the paint on the top near the headlights and which later develops into the mis-shaping of the panel at its furthest point where it meets the front wing. The root cause is damp getting into the folded area of metal underneath, clearly visible when you open the bonnet.

Another area of concern on the bonnet is the lip which forms the profile around the grille area. This corrodes from underneath where it can't be seen, unless you are looking for it specifically when the bonnet is open.

The only remedy is either to fit a new bonnet or have the old corroded metal cut out and replaced. This is not very expensive, and can be done in situ, but the cheaper, ineffective way is to clean the area up, fill and paint it, so look at this area closely on any intended XJ40 purchase.

The bonnet support struts can either weaken over the years causing the bonnet not to stay in the 'up' position, or they stiffen to the point that raising the bonnet from its rearward lip will cause it to strain and

A typical XJ40 bonnet that has been repaired. The metal has expanded causing it to mis-shape and the bubbles clearly show where the corrosion is, which will have extended right through the metal by this time.

The same bonnet and not much pressure was needed on this screwdriver to go right through.

A bonnet from the inside clearly showing the way corrosion has spread along the bottom edge, which means that this particular bonnet is probably too far gone for economical repair.

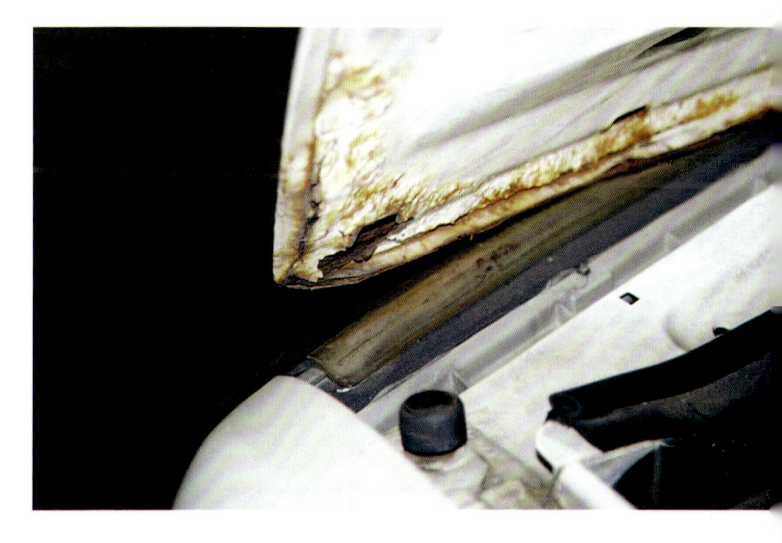

A typical front wing bottom that has corroded through ingress of water. The rust will already have extended beyond what can be seen.

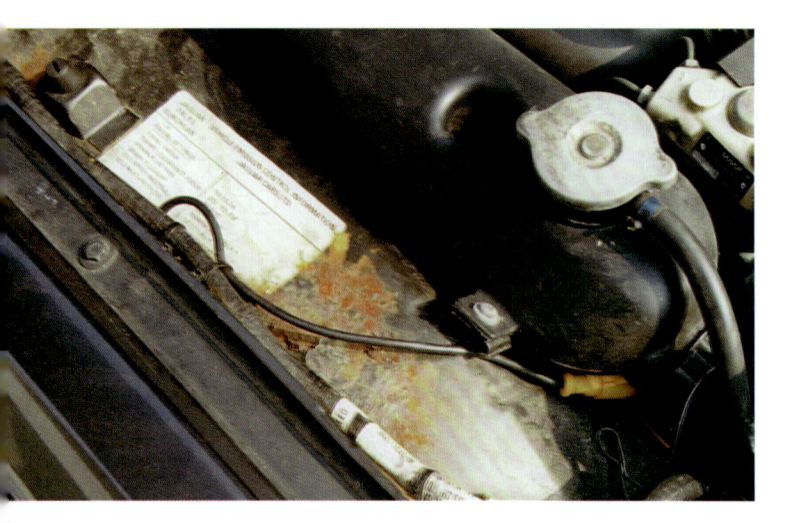

Even more important at the front are the inner wings which are a well known area of concern. This amount of corrosion is not unusual in the earlier cars and usually means a complete new inner wing is required.

With the outer wing removed, the inner corrosion was found to be so bad that the whole inner area had to be cut away, eventually leading to a complete new wing.

actually damage it as mentioned earlier. Either way, the struts are not expensive to replace and are readily available.

Front wings

The front wings are arguably more resistant to corrosion than those on earlier models or indeed other makes of car. The wheelarch lip can fill up with dirt and mud over the years which, if not cleaned regularly, will cause mild corrosion here and the rear bottom edge of the wings will rust out through ingress of damp from the inner-wing area. These are bolt-on items so are readily replaceable if severely damaged.

The inner front wings are very prone to corrosion, particularly on the earlier cars. They can corrode on top of the wheelarch area, around the seams, shock-absorber mountings and at the rear edge. This type of corrosion can be spotted easily with the bonnet open

With an outer wing removed the extent of corrosion inside can be seen, which is usually caused by water ingress thrown up from the wheels.

but is difficult to repair because of the proximity of equipment and the need for extensive welding to replace the whole panel. The design of the inner wing changed just before the V12 models were introduced (around late 1992) so there are two types, both of which are inter-changeable although the later type only fits V12-engined cars.

Doors

Doors are one of the lesser problems with the XJ40. On the earlier cars however, they will inevitably rust out at the bottoms and halfway up the doorskin while on all cars some minor rust will appear around the seams, no different from any other car.

Whilst on the subject of doors the most common problems affecting pre-1991 cars are the locks. Made from Mazak the mechanisms are brittle and after some use will become stiff to operate (more on this in the next chapter). A new style of lock was produced for later models which can still be bought, but it won't fit the older models. Repair kits are now available for the older locks.

Bulkhead/roof

The internal bulkheads on XJ40s are known to corrode, badly in some cases. This seems to be caused by ingress of water from the scuttle area and doesn't manifest itself without a thorough inspection from inside the engine bay with much of the area covered in pipework, ancilliary equipment, etc. This corrosion is inevitable but is rarely terminal although it requires extensive treatment which, in most cases, involves removing the complete dashboard. In some cases the air conditioning/heating system also has to be removed so it can be very expensive in time.

XJ40s are also prone to corrosion in the A post screen area. This is either through improper protection when new or ingress of water over the years, coming down the drain channel, the rust eating its way through. This is easily identifiable and usually necessitates the windscreen being removed to rectify it properly.

The roof panel rarely rusts except for around the sunroofs and the base D post area where it is welded to the rear wing with the weld covered by the chrome (later painted) finisher. Rust festers under this area and reveals itself in the form of rusty water marks running down the wing. The area around the rear screen can also be vulnerable to corrosion particularly if any paint was removed when the screen was fitted or during a subsequent refit.

Corrosion in the A post between the windscreen and front door is also common and can be expensive to repair because of the strip-down work needed.

Corrosion is also a problem around the front bulkhead which manifests itself in two ways. First, like here under the plastic scuttle finisher the surface corrosion, once cut away reveals further extensive damage inside. Also, it is common for the bulkhead itself to corrode from behind the engine area, again caused by water that has seeped through. This is very expensive to repair because the whole dashboard assembly has to be removed.

Choosing and buying an XJ40

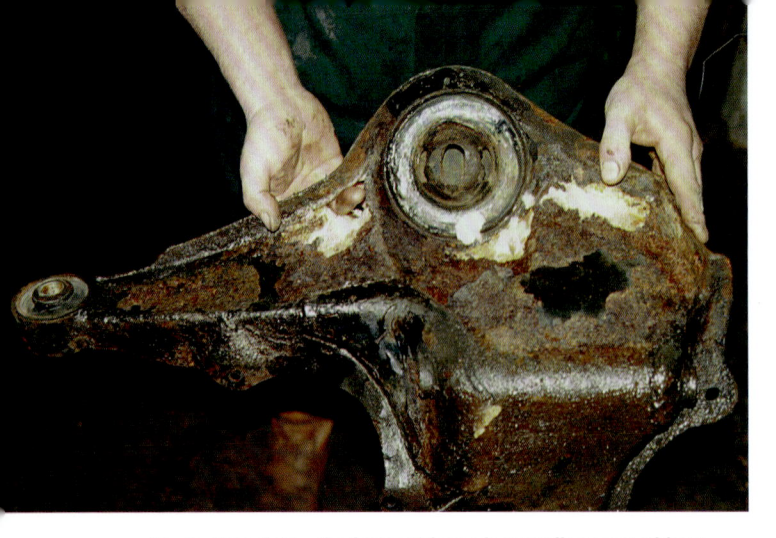

An alarming sight – the front subframe is corroding away without anyone realising. The severity of this example is quite normal and great care is needed to inspect this item before purchasing a car. They are expensive to replace and cannot be welded.

Sills/floorpan/underside

Inner and outer sills rust out as on any car and this can be a major problem on earlier XJ40s. However, it is certainly not uncommon to find the floorpans corroding badly at the front or along the length of the seams with the inner sills. This area is best checked by lifting the carpets inside the car.

A vital aspect for which we make no apology for treating it separately, is the condition of the front subframe on the six-cylinder models.

It is an important issue that should be checked before you consider buying any car, regardless of its overall condition in other areas. Corrosion is bound to be there to a greater or a lesser degree, dependent on the age of the car and the way it has been looked after. However, this is not a specific pointer about the owner of such a car merely the fact that the corrosion damage can often not be seen easily. It is not unknown for these cars to carry a new MoT certificate because the tester has not identified the problem, yet the car could be very unsafe indeed, such is the importance of this one particular aspect of the car.

The subframe is a welded steel unit filled with expanding foam. The actual location of corrosion can be difficult to identify, much of it hidden by the engine and other aspects of the car's mechanicals. As a guide they normally corrode in the following places and, apart from visual inspection, tapping the subframe sharply with a hammer can reveal the overall condition, by a changing tone with a distinct 'ring' to a dead sound.

The main culprit is on either side at the top where the top wishbone fulcrum pin is located and another is the aperture into which the top of the coil spring fits. The other main areas of concern are along the legs where they sweep back to the rear subframe body mounts. These are a costly but necessary item to replace when corrosion has eaten into them and they cannot be welded because of the expanded foam inside. There has, in the past, been a good supply of secondhand subframes but these are now running short and the only other option is to buy new from Jaguar, a very expensive item and, of course, a not insignificant job to carry out.

The V12 XJ40s do not suffer this problem as their subframe is of an entirely different design which doesn't corrode, but this is not interchangeable with the six-cylinder cars.

Probably the best-known area of corrosion on the XJ40 is the boot lid, and this is a particularly bad example.

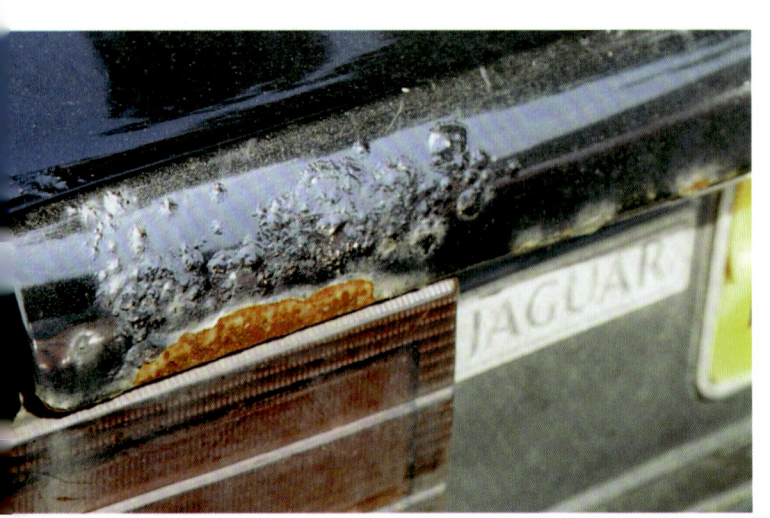

Corrosion will gradually eat its way through the whole boot lid, all along the lip securing the boot lock and number plate lights and, if not caught early, will result in a completely new lid being needed.

Boot

The boot area is particularly prone to corrosion. First the boot lid, particularly on pre-1991 cars suffers badly with corrosion on the lip, under the double-skinning where the lid closes on to the rear wings, the folded area along the numberplate light area and at its extreme edges. This can be severe and affects all these cars, but through better preparation, was nowhere near as bad on later models although some aspects of the rust can still appear.

The inside of the boot is prone to water ingress, usually coming from the rear valance area (more on this in a later chapter). This results in damp carpets, a musty smell, damp patches or even mould on the boot lid board finisher panel, and in severe cases, corrosion of the rear valance and boot floor itself.

The overall problem here is in many cases curable and if major corrosion has not attacked the area, it shouldn't deter you too much from considering one particular car to buy.

Other areas

The rear wings are not usually affected by bad corrosion although the wheelarches will inevitably suffer like the front ones. The rear valance has already been mentioned above, while the front valance is more likely to suffer damage from high kerbs than corrosion. It is not unknown for corrosion to appear around the sunroof where fitted.

This plastic finisher is self-tapped into the rear boot panel and is notoriously a place to harbour damp. In this case the strip has actually lost its shape and water will get beneath it easily, causing it to fester.

Removing the strip will reveal more damp, here seen after two days left to dry.

The damp has found its way into the rear valance and has gradually soaked through the seams into the boot area, soaking the carpet.

A quick reference point to identify this problem is to smell inside the boot and check the inside of the boot lid which will have turned musty and mouldy in the confined area.

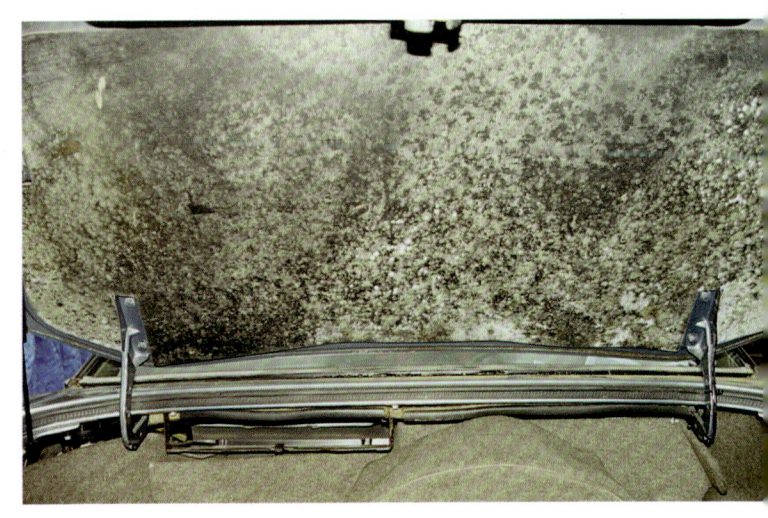

Choosing and buying an XJ40

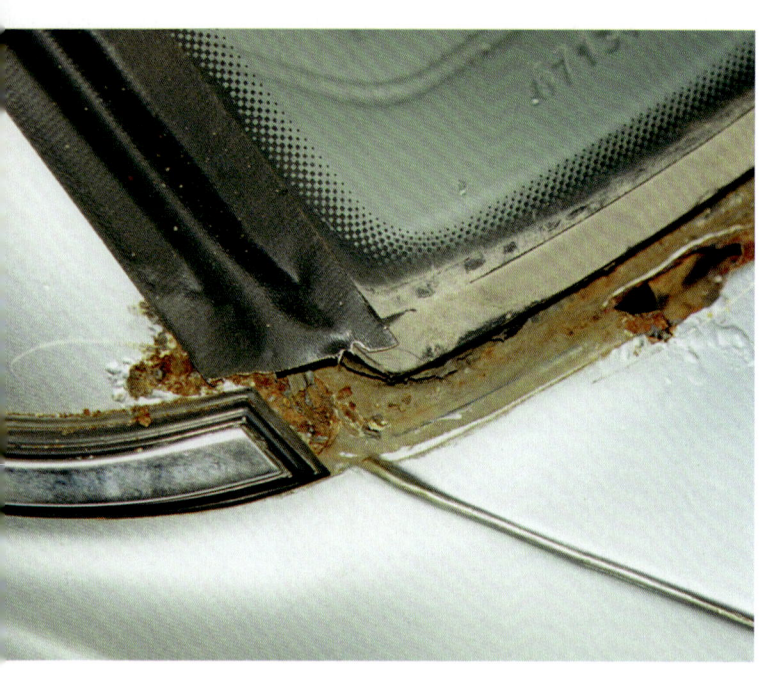

Not so common now, but it can be on the earlier cars. This is the base of the rear screen with the finisher removed revealing corrosion that has gone right through the body.

Exterior chrome/trim/wheels and tyres

The chromwork on XJ40s is relatively hardy and there is little of it to worry about as many items such as the window surrounds are stainless steel. Bumper bars are the most likely cause of concern as they will pit and tarnish in the usual way and can be expensive to replace as they are both one-piece items. The bumper bar

Another common problem which shows neglect in the upkeep of a car is water collecting in the fuel filler which will eventually corrode the hinge and cause water ingress into the petrol tank and boot area.

rubber trims are prone to accidental damage over the years and again can be expensive to replace with new.

The rectangular headlights of some models are prone to ingress of water to a lesser extent than the conventional round style, the former are being expensive to replace. Rear light clusters do lose their brightness after a while and also seem to suffer cracks and crazes more than many other contemporary cars. This is often because the boot lid seal fails, so the lid actually catches the lights as it closes.

Plastic and rubber trim is generally good although some areas will suffer from the ultra-violet rays over the years such as the scuttle finisher and, in particular, the screen-wash jets.

The boot badges are a common source of problem, particularly the rectangular styles which get water trapped in them and look very unsightly after a few years. All the boot badges are applied to the panel with self-adhesive tape and are an easy replacement, after which the whole car looks instantly better for it.

Cars equipped with steel road wheels use a plastic rimbellisher trim. On the earlier cars these were vaned with a separate push-on plastic centre to cover the wheel nuts. This type of trim discolours with age and the clips that hold the centre section on become brittle and break off. Far better are the later style, one-piece trims which don't seem to suffer any real problems.

There were several different types of alloy wheels used over the years, but the most common is the 20-spoke with revealed wheel nuts. On the earlier cars these are of metric size, but later the same style of wheel was produced in non-metric making it more economical when buying replacement tyres.

All-alloy wheels suffer from corrosion normally caused by the hot brake dust (particularly on the front wheels) which settles, stains and eventually wears through the top alloy coating. They can all be refurbished, but at a cost. Particularly bad are the diamond-turned alloy wheels (like the Kiwi) design that require much more regular cleaning to prevent damage.

A complete list of the alloy wheels fitted to the XJ40 is provided elsewhere in this book, with comparison photographs. The aspects of metric-sized tyres and the alternatives are also discussed elsewhere.

Interiors

The interior aspects of the XJ40 models can be split into two categories: leather and non-leather equipped cars, but all seem to wear better than on previous Jaguar models.

First the cloth/tweed upholstered cars, the seats of which wear very well but are prone to 'pull' in the fabric from trouser buttons and sharp objects. The lighter colours can also prove more difficult to keep clean. On the leather-clad cars seat facings always wear well, but the driver's seat in particular is prone to scuffing, also from trouser buttons and the like. The seats rarely sag and a badly worn driver's seat is a sure sign of irregular cleaning and a very high mileage.

Most other interior trim is either leather or vinyl and some vinyl areas are prone to drying out over the years leading to cracks and a hardening of the material which eventually results in it breaking up. Door armrests and the centre console armrest are particularly prone to this problem.

The door trims, especially if they have been removed and refitted a few times for various reasons, will become a sloppy fit and in particular, the top edge will 'sag' in the middle where the clips have not been applied or have become dislodged over the years. The under-dash trimmed panels are also prone to damage over the years and are now difficult to find in good condition as a replacement, unless you are prepared to buy another colour and dye it.

Headlinings and carpets are generally very good although the latter will inevitably suffer if the floorpan gets damp and starts to corrode. The headlining is a one-piece item and is known to sag after a few years, particularly if cleaned constantly with a lot of water.

Woodwork is usually very good with few problems of cracking associated with earlier Jaguar models. The 'ski-slope' area on the centre console is somewhat prone to cracking however, particularly around the ashtray area which is also likely to fade quicker than other parts of the wood trim because of exposure to UV light. There are plenty of cars around that have finished their useful life to provide a good source of supply in case a replacement is needed.

Mechanics

Engines

Specific pointers to look out for with engines are as follows:

Starting with the larger, six-cylinder engines, removal of the oil filler cap will often reveal heavy deposits of a mayonnaise-like substance, which on many engines is indicative of a head gasket problem, but on these engines it is more likely to be due to long periods of short-journey running. Head gaskets normally show failure in one of three ways.

It is always worth seeking out a car with a good interior. XJ40s don't suffer badly so if the one you are looking at has, then it is worth thinking about how well the rest of the car has been looked after.

The most common is severe engine oil leakage from the rear right-hand side of the cylinder block head gasket joint, or from around the distributor area which can indicate a head gasket problem where the clamping pressure of the gasket around the oil returns is failing. This will not normally prevent a car from performing adequately though.

Preformed trim areas like the door armrests and the centre console glove box lid are well known to deteriorate over the years, and under excessive heat will crack like this.

Secondly, the head gasket will blow out between two adjacent cylinders so creating a misfire and/or pinking and does requires immediate change as driving in this condition can melt a piston.

Thirdly and not so common, there is a failure from the water jacket to the combustion chamber via the head gasket whereby the engine can hydraulic. Heavy water consumption, white smoke from the exhaust, overheating and failing to turn over when trying to start an engine are all indicative of water in the cylinders.

The cam cover gasket's U section can harden and split with age causing quite dramatic leakage of oil, normally on the exhaust side of the engine with the consequential problems of oil leaking on to the exhaust creating smoke or even a fire hazard, indicative of poor maintenance.

Common to all the bigger, six-cylinder engines is a problem with the crankshaft pulley which can work loose causing an adverse effect on the engine's running. If you hear a heavy hollow knocking from the engine when it is coming on or off load, this is usually the cause. The simplest way of detecting this is to grasp the water pump pulley and try to rock it backwards and forwards. If it rotates in this way, then the crankshaft pulley is also loose.

HT leads need changing after about 60,000 miles and as these start to break up, the carbon will build up on the legend strip under the bonnet and on the rocker cover, again not a major problem, but also indicative of poor servicing.

A good clean engine bay is a sign of a well kept car. Check items like coolant hoses, oil leaks etc. and in this engine bay note the corrosion on the inner wing.

On the 2.9-litre engines cross threading of spark plugs in the cylinder head is quite common because of their awkward position and difficult access (see maintenance chapter). This will result in the head needing helicoiling.

Engine breathers block up easily on the 2.9-litre units and can cause heavy oil smoke from the back of the car, again indicative of bad servicing. Listen carefully to a 2.9, if there are any peculiar noises from the front of the engine it is almost certain that the top timing chain tensioner will be broken, which is expensive to replace. If there is a low frequency buzzing noise it is still possible that it is the timing chain tensioner which has broken and may have been bodged to quieten it. The way to ascertain this is to feel with the finger in the base of the shoe that protrudes from the cylinder head behind the distributor. If you feel a bolt inside the hole which is just a machined flat finish, then it has been bodged and this surely indicates a bad engine, and maybe car.

Thirdly, piston ring failure is quite common on these engines and will be easily identified by plumes of blue smoke from the exhaust, or heavy oil consumption but don't confuse with a breather problem.

Head gasket failure on the 2.9 is not that common, but when it is problems must be considered when trying to remove the head. As it is secured by studs, the head can stick severely to the block, unlike the other six-cylinder engines which are secured with bolts.

V12 units are particularly trouble free. Regular maintenance will easily show through on these units by the condition of things such as the general engine bay cleanliness, condition of water hoses, coolant and the engine oil in the sump.

Look for signs of anti-freeze splatter over the engine indicating blown hoses and check if there is any record in the service history relating to the radiator having been removed and thoroughly cleaned. Small bleed pipes and vacuum hoses can split under the manifold, all down to careless maintenance. HT leads and the distributor cap are rarely looked at – out of sight and out of mind – so again can be indicative of a poorly maintained car.

The problem of cross-threaded spark plugs applies to the V12 engine as do sticking heads if a head gasket needs to be replaced. The cooling system on the V12 is always marginal so it is vital that it works efficiently with the correct mix of anti-freeze to water, that all hoses are in good condition, the correct thermostats are fitted, etc. In short, good regular maintenance is essential.

Transmissions

The Getrag manual gearboxes are pretty strong and last well, although many still complain about the stodgy gear change and sometimes a heavy clutch pedal, associated with the damper on the master cylinder applicable to earlier cars. It is not realistic to repair a Getrag gearbox if it fails, and its is preferable to buy another as parts are not readily available any more.

All the automatic transmissions are pretty much bullet-proof provided they are maintained well. A typical aspect of poor maintenance is a sluggish or notchy gear change, normally caused by dirt in the system and the filter not being changed regularly.

On the 4.0-litre automatic cars equipped with the Sport gearbox, where the changes are controlled electronically, a multi-pin connector which passes into the gearbox underneath the car can become corroded. This is often a source of 'limp home' mode problems. There can also be problems with the failure of the relays on the bulkhead with the later cars; all identifiable by problems with the gearbox and the 'limp home' mode.

A common fault associated with the XJ40 is a noisy differential which is normally attributable to bearing wear or pinion whine. Although not an insurmountable task, there is nevertheless, a lot of time involved if you wish to carry out the work yourself so the price should be adjusted on such a car if you intend to buy.

Electrics

The electrical system has always been an Achilles heel of the XJ40. In its day it was very advanced, but after so many years in use it is now considered old-fashioned and troublesome. The subject is too large to go into in this buying chapter thoroughly, but the regular items of concern are bulb failure and ABS notifications on the vehicle condition monitor, and the inability to start the car with a partially flat battery.

All these and much more are covered later in this book, but suffice to say at this point, that most of the problems are neither insurmountable nor necessarily expensive to put right.

Most XJ40s are very well equipped with electrical gadgets. The best suggestion is to try everything to make sure it all works – not just the wipers, washers, etc. but the sunroof, electric seats, cruise control, air conditioning, etc. Any failures should have an effect on the end price you pay for the car.

In particular, check items such as the air conditioning and sophisticated heating systems on these cars which are prone to many 'messy' problems. In the main they are not major problems but you will have to address them later once you have purchased the car and they can prove expensive if replacement parts are required. So, the moral is, make sure everything works on the car you intend to buy, or adjust the price accordingly.

Steering and suspension

Again, there are many things to consider, but the most common areas to show poor regular maintenance are worn-out shock absorbers causing the ride to be flawed or bouncy, and knocks and moans from the suspension, generally caused by old bushes which need replacing. On steering, tramlining will show worn bushes, as will irregularly worn tyres.

Wheel bearings can be a common problem on the XJ40s, more on which is explained in a later chapter. When buying a car listen for noises from the wheels, particularly when cornering, and if very noisy, be aware that if the bearings have gone, this can prove very expensive.

Springs weaken over the years as do the shock absorbers, leading to a bouncy ride or knocks created from the underside resonating through the body. This also applies to the many bushes fitted to the car, again, usually caused by poor or irregular maintenance.

The main problems here are, that if you are not used to the refinement of a Jaguar, any Jaguar, then you will find it difficult to associate concerns in this area as a badly maintained car in the suspension department as it is still likely to drive better than many other contemporary models in good condition.

Brakes

The braking system should operate smoothly without excessive pedal travel, the handbrake should be efficient and any signs of vibration through the pedal will normally be associated with poor-condition discs.

Watch for any warning signals from the on-board computer and when the engine has been running, switch it off and try to depress the pedal several times to see if hydraulic pressure is still being held in the system. If it doesn't, this relates to a problem with the sphere which may also lead to other faults.

Conclusions

The XJ40 is a highly complex motor car and it cannot be stressed too much that great care is needed when purchasing one of these models. If, however, you make the right decision, an XJ40 can provide many thousands of happy motoring miles.

Chapter **Ten**

Owning, running and maintaining your XJ40

This chapter looks at what is involved in running an XJ40. It is not the intention of this book to cover all aspects of maintenance in every detail and for further, in-depth information we suggest the purchase of the relevant manuals including the step-by-step, easy-to-use *Haynes Service and Repair Manual No. 3261, Jaguar XJ6 and Sovereign (October '86–September '94)*. Then there are the factory-produced workshop manuals, copies of which can still be found at Jaguar-orientated autojumbles and in the 'for sale' classified advertisements of magazines like *Jaguar Enthusiast*. You can also purchase one of the CD-ROMs now produced by the Jaguar Daimler Heritage Trust on this model, but these are not comprehensive, but help and advice can be sought from other owners, the Jaguar Enthusiasts' Club experts, and at seminars on the model held annually by that club.

General maintenance

Dependent on the age of the car, servicing intervals are at 7,500 and 10,000 miles (see earlier chapters for changeover points). It should be stressed however, that the change to the longer servicing interval was very much a marketing ploy to match other manufacturers and it is probably best to adhere to the former, lower mileage figures, particularly now the cars are getting older.

The service procedures for the various engine sizes comprises up to 52 different attention points made up as detailed in Appendix E.

It is strongly recommended that only Jaguar-branded parts are used wherever possible. A service kit for any of these cars can still be purchased from your local Jaguar dealer and it is not extravagantly priced for what you get (air and oil filter, plugs, washers, split pins, etc, and even includes disposable seat covers and lubricant for the radio aerial).

A minor point to watch when servicing an XJ40 is to check the battery which can overheat because cars charge them at a very high rate and this tends to dry them out quickly. This affects all cars. So it is always worth keeping a check on the battery water level more often than with some other cars.

Coolant loss should be checked on all these engines. The AJ6 engines are particularly prone to head gasket failure which can be identified by the loss of coolant. White stains appearing down the cylinder block, however, do not always identify the start of head gasket failure. More often this is due to minor leakage of water through the gaskets to the outside of the engine. All engines should maintain a minimum 50/50 mix between water and rust inhibited anti-freeze so never top the header tanks up with plain water unless in an emergency.

Coolant loss can also occur through leakage from the joint between the water rail and the cylinder block. This is the output from the water pump into the block. Early cars used gaskets at this joint but later ones used RTV sealant only.

The power hydraulic system on the earlier XJ40s is complex and levels can be checked via a sight-glass at the front offside of the engine bay which should always show green, red indicating the need to add fluid. Only Castrol-Girling mineral fluid should be used and filled via the special feed bottles supplied. For brake systems only DOT 4 hydraulic fluid should be used which can also be used in the clutch reservoir where manual transmission is fitted.

Checking the condition of wheel bearings is vital as both front and rear are of the sealed-for-life variety. This doesn't mean they should be ignored. Properly packed front wheel bearings will last up to 30,000 miles before running dry. If not checked and repacked with grease they will need replacing, but if they start to make a noise, they will quickly wear to the point that the stub axle, callipers, discs, etc. can be damaged beyond repair.

The rear wheel bearings are claimed to last up to 90,000 miles before inspection and repacking although it is better to do this at about 60,000 miles, to be on the safe side.

Shock absorbers are notorious for leaking and/or just wearing out under the strain of a heavy car. They should never be replaced as single units as the ride and handling will be adversely affected.

At the rear of the car, underneath, there are a lot of cables for items such as the ABS speed sensors, pad wear sensors and flexible brake pipes so, whenever checking this area ensure nothing has become fouled in the suspension and that they are all securely tied to their correct points.

There are no grease points on the front suspension but there is one on each of the four UJs on the rear half shafts which need regular attention as do their gaiters to avoid ingress and damage. Differential pinion seals are also prone to leaking on the XJ40 so again these should always be checked at service time.

On post-1987 cars the propshaft is connected to the differential via a Jurid coupling. This rubber and Rayon composite coupling should be checked for cracks and replaced accordingly.

A point worth mentioning is that all XJ40 engines have a huge oil capacity and the coolant systems are large, so whenever draining a car ensure you have a good-sized receptacle in which to collect the used fluids.

An often neglected point is that all road wheel nuts, when replaced on a car after work done, should be torqued to 75lb ft and not just tightened by hand. On a similar note it is always recommended, when replacing alloy wheels, to apply copper grease liberally to the inside of the wheel where it mates with the hub. This will prevent the wheel 'sticking' to the hub and therefore being very difficult to remove at a later date.

A simple point on the radio antenna is that, because of its position on the rear wing it is susceptible to collecting dirt and road grime. A Jaguar service kit includes special lubricant which should be applied at each service to avoid damage. If you don't use the Jaguar kit, then cleaning the mast with WD40 or a similar compound will also help, but do not use a light oil as this will aggravate the problem by attracting more dust.

An example of an XJ40 rear hub assembly where the wheel bearing has not been checked, so it has worn through destroying the surface of the hub, seen here as the very shiny area in the centre.

In the following pages we will take you through as many specific pointers on the cars and engines as we have space for. By necessity, work is split up by either engine size or type of model.

Another common item to keep a check on is the Rotoflex coupling in the drivetrain to the rear axle. Over the years it degrades and eventually splits like this. It must fit in one orientation only, as explained in the instructions that come with the new part.

V12-engined models

Parts availability
Parts in general are not a problem at all for the 6.0-litre V12 engine as fitted to the XJ40. All drive belts (and there are three) are readily available although the multi-groove alternator drive belt can be spasmodic in supply. The oil filter on these later units is exactly the same as used on the six-cylinder engines.

Oil leaks
The V12 engine can be prone to oil leaks from a number of areas including the cam cover gaskets, which are a particularly weak point. It is difficult to change these because of the necessity to remove items such as the inlet manifolds, so if a car has not been well serviced this is a telltale of the problem. The oil gauge and warning light transmitters (situated at the rear of the engine behind the throttle pedestal) are also prone to leaking, but this is not a major problem to rectify.

The front crankshaft oil seals are quite prone to leakage but this doesn't require many specialist tools and although it looks quite daunting, it is a relatively easy DIY job to rectify. Changing one of these seals involves removing the front crankshaft pulley set. To do this you remove all three drive belts, the outer one first, inner last, simply by undoing the respective belt tensioners. Then the viscous cooling fan can be removed by undoing the four nuts holding it on to the front of the drive. Access to the front crankshaft pulley is tight because of the proximity of the radiator and cooling cowl although the cowl itself can be easily removed if necessary.

Four bolts hold the outer pulley set on the rear pulley. This also brings off the $7/8$in AF stud. There is a 1 $5/16$in AF bolt which holds the innermost pulley on the crankshaft. This is always very tight and requires the locking up of the pulley itself to prevent the engine from turning during removal.

Once removed, the inner pulley has a coned sleeve located in a specific position with a Woodruff key. With everything out of the way the crankshaft seal is revealed. Genuine Jaguar replacement seals come with an inner seal race which must be replaced as this is the area which causes most of the oil leak problems. In order to remove the old race the Woodruff keys from the crankshaft also have to be removed. These will also be very tight and, dependent on the age of the engine and previous work carried out, can be damaged, so it is advisable to carry new spares just in case.

A blocked engine breather can cause oil to be blown out from either the sandwich plate gasket or the rear crankshaft oil seal. If an engine leaks significantly from either of these areas, the first thing to check is that the breather is free. Replacing the sandwich plate gasket is difficult because the front subframe has to be dropped as it runs the entire length of the engine. If the rear crankshaft oil seal is leaking badly this used to mean the removal of the engine, but with the 6.0-litre engines in the XJ40 it is a much easier task of removing the gearbox and fitting a new lip seal, a matter of seven to nine hours work for an experienced mechanic.

General maintenance tips
The V12 engine responds well to regular, quality servicing. Service work is not as daunting as one would think and is certainly not beyond the realms of the DIY mechanic, providing they have a basic understanding of how everything works and have access to a good and relatively comprehensive tool kit. A good quality $3/8$in drive socket set is needed but there are no special tools required for regular maintenance.

Care, however, should be taken when working on one of these engines because of the complex nature of the installation and associated wiring, ancillaries, etc. This applies in particular to the front of the engine when working on the first plug on each bank. The type of plug recommended for the 6.0-litre is the NGK BR7EF.

To carry out the average major service on the V12 engine will involve many tasks all of which will take the average, competent DIY mechanic about four to five hours to complete.

A good-quality semi-synthetic 10W40 oil will suffice and it is a characteristic of V12 engines that when hot, oil pressure can fall as low as 15–20psi at idle. A good measure of the engine, however, is that oil pressure should recover very quickly to above 50psi at only 1,300rpm.

Having said this, the oil gauge sender units are notoriously unreliable. If the engine sounds clean without any undue noises or oil usage, but with apparent low oil pressure, it is suggested that the oil pressure is tested with a master wet line gauge.

All V12 engines should be quiet in operation without undue noise levels. The ticking of the fuel injectors should be the overriding noise at idle. Holding the engine at around 1,200rpm then backing off the throttle can occasionally cause a slight timing chain rattle. This usually means a slightly worn chain and/or tensioner, but the engine can carry on for many more thousands of miles without direct concern.

However, when the time comes to address this problem, it is a major job to change the timing chain and one you should consider very carefully, or enlist the help of an experienced mechanic with the V12 engine. It is not the cost of parts that should be of concern but the work which is extensive and includes the removal of the air conditioning compressor, the cam covers, inlet manifolds, water pump, alternator, power steering reservoir and, if done with the engine in situ, the radiator as well. It also means either taking the cylinder heads off the engine or dropping the sump from underneath. The latter is a lot easier, but still means dropping the front suspension subframe.

When carrying out this much work to change the chain it is strongly recommended that the tensioner and dampers are also changed as well as the chain. The former may still look in good condition but over the years will become brittle with the heat generated inside the engine. It is not unknown when retensioning the chain upon reassembly for this to break, thus rendering the work to be done all over again!

Another common problem relates to the throttle capstan and rod adjustment. Primarily, when one presses the accelerator pedal the idea is to open the throttles to each cylinder bank simultaneously. However, this does not always happen as the throttle rods go out of adjustment regularly due to wear appearing in the small ball joints and in the rod bushes.

The bushes are located in a carrier bracket to the rear of each butterfly housing. These are rubber and are still readily available. Continuous movement and oil contamination from the engine will cause these to go brittle, eventually breaking up and falling out, resulting in excess movement of the accelerator pedal in relation to the movement of the throttle rods. To replace these bushes involves undoing the end plate which carries them, from the inlet manifold and simply pressing replacement bushes into place and reassembling.

Adjusting the throttle operating rods is best carried out by working with only one bank at a time. Unclip one throttle rod from the capstan; these rods have a left-handed thread at one end and a right-handed thread on the other. Slackening off the 5/16in AF locknut allows you to increase or decrease the length of the rod accordingly such that with the capstan closed properly the butterfly is just about to open (i.e. there is no free play at all). Repeating the process on the other rod, not forgetting to lock up the locknut again, finalises the job.

The correct adjustment of these throttle butterflies on a previously incorrectly adjusted engine can improve fuel consumption by 1mpg to 2mpg as the throttle capstan also controls part of the fuel injection control system (via the throttle potentiometer). This instructs the ECU on the position of the throttle at any one time, so wrongly adjusted the accelerator is pressed further than normal for a given engine load, sending the wrong message to the ECU which then over-fuels the engine.

It can be clearly stated that all 6.0-litre V12 engines fitted to the XJ40 were built to accept unleaded fuel and shouldn't be run on anything else.

Engine management

Control of engine management is achieved by a Lucas fuel injection system interfaced with a Marelli ignition system.

The manifold pressure sensor is incorporated within the ECU which is situated under the dashboard. This takes the form of a piezo-electric cell (non-vented to atmosphere). To compensate for changes in atmospheric pressure and engine load the fuel pressure regulators are modulated according to the above by means of a vacuum connection to the manifold.

On the subject of fuel distribution, petrol is supplied to the engine by an in-tank fuel pump module incorporating a number of first stage filters. The second stage (disposable) fine filter is located in the fuel line under the left-hand side of the car just forward of the rear wheelarch. In the engine bay, fuel passes through the fuel rail, the pressure being controlled by a fuel pressure regulator at the side of the fuel rail. Excess fuel is then returned to the fuel tank.

There are also various temperature and load sensing devices around the engine and all models use the same principles of sensing. The 'limp home' facility will allow the car to continue running, even if one of these important sensors should fail.

The Marelli ignition system can be problematic for the following reasons – bad connections at either of two ignition amplifiers, especially if they have been disturbed, and either of the ignition coils can fail spontaneously, the two-stage rotor arm can burn through between contacts. Any of these can produce cronic misfire symptoms with possible catalytic damage.

Cooling system

The cooling system of the V12 engine must be maintained in pristine condition as the whole system is rather marginal in its capabilities, and this applies in particular to the 6.0-litre XJ40s. The V12 is such a strong engine that it can be run virtually with no oil in the sump for short periods. This is not recommended, but add some oil and you are unlikely to experience any long-term problems. However, if you allow these engines to become overheated, the damage can be so great that the engine will possibly have to be replaced.

This means *always* running with the correct 50/50 level of anti-freeze to water to prevent the build up of corrosion inside the engine. When this happens the composite head gaskets also corrode as the engines are of a wet liner design with no block face. Both surfaces of the head gasket are in coolant and when corrosion starts on the outer edge behind the seal to the combustion chamber, the bridge that this part of the gasket forms will disappear allowing the gasket to 'blow' comprehensively.

Changing the head gaskets is not normally an easy job on the V12 engine as very often when corrosion has taken place, the heads will seize on. It is often possible to suspend the whole weight of a V12 engine by its cylinder heads, and they will still not free off.

Filling the cooling system is a slow procedure which must be followed to ensure there are no air locks. On all the V12 cars there is provision to automatically bleed the system of air. The engines take a total of around four gallons of coolant and when empty, it must be ensured that four gallons actually go in.

The efficiency of the cooling system also means checking that the two thermostats fitted are of the same make and grade and are in the right position. The correct, 82° thermostats for these engines should have a small bleed hole (called a giggle pin). This bleed hole should always be fitted at the 12 o'clock position – i.e. at the uppermost point. This is to allow air to be purged from what could be an empty, four-gallon capacity cooling system. Failure to fit this type of thermostat or to fit the right type the wrong way will cause major air locks inside the engine with disastrous results.

The radiators, due to the design of the oil cooler, the air conditioning condenser and their prominent position at the front of the car, are prone to exterior blockages. This comes from debris and road grime, all of which can cause overheating problems. Equally the automatic transmission and power steering cooler pipes enter the radiator on each side. These tend to weep and oil can stick to the radiator matrix and create a magnet for dust and dirt further hindering free flow of air.

The radiators therefore need to be cleaned fairly regularly to ensure total efficiency. The use of a simple jet-wash through the grille is insufficient for this purpose. The only satisfactory way of cleaning these radiators is to remove them from the car about once every 12 months to thoroughly inspect and clean them out.

Removal of the radiator is relatively easy, but there are a lot of nuts and bolts and there is a definite procedure to be followed. It requires some thought before starting the job and you need to be methodical to avoid leaving some aspect of wiring disconnected and causing problems afterwards. The radiator is a very heavy item and it is strongly recommended that it is lifted out by two people, not only to prevent damage to the surrounding area and/or the radiator itself, but also for safety reasons.

There are more than 15 different coolant hoses on the V12 engine. At the very least, if taking the radiator out, it is advised to change the bottom and heater return hoses because they are so difficult to change in situ. V12 engines are prone to blowing their top hoses and if one does go, then it is also advisable to change the other at the same time. Fortunately this is not normally a sign of a damaged head gasket but a merely a weakness in this area.

There are also three hoses that form what is called the water rail hose assembly. This is where the outlet from the water pump splits off to a T, going to the right and left cylinder heads. They are very difficult to see and so are 'out of sight, out of mind', but they should be checked regularly as they are not easy to change. To change them involves removing some of the three drive belts.

Exhaust system

All the 6.0-litre XJ40 models are fitted with catalytic converters. These are situated in the down pipes and intermediate sections. They are not prone to any problems but are bulky so ground clearance needs to be watched. The exhausts themselves are long lasting and there are no known common problems.

Transmissions

The automatic transmission fitted to the 6.0-litre cars is extremely reliable and it will respond well to regular maintenance. Every two years or 30,000 miles the sump pan should be removed, the oil changed and the filter discarded and replaced with a new one.

To identify the condition of the oil and therefore perhaps the gearbox, the dipstick is removed and if the oil is found to be brown and tarnished and/or smells burnt, then not only has the oil not been changed regularly but the gearbox may be in need of refurbishment.

A particular problem associated with V12-engined cars relates to the bolt which holds the output shaft flange on to the output shaft of the gearbox. It works loose, eventually becoming undone completely. When this happens it allows the output shaft flange to move in and out from the gearbox on its splines, thus increasing wear. To check if this is the case, use a crowbar to try to move the flange forwards and/or backwards. If there is any movement then the propshaft will need disconnecting, the bolt removing (if not already off) and thread-locked back into position.

Six-cylinder models

The AJ6 engines fitted to the XJ40 were of 3.6-litre capacity and then upgraded to 4.0 litres in 1990. Most of the following applies to both types of engine unless otherwise stated and also includes the 3.2-litre unit. Specific comments relating to the 2.9-litre engine are given separately.

Parts availability

Parts availability for the six-cylinder engines is exceptionally good. The only problems at present maybe with the early cars in that piston rings or pistons are no longer available. This means that any problem, for example, with a burnt out piston may necessitate the changing of all six pistons for the later type which are a direct replacement, to ensure correct balance. This same scenario applies to the exhaust valves.

These engines are very reliable and capable of huge mileages as far as the bottom end is concerned. They are not known for oil use or loss although the 4.0-litre engines will often use more oil than the 3.6-litre units. This is mainly due to a change in piston design. Both types of engine are prone to blowing head gaskets at anything over 50,000 miles and equally, a poorly tuned engine can easily burn out its valves. This is most common to 4.0-litre engines and is generally caused by hot spots often due to faulty thermostats or blocked radiator, air leaks from a leaking manifold gasket or incorrect timing.

General maintenance tips

All jobs can be carried out by a competent DIY mechanic and the use of special tools is again limited, but as before, a comprehensive tool kit is a big advantage although access to the engine and ancillaries is significantly easier on these cars.

Regular maintenance will always pay off as with any engine, and one of the often-neglected items on the 2.9-litre engine is cleaning the engine breather system. This helps to prevent sludge build-up and will help engine life and not least fuel economy.

One of the most common issues discussed by owners of these cars relates to the use, or not, of unleaded fuel. Whilst factory unleaded conversions have been available for all engines in one form or another, the life and performance of a well-maintained unit seems to be unaffected by the use of unleaded fuel.

As mentioned earlier, a common problem associated with the 2.9-litre engine is the cross-threading of spark plugs in their holes because they are fitted in at an oblique angle and access is a little difficult.

We have also already mentioned the risk of the cylinder head gaskets blowing on the six-cylinder engines and the replacement of the gasket is not a major problem for a competent DIY mechanic with good quality tools.

It is not vital to completely remove the inlet manifold but it has to be disconnected and moved away from the head. This in itself necessitates the removal of other items initially, such as the air flow meter and the engine and gearbox oil dipstick tube securing bracket. Hoses to be removed include the one from the thermostat housing, a small heater supply hose from the cylinder head to the heater unit, which is very difficult to access in the engine bay.

The throttle linkage has to be dismantled, but not removed, and if the car has automatic transmission a similar action has to be taken to undo the kickdown cable. The top 13mm nuts on the head also secure brackets supporting the fuel injection wiring loom and have to be disconnected. On the uppermost front nut there is either one or two earth connectors to be disconnected.

There are six 13mm manifold securing nuts visible from the top and a further seven 10mm headed bolts at the base. It is recommended that the centre top 13mm nut is left in place until the very last to help secure the manifold in place. Two further 10mm long bolts hold the thermostat housing in position, which has to be removed from the head.

The manifold, when free, can then be moved across lightly to make room for the removal of the cylinder head. A new inlet manifold should be used when reassembling.

After removing the chromium-plated heat shield from the offside, the two exhaust manifolds can be removed from the head quite easily, although on the 2.9-litre engine they are known to be difficult and can shear the studs if you are not careful. It is not necessary to remove the manifolds or exhaust, but merely move them away from the head which should reveal a good view of the block itself which will show signs of water seepage from the head gasket. Again, as with the inlet manifold, it is strongly recommended that all gaskets are replaced on reassembly.

Next off should come the plug leads, distributor cap and the camshaft cover. Turning the engine over to TDC with the aid of a 1 5/16in AF spanner on the crankshaft pulley nut, the position of the rotor arm in the distributor body can be marked with Tipp-Ex or similar, then the distributor and shaft can be removed from the engine. This allows access to remove the timing chain adjuster.

The top timing chain requires disconnecting from the camshafts. This is achieved by removing the four bolts which hold each sprocket on to the camshafts and allowing them to drop down. Once the sprockets are removed the chain can be carefully laid down inside the timing case.

Finally, three 10mm headed bolts right at the front of the timing chain case, one of which on many models secures a hydraulic pipe bracket, must also be removed. This now just leaves the 14 17mm bolts securing the head to the engine, which after removal, are discarded as they *must* be replaced with new ones. The cylinder head is a heavy unit and so two people should lift it clear of the engine to avoid damage and injury.

After removal, the head must be cleaned thoroughly and checked in case it has warped. This is not usual on these heads but it is always worth checking, and before refitting the head the timing chain tensioner blade needs to be secured in an upright position with a cable-tie to below the head, to pass over it.

Apart from the following components a complete Jaguar head gasket set will provide all the parts required. The additional parts are the cylinder head stretch bolts and the four camshaft lock tabs as well as all fluids, etc.

The replacement head gasket only fits one way and should always be assembled *dry*. The new head stretch bolts should be torqued up between 59 and 61 Newton metres (45lb ft) starting from the centre and working outwards on both sides. After this, each bolt has to be turned through 90° clockwise preferably using a dial gauge for accuracy.

Finally, timing chain adjustment must be confirmed with the aid of a special tool, originally manufactured for Jaguar by Churchill and now available through the Jaguar Enthusiasts' Club. The use of the tool is as follows.

Top dead centre (TDC) is determined by rotating the crankshaft until the tooth on the toothed wheel identified by a small embossed triangle is in line with the timing marker on the timing case. With the engine at TDC, place the tool over each camshaft in turn so that when each end of the tool rests on the machined face of the cylinder head top, the lug fits exactly in the slot in each camshaft.

Reassembly is the reverse and it is always advisable to replace the seal sets in the cam covers (which are reasonably priced) as they do become hardened with age and will inevitably cause oil leaks.

Returning to the issue of normal maintenance, regular oil changes are essential, otherwise a

The special timing chain tool required to adjust the timing on the AJ6 engine. A similar concept (but different) tool also needs to be used on the V12 engines.

significant build up of oil sludge will take place. This builds up in the sump and can cause problems with oil pick-up leading to oil starvation.

It is always a good policy to keep the rotor arm and distributor cap clean and it should be checked regularly for damage caused by corrosion and erosion. It is the nature of this type of ignition system that these parts will deteriorate quicker than with others. All cars have the digitally controlled ignition system with just the rotor arm within the cap.

During regular service intervals, it should be ensured that electrical contacts to fuel injection and ignition sensors are clean and lubricated. Using a proprietary contact cleaner, remove the connectors to clean them and spray the contacts.

Cooling systems

The drain screw on XJ40 radiators is made of plastic situated on the right-hand underside of the radiator and often becomes damaged over the years if too small a bladed screwdriver is used.

The condition of coolant hoses on all engines is important and because of the position of some of them, they are often neglected. A particular example is the heater return hose which runs the entire length of the engine underneath the inlet manifold which can swell in its retaining bracket. To access this the heater valve hose has to be disconnected (a push fit and jubilee clipped) *but* it is pushed over a very thin pipe which is screwed into the heater matrix. Violent movement when disconnecting the hose could dislodge or crack the pipe. The heater return hose is also disconnected from behind the heater valve.

It is strongly recommend that, like the V12s, the radiator is removed and cleaned thoroughly at least once every two years.

There is a general weakness in XJ40 water pumps which normally start to weep from about 70,000 miles. Renewal is quite straightforward, if a little fiddly. The fan-drive viscous coupling and cowl require removal followed by disconnection of the many hoses from the back of the water pump, these in turn being accessed by removal of the air flow meter, etc. The drive belt must also be removed by detensioning the tensioner. The water pump is held to the block by bolts which, after removal, allow it to be withdrawn.

Electrics

One of the most common problems is the inability to start the engine from cold on a partially flat battery. Constant attempts to start the car will result in flooding the engine and the only answer is to remove all the spark plugs, clean them and heat them up (perhaps in a kitchen oven). When thoroughly dry and warm refit them in the engine and, ensuring the battery is fully charged, the car should start after some cranking.

Severe damage can be caused to the electrical system on the XJ40 by attempting to jump-start the car from another vehicle. One of the most common problems is blowing the over-voltage relay fuse, found in the boot area of the car (pre 1990 cars). The moral with these cars is to either charge the car's battery *off* the vehicle or with the terminals at least disconnected or, if you have to jump-start from another vehicle, never have the other vehicle's engine running, or its ignition switched on.

Transmissions

The manual gearboxes are very reliable in service although parts are now difficult and in some cases almost impossible to obtain. It should be noted that the oil originally specificied for the manual gearbox was SAE 80. However, particularly when cold, this can make the gear change stiff and notchy. Later cars were specified with automatic transmission fluid and it is perfectly acceptable to use this in the earlier

There is a maze of electrical wiring, relays, etc. both inside the car and under the bonnet. This array of blue relays on the bulkhead under the bonnet can, over the years, be ingressed with damp and if the contacts are not kept clean, will result in many symptoms of failure.

gearboxes which will ensure a lighter and smoother gear change.

Flywheels on manual cars are prone to some distortions leading to cracking, particularly when the clutch has had heavy use. If the clutch is juddering under take-up and operation, this is indicative of distortion. Removing the gearbox and clutch will show if the flywheel has gone 'blue' or has cracks. If not too heavily cracked it can be removed and skimmed, which will alleviate the problem. If it is too bad, then the only solution is to replace the flywheel.

The ZF automatic transmission is not known for problems and can be easily rebuilt by experts but will be expensive. As usual with transmissions, they respond well to regular maintenance and incorporate a renewable oil filter. Again, the same checks apply as with the V12 transmissions.

The later, 4.0-litre-equipped 'sport' boxes have a multi-pin connector entering the gearbox underneath the car. This can corrode through damp ingress which causes false electrical signals to be transmitted. Undoing, cleaning and replacing the connector will usually cure this problem.

The gearbox mounting is similar in concept to the V12 models, but it rarely causes any problems.

The automatic transmissions are also trouble free if maintained properly and that means having the filter changed at the recommended intervals. This is a relatively simple job; first draining the fluid and remove the six bolts holding the sump to the box. This will then reveal the filter held in place by three torx-headed bolts. Discard the filter and replace ensuring a new O ring is fitted to the filter, clean the sump and fit with a new gasket and then carefully bolt back into place and refill with oil.

A problem associated with the ZF gearboxes on the six-cylinder cars is a sticking shift lever that doesn't want to move from 'Park'. Much of this is down to the J-gate cover and wear over a period of time. By removing the centre console surrounds and gaining access below the J-gate panel there is a sliding metal plate dust shield, the edge of which will wear a groove in the shaft causing the rough movement and, in some cases, completely restricting it. Adding a radius to that shield will smooth the flow of the shaft again and prevent the problem.

Engine management

XJ40 cars used the micro-fuelling Lucas system of fuel injection which incorporated a hot-wire air flow meter as opposed to a pressure sensing system. This same system continued virtually unchanged to the end of production in 1994. These systems are extremely reliable, the only problems being the aforementioned cold start flooding with a flat battery and the spontaneous failure (and self rectification) of the crankshaft speed sensor. If a car has a history of periodically not starting and then being OK for a few days, changing this sensor will often cure it (not affecting 2.9-litre engines).

For some reason, 2.9-litre air flow meters are more prone to failure than the others and it is worth noting that the ECU coolant temperature sensor is the same for all twin-cam engines and many other Jaguar applications, but the 2.9-litre sensor is unique to this engine. If the incorrect one is fitted, this will create problems.

Not associated directly with fuel injection, but having a bearing on it if it fails, is the problem with the left-hand fuse box on post-1993 model year cars which is located in the A post. Failure of electrical joints in this fuse box causes low voltage signals to be sent to the coil and this will prevent the engine from starting.

Exhaust systems

The system, although different from the V12-engined cars, is just as trouble free, remembering that only certain models had catalytic converters which inevitably will be more expensive to replace in due course, but are extremely durable.

XJR specifics

Some of the genuine XJR models from TWR and JaguarSport have mechanical differences to standard production vehicles. This, however, very much depends on what the original owner specified at the time of purchase.

Technical information on these cars is scant to say the least with nothing actually available from Jaguar themselves, and it would appear that little information is held by TWR who modified them when new.

Maintenance issues affecting all models
Rear axles and the drive train

Differentials on XJ40s are known for becoming noisy after about 80,000 miles. This is a common problem, also associated with some later Jaguar saloon models. The cause of this is worn bearings and the only answer is to remove the differential from the axle, which is a

The rear axle and suspension assembly on the XJ40 is a daunting sight: it is heavy to remove and costly to completely refurbish.

Rear A frame bushes are relatively easy to replace and their condition (as with other bushes used around the car) can make a world of difference to the ride quality. The one on the right is taken from a car with a current MoT, but compare with a new one, on the left.

major task, and review the condition, replacing bearings as necessary. Pinion seal oil leaks are also not uncommon but the replacement of these is a relatively simple operation and can be dealt with at the same time as the differential.

To carry out any work on the differential requires the complete rear axle subframe to be removed from the car. Whilst not technically difficult the problems encountered are due to the sheer weight of the components and the amount of corrosion, which over the years, will have caused nuts, bolts, etc. to seize. It is for these reasons that such work should not be undertaken lightly by the DIY owner.

Brakes

All XJ40 models are equipped with four-wheel disc brakes, servo assistance and, on the majority of cars, ABS. The earlier, pre-4.0-litre cars used a conventional dual circuit master cylinder using pressurised mineral oil from an engine-driven pump, commonly known as the Jurid system. Later cars used brakes of Teves manufacture with a master cylinder assembly incorporating the ABS. Both are very safe and competent systems in general although, as with any other mechanical aspect of a car, they are subject to the usual problems of age, like worn discs.

Jurid brake callipers have problems relating to the slides seizing which will cause excessive pedal travel whilst Teves front brake callipers (particularly on the right-hand side) will often suffer from a seized piston. In each case, the calliper is of the single-piston floating variety.

One of the most common brake problems is with the ABS. Each wheel has a speed sensor and these relate wheel speed to road speed. On the pre-1990 cars the rear-wheel sensors suffer from crushing as corrosion in the alloy housing expands and collapses the thin outer wall of the sensor. The ECU then picks this up and will flash up a warning on the VCM and stop the ABS working. To identify which sensor is at fault remove the boot bulkhead interior trim and disconnect each sensor from the main body wiring loom. Using a digital ohm meter (it is important to avoid damage to the electrical circuitry of the car), attach one lead to a suitable earth on the car and the other to each of the pins to the sensor in turn. If there is any continuity at all, however high the resistance, the sensor will require replacement.

The sensors can easily be accessed on the hub and at first glance may look in good condition, but internally one or both of them may have imploded preventing them from working and therefore activating the computer warning system on the dashboard.

The old sensor may be difficult to extract because of corrosion, but once it is and its accompanying wiring removed, a new one can easily be installed, but not before the orifice in the hub has been cleaned of all debris and corrosion. Copper grease should be used to lubricate the sensor.

An interesting 'knocking' sound from under the bonnet area on pre-1990 models can come from the braking system valve block on the inner wing. This also applied to later cars still equipped with self-levelling equipment. It comes from the valve block not relieving pressure correctly, which will therefore need replacement.

The hydraulic system accumulator sphere will, over time, lose its pressure capacity (of up to 1,350psi when new) but should still last to over 100,000 miles. To test its ability to hold pressure run the engine until the warning lights are extinguished. Switch off the engine, turn the key back to the '2' position so that the dashboard warning lights will illuminate again. Pump the brake pedal, counting the number of times you press the pedal hard to the floor, until you see the 'low brake pressure' warning come on. Normally this should be after at least eight pumps; if less than five the sphere is getting near the end of its life.

When it is necessary to bleed the brakes on the XJ40, because most are ABS-equipped, it involves a totally different procedure to conventional systems. A full understanding of the ABS system is needed and involved procedures must be met to eliminate the possibility of expensive and dangerous problems. It is suggested that anyone wishing to bleed these brakes consults the appropriate Jaguar workshop manual and follows the procedure to the letter.

Brake fluid should be changed every two years or at 30,000-mile intervals and a quality DOT 4 fluid used.

The earlier cars with the commonly referred to Jurid brake system, used this type of hydraulic master cylinder arrangement.

The later Teves-equipped cars used this type of combined master cylinder/ABS modulator system.

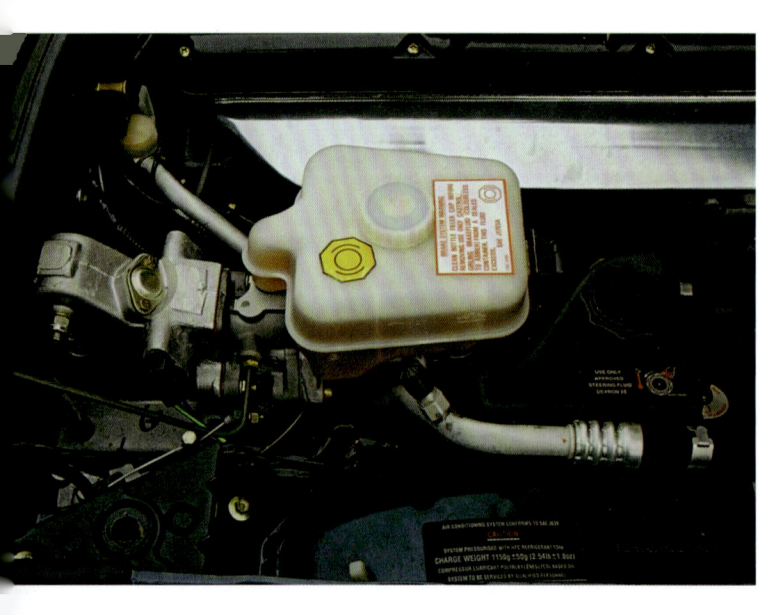

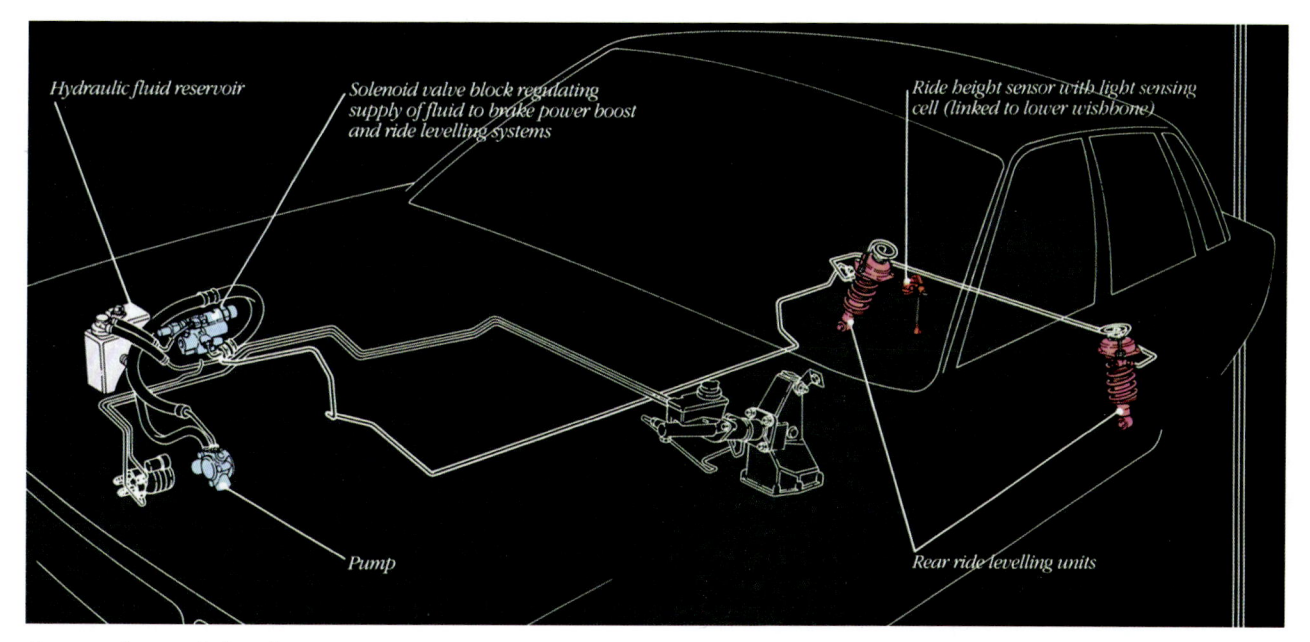

This is the layout of the self-levelling system on the XJ40.

The layout of the front and rear suspension shows the integrated nature of the rear damper/spring unit.

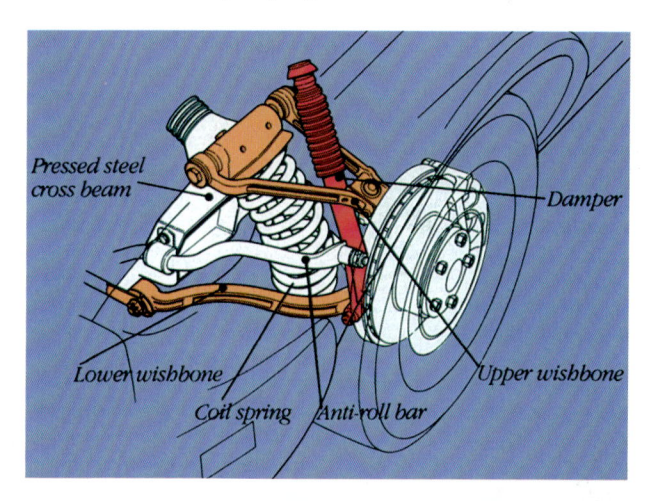

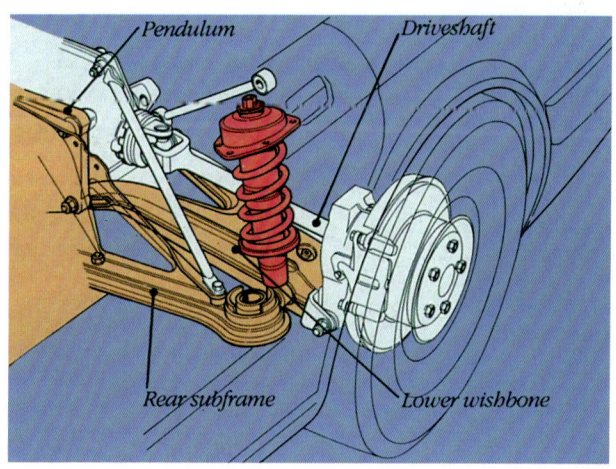

Suspension and steering

On the issue of suspension we must mention the self-levelling system which was later discontinued from all production cars. The system, although good in theory, never worked at its best and gave a lot of problems in use.

Once this system shows up faults, it is strongly recommended that it is decommissioned from the car which results in the need to fit a different type of rear spring and shock absorber arrangement. In terms of expense this is minimal compared with the constant work necessary on the ride height system, if left so equipped.

One of the most common problems with a heavy car like the XJ40 is that the shock absorbers will need replacing. At the front this is a simple operation, but at the rear, this requires the removal of the spring from the shock absorber assembly and therefore the use of specialist tools. It must also be noted that the very last of the XJ40 models had a revised rear suspension system whereby the coil springs had to be compressed on the car before the shock absorbers could be removed. All shock absorbers should be replaced in axle pairs to ensure safety and the retention of good ride and handling.

Steering on all cars is by rack-and-pinion with power assistance and is generally reliable, although flexible hoses are prone to failure, this usually due to incorrect or careless fitting at some time. There are many flexible joints and sharp objects to foul them which will cause problems if care is not taken in fitting.

The track rod ends come in for a lot of work and

Owning, running and maintaining your XJ40

This is an example of how badly corroded the front subframe can become on an XJ40.

The right-hand side of the front subframe (looking from the front of the car) showing its relationship with the suspension unit. Much of the corrosion will not be seen without very close inspection.

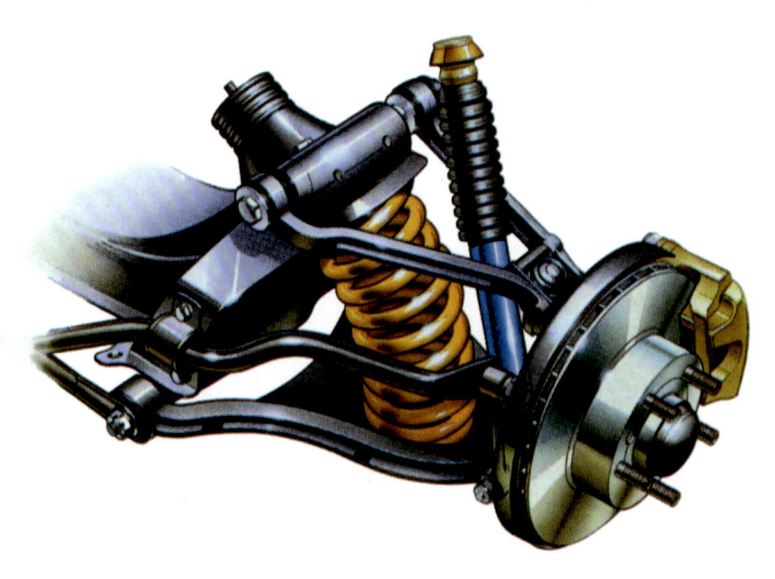

wear due to hauling around such a big and heavy car. They require regular checking, and when worn, are a not-serviceable item so total replacement is needed.

Other mechanical aspects

On the earlier cars which have an axle-mounted fuel pump it is not unknown for the fuel non-return valve to fail. The function of the valve (which screws on to the end of fuel pump) is to prevent the loss of fuel pressure back to the tank via the supply system. Over time, the spring-loaded valve will degrade and the only solution is to change the valve itself, not an expensive item although later valves have a slightly different spanner size fitment.

Front subframe and rear A frame

The importance of the front subframe condition was mentioned in Chapter Nine, Choosing and Buying. To undertake such work is expensive and involves amongst other things, supporting the engine so that the subframe can be withdrawn.

The rear A frame carries the diff and fits across the width of the rear axle. Located to the body by two bushes (see previous picture on page 139), changing bushes is not difficult, only complicated by the possible seizure of bolts and the need to access a press to insert them.

Electrics

Many consider that the XJ40 electrics are notorious and complex but once understood there is no need for any aspect to be considered daunting. A basic understanding of car electrics and electronics is essential and in some cases specialist equipment may be needed, which is not always available to the DIY mechanic.

A simple fault which is easy to rectify is the inability of the single windscreen wiper to park correctly. This is nearly always down to either a 7.5 amp fuse blowing which is accessible under the passenger side dash liner, (very early cars did not have an in-line fuse fitted and Jag themselves upgraded subsequent fitment of a 5 amp fuse to 7.5 amp.) or failure of the micro-switch within the wiper motor itself.

Bulb failure warnings are common and if this is not down to a specific bulb not working, it usually occurs because of a bad earth somewhere in the system. The most common faults here are associated with the front wing-mounted indicator repeaters (European cars). Another component to cause this problem is the 'dummy plug' which is substituted for a fog lamp when these are not fitted to the cars. These plugs incorporate a resistance which simulates the fitment of a bulb and are situated just behind the front valance, and over the years will corrode due to ingress of water.

Many common electrical problems with the XJ40 relate to printed circuit boards and dry joints. For example, in the headlamp modules there are two boards in each and a sure sign of a broken joint is found when turning on the sidelights and one of the dim-dip bulbs will flash on and then extinguish, often resulting in the bulb failure warning light coming on. The problem is, however, often caused by a broken joint on one of the two circuit boards within the modules, which are easily accessible by straightening out the tags that secure the lid of the module in position. An easy repair can be accomplished once you have found the 'break' which is far less costly than buying a new module at not much under £200.

A minor problem associated with many cars, where the radio antenna is situated at the rear, is a sticking mast. Luckily on the XJ40, this is not usually an expensive problem. The motor works on overload sensing which prevents the mast from moving up or down beyond its locking points. It will therefore also stop if the mast sticks at any point because of dirt trapping it. Sensing the stop position, thereafter whenever the motor is activated by turning the radio on, the mast will always stop in the same position.

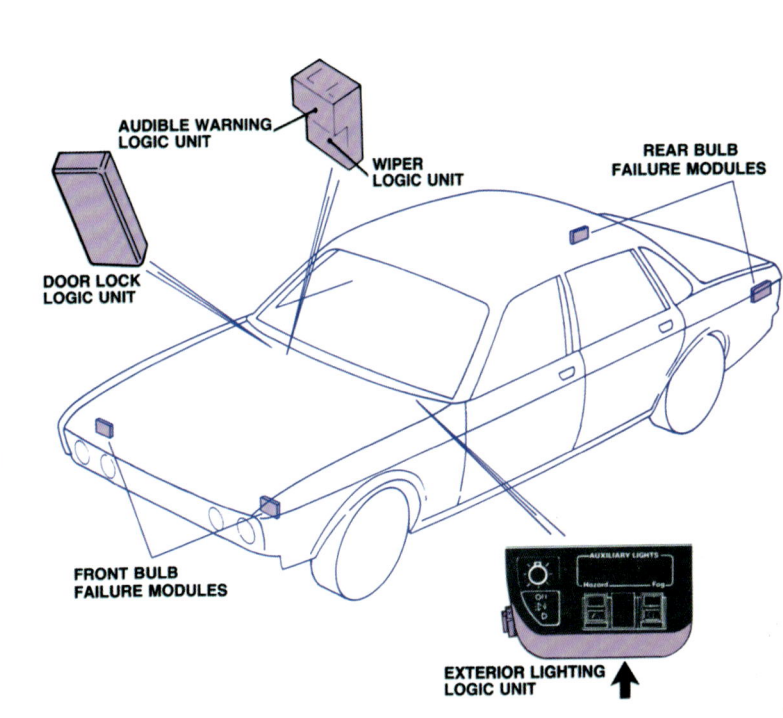

The XJ40 electrical system incorporates several logic units within the circuits to provide feedback on information to the central microprocessor.

By releasing the retaining nut on the rear wing, turning on the radio will cause the mast to raise, and holding it will allow it to continue to be extracted from the body with its toothed-nylon cable. If the mast and its cable are still in good condition (the mast not be

A typical printed circuit board used in the XJ40 which can, over time, collect damp and corrosion and the joints will dry out. The technology is now relatively simple and these boards can be cleaned and resoldered successfully.

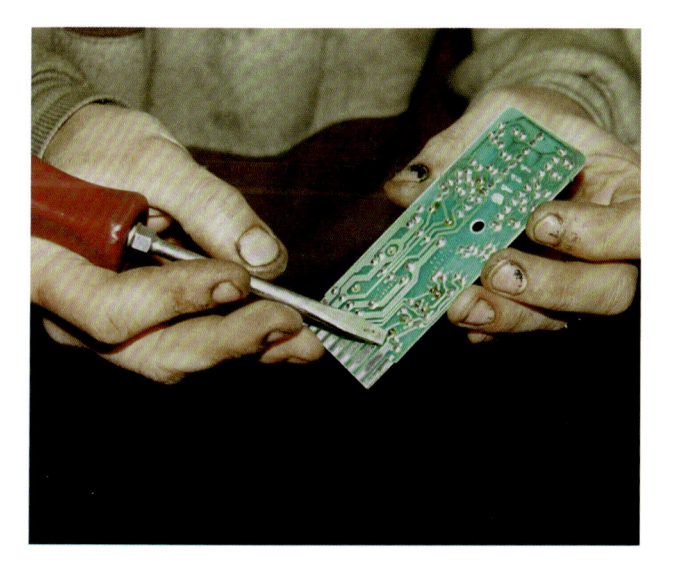

The central processing unit on the XJ40 monitors the functions of many systems. Simultaneous failure or erratic behaviour of many apparently unassociated systems can often be traced to a problem with the CPU, quite common on 1990 to 1992 model year cars.

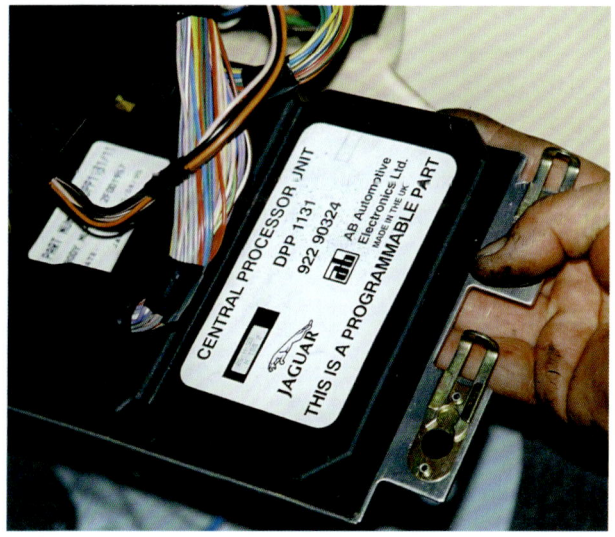

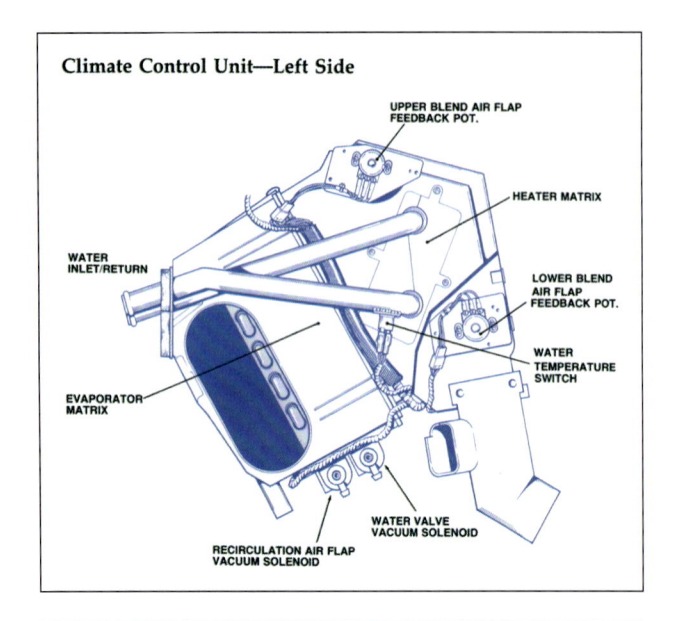

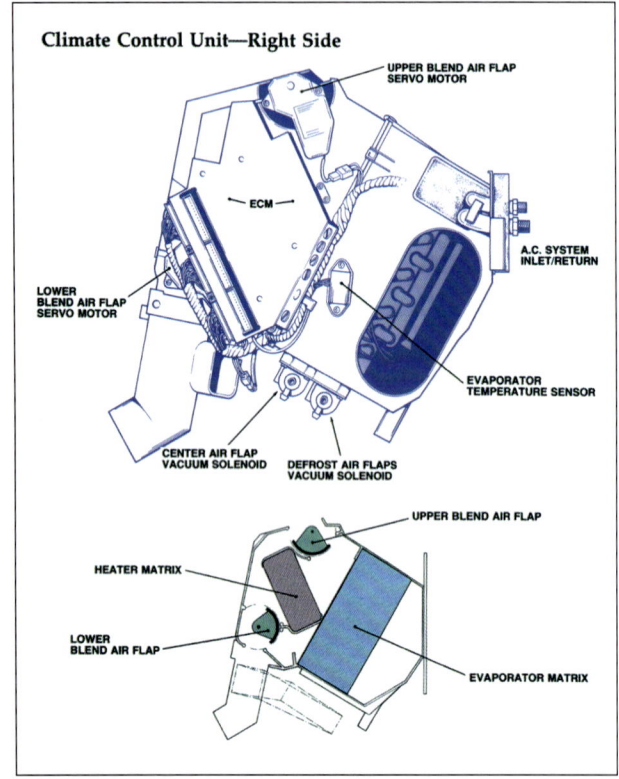

Both side views of the complex climate control unit as fitted to the XJ40 models.

bent or the cable frayed) reinsert it with the teeth towards the front of the car, then with someone to turn the radio off, after about 15 seconds the cable should start to reel in. Even if the cable and aerial do not fully retract first time, the motor will reset itself on a second operation.

There is a set of fault codes identifying electrical problems which affect the running of the car, and these are shown in Appendix F. These should be referred back to a Jaguar workshop manual or a specialist for diagnostic appraisal as the work is too extensive to be covered in this book.

Heating and air conditioning systems

There are many problems associated with this area of the XJ40, but in essence, the system developed for the car was well conceived and is not as complex as it seems once you get to know it.

Most of the problems are caused by the ingress of water caused either by the blocking of the air conditioning drains, blockage of scuttle plenum drain, leakage of the windscreen and leakage of the heater matrix. The electrical faults on these systems commonly fall into one of three areas:

1. Failure of any of the air conditioning controls to respond, which is normally down to a micro-switch in the air conditioning control module.
2. The propensity of the system to deliver either permanently hot or cold air at either foot or face level regardless of the temperature selected. This is due to the failure of the relevant flap motor which incorporate nylon gears that often bind.
3. The two fans are known for either failing to work or 'locking' on to a permanent speed. This is due to a fault with the transistors as fitted to the control modules within the fans themselves. Removal of the fans and replacement of the transistors will usually cure the problem. Prolonged and heavy water ingress will eventually cause the fan motors to seize up and burn out.

There are other non-electrical aspects to also consider. For example refrigerant can be lost through a variety of reasons. There are various O rings and joints which can leak or even perforation of the air conditioning condenser can take place. This latter item sits right at the front of the car just behind the radiator grille and therefore bears the brunt of road debris which impacts on to it over the years.

It must be stressed that any loss of refrigerant is a safety aspect. Most XJ40s will still be using freon R12 gas which is now illegal to release into the atmosphere. In fact, it is now illegal to release any refrigerant gas into the atmosphere even on later cars (from about 1993) that use R134A gas which, although environmentally safer, should still be captured upon release. There are now various substitute gases which replace the old R12 gas, such as R49. In all cases, it is suggested that an approved air conditioning specialist deals with such aspects of the car.

Another weak point is the expansion valve, a metering unit from the compressor to the evaporator, situated at the evaporator. These can shut down and therefore be the cause of numerous problems such as a compressor burn out. Again such matters need to be dealt with by air-con experts because of the need for proper diagnostic equipment. This expansion valve is much easier to remove than on previous models, but any ham-fistedness around this area can damage the evaporator itself.

The cruise control system fitted to the XJ40 models is of the Kiekert design using a microprocessor-controlled system. The bellows and allied items are more reliable than earlier types and the vacuum was created by a pump which is also very reliable.

There is a safety 'dump-valve' on these systems situated near the vacuum pump (on the inner wing) which will cause the vacuum to permanently release into the atmosphere if a problem is noted with the cruise control system. It is not unknown for this valve to hold open due to a fault within the valve. Therefore the system won't operate. Again, proper diagnostics are really necessary to determine where the problem lies, which is beyond the realms of DIY maintenance.

Bodywork

It is not within the scope of this book to cover all aspects of body repair. Suffice to say that many panels are still readily available for the XJ40 and all the original tooling has been retained by Jaguar. XJ40 body parts will therefore form part of the Unipart/JDHT Classic Parts Scheme in future and, although at times, there will inevitably be shortages, most parts should continue to be available.

Water leaks are one of the major problems, particularly around the boot area but can be cured by removing the plastic finisher panel on the rear valance boot lid shut-face. Then after drying thoroughly, applying mastik to the whole area including the self-tapper holes, then refitting the plastic finisher and applying more mastik.

The door locks are a common area of concern on the earlier cars, caused by poor design compounded by seizing of the mechanisms due to lack of use. As the mechanisms became harder to operate, so occupants pull harder on the handles, exerting more strain on the

This clearly shows the problem associated with the earlier door locks on the XJ40. When the 'pull' has gone off-centre like this then the lock is beyond repair.

metal. The only cure is to keep the mechanisms well lubricated which means removing the door panels and setting the link rods so that there is little free play between the operation of the door handle and the actual opening of the door.

Post-1990 cars have a non-interchangeable style of handle mechanism which is generally more reliable, but these are not unknown to break either.

The mazak moulding has split on this lock assembly, due to previous incorrect adjustment resulting in the occupants having to pull harder on the door handle and thus causing the damage.

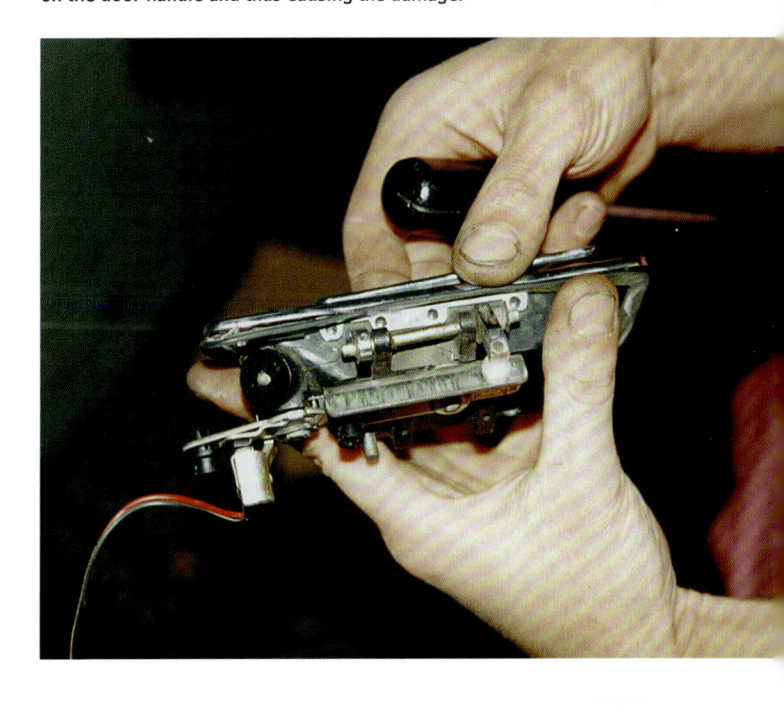

Chapter **Eleven**

Modifications and improvements

There are lots of 'easy fixes' to upgrading the looks or performance of an XJ40. With so many built and many now in the hands of dismantlers, as well as some very cheap and cheerful examples still around to buy, there is ample opportunity to improve your existing model even if you don't want to go to major expense, particularly if you carry out much of the work yourself.

Let's start with enhancing the appearance.

Exterior

For example it is down to personal taste as to whether you prefer the four headlamp treatment or the rectangular units. Either way, these can be changed around, the only proviso being that all the corresponding mounting brackets and bulb failure modules must be changed as well. Both styles of bulb-failure modules will fit into any main wiring loom regardless of car.

Next the wheels and tyres. We have already mentioned that most cars are better shod with non-metric versions these days and from thereon in there is a host of alloy wheels to choose from. All of these will fit with no problems, although you should be sure that any second-hand wheels you buy are not only undamaged and safe to fit, but that also they do not come from another Jaguar model such as the XJ-S or Series 3 XJ saloons which, in some cases, have a slightly different offset to the wheel centres. Wheel changes do not affect the calibration of the speedometer as the drive for this comes from the gearbox, and not through the wheels.

Disregarding the earlier metric and later 20-spoke (teardrop) exposed wheel nut type (the most common found on XJ40s of any age), there are lots of original Jaguar fitment XJ40 wheels to choose from:

Also, some of the later X-300 wheels will fit the XJ40,

such as the Aero, Dimple and Sports. If you wish to retain steel wheels, then certainly the later directional type plastic rimbellishers can still be quite easily found and, of course, are easily painted if scratched.

A cosmetic change could incorporate the colour-coding of trim like the S models or even go a stage further such as the prototype Coupé in an earlier chapter. Jaguar used to produce rubber/chrome body side mouldings which fitted along the bottom swage

The original metric TD wheel specially designed for the XJ40.

The later equivalent to the TD, in non-metric size.

The early JaguarSport fully enclosed wheel.

This wheel was only used on the Daimler Double Six in the UK/Europe and on some US models.

The later JaguarSport wheel as fitted to XJR models.

The Roulette wheel featured on some Daimler models and US cars.

The lattice wheel, of which there were two sizes.

The Kiwi wheel, first seen on the Gold model.

The five-spoke wheels, originally produced for the S models.

The 12 duo-spoke wheel was fitted to the later Sovereign models.

Modifications and improvements **147**

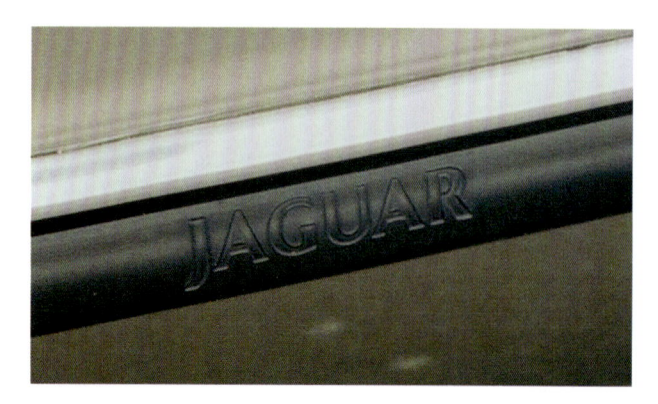

Jaguar produced their own side mouldings as an accessory with the Jaguar name embossed in the rubber.

line of the car. These are not only useful in preventing accidental damage, but look good and although you can no longer buy them new, again visiting dismantlers who have XJ40s may reveal a complete set.

The later chromed surrounds finish off the rear of any XJ40 model.

Alternatively, aftermarket companies still produce this type of thing, although it will not carry the correct Jaguar name.

At the rear, the fitment of the later chrome surrounds to lights and boot lid can help take away some of the bland look of the earlier models, and you might also consider fitting one of the plastic in-fill panels such as on the S model.

Some highly specified cars had such items as headlamp high-pressure wash systems, which are not difficult to retro-fit from another car providing you replace the bumper blade if the car was equipped with round headlights before, the same applying to integrated fog lamps. The sunroof panel is an easy item to remove and refit, but if your car hasn't had one fitted previously, then there is much more work involved of course.

A full list of the accessories that were produced by Jaguar during the production years of the XJ40 are shown at the back of this book, Appendix D.

The Custom Cabrios lookalike conversion to X-300 style for the XJ40 models.

Just Jags produces a range of bolt-on body kits for various models including the XJ40, as shown here.

Putting on a front

It is arguable now, whether the owner of an XJ40 would want to turn his car into something it isn't, but a company in Norwich (Custom Cabrios) produces a body styling kit to turn your XJ40 into a look-a-like X-300 (the replacement model).

Comprising replacement panels for the front wings, valance, bumper, bonnet and boot/lights, many XJ40 parts have been made to be interchangable such as the indicator lights.

As well as this, Custom Cabrios also produce cabriolet conversions for the XJ40 models (similar to the ones mentioned in a previous chapter), by cutting off the roof, strengthening the underside of the car and adding targa roof panels at the front and a rear hood section over the rear seat. Perhaps ideal for wedding cars.

Body kits

There have been numerous body kits around for the XJ40, the most famous of which is probably those of JaguarSport, discussed in a previous chapter. Although no longer officially available from Jaguar or TWR, most aspects of the kit can still be acquired from the company who originally designed and painted them, QCR Motors in Nuneaton.

From the late 1990s, a company called Just Jags in the West Midlands designed and still produces specialist body kits for the XJ40. Made of glass-fibre the

Modifications and improvements

Genuine TWR body kits have their name embossed on the bumpers.

panels are easy to fit and many would say modernise the exterior look of the XJ40. The bumper bars, painted to body colour, and sculpted like the X-300 type, replace the existing rubber-faced bumpers. The front valance incorporates X-300 driving lights and a rear in-fill panel is not dissimilar to the type fitted by the factory on the S models. A stylised rear boot spoiler incorporates a high level LED brake light. The company also still produces door mouldings and oversills.

The later JaguarSport kits had sculpted sills fitted.

Interior

Internally, much depends on the model you own. For example, if you do not have leather upholstery, the fitment of a complete leather set from a scrapped car can certainly enhance the quality feel of the car. Similarly, if you do not have veneer with boxwood inlays, it is an easy matter to change this over or even buy a complete new set from Jaguar as they still retain much of the original stock in the Unipart/JDHT Classic Parts Scheme. Apparently they can also still supply some of the specialist Insignia colour schemes if required.

Other items, such as electrically adjustable seats, Daimler seating, etc. can all be taken from another car and fitted without much concern as the same wiring is built into all the cars. It must be noted, however, when changing seats that the very early cars had a different seat fixing style to later ones. This changed (about 1987) and is identified by the seats being held on to the floorpan by four bolts. The two at the rear are the same on all cars, but the front ones on early cars fit down vertically whereas the later ones are screwed into the strengthening beam, horizontally.

The electrical link leads must be purchased with any seats bought and the relays will need fitting into the blocks, these being situated under the ski slope attached to the support bracket for the main air conditioning box, in the centre console area.

One area which does require serious consideration is the fitment of air conditioning as not all cars had this feature from new and it is now of greater importance to modern day owners. Jaguar used to offer a conversion kit, quite extensive and expensive at over £1,000 to buy, which replaced the existing heater unit, radiator and all the other equipment needed. Nowadays, these kits are no longer available which would mean the removal of same from an older car, which in itself is not a quick job. Also, to fit air conditioning to a non-air-con model requires major surgery in that the whole dashboard assembly has to be removed, there are alterations to the wiring harnesses, and much more – not a job for the faint-hearted.

Most people prefer the later analogue instrument binnacle as fitted from 1990 and it is often asked if these can be changed over for the earlier dashboard. Unfortunately, they cannot because the wiring loom is completely different and the instruments received messages in a different manner.

Performance and convenience upgrades

If you own a 2.9-litre-engined model, the easiest way to upgrade performance is to fit a 3.6-litre or 4.0-litre engine. The basic principle applies to any engine change and a short list of what is involved indicates that you would probably also need to change the gearbox as one for a 2.9-litre car will be calibrated differently. Secondly, the fuel injection wiring loom must also be changed as will the ECUs and the front coil springs because of the difference in weight distribution. The differential ratio may need changing to accommodate the more powerful engine. If you do change an engine over, don't forget to tell the DVLA and your insurance company!

There are simpler and very effective ways of boosting performance including the modifications suggested by AJ6 Engineering of Stockport in the UK, ideally suited to the 3.6-litre and 4.0-litre engines. They can recalibrate ECUs and modify inlet and exhaust manifolds to improve brake horsepower. Such changes don't show in appearance but are very effective and make a significant improvement in power for very little money.

If you want to change the tone of your exhaust system, the two rearward silencers can be removed and replaced by standard pipes. This increases the air flow which will be adjusted automatically by the engine management system and give you a little more 'rasp' to

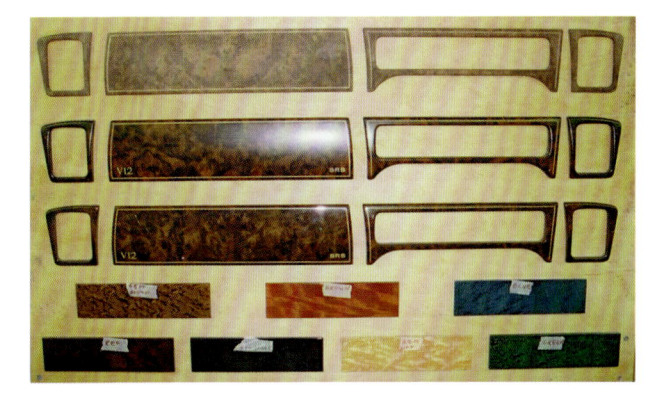

Surprisingly, a lot of XJ40 woodwork is still available from the Unipart/JDHT Classic Parts Scheme through some Jaguar dealerships; even Insignia woodwork can be purchased.

the exhaust note without being obtrusive.

The fitting of better quality shock absorbers is also very worthwhile. For example, either the JaguarSport type or those produced by Bilstein, or even adjustables, all of which will improve the handing without affecting the ride too much.

The choice of manual or automatic transmission is another consideration. Although in their day few people actually preferred the manual gearbox, these days, particularly for the real motoring enthusiast,

To consider fitting air conditioning to a non-air con model is a daunting task, particularly now that no factory kits are available. This is some of the dis-assembly required to make the change!

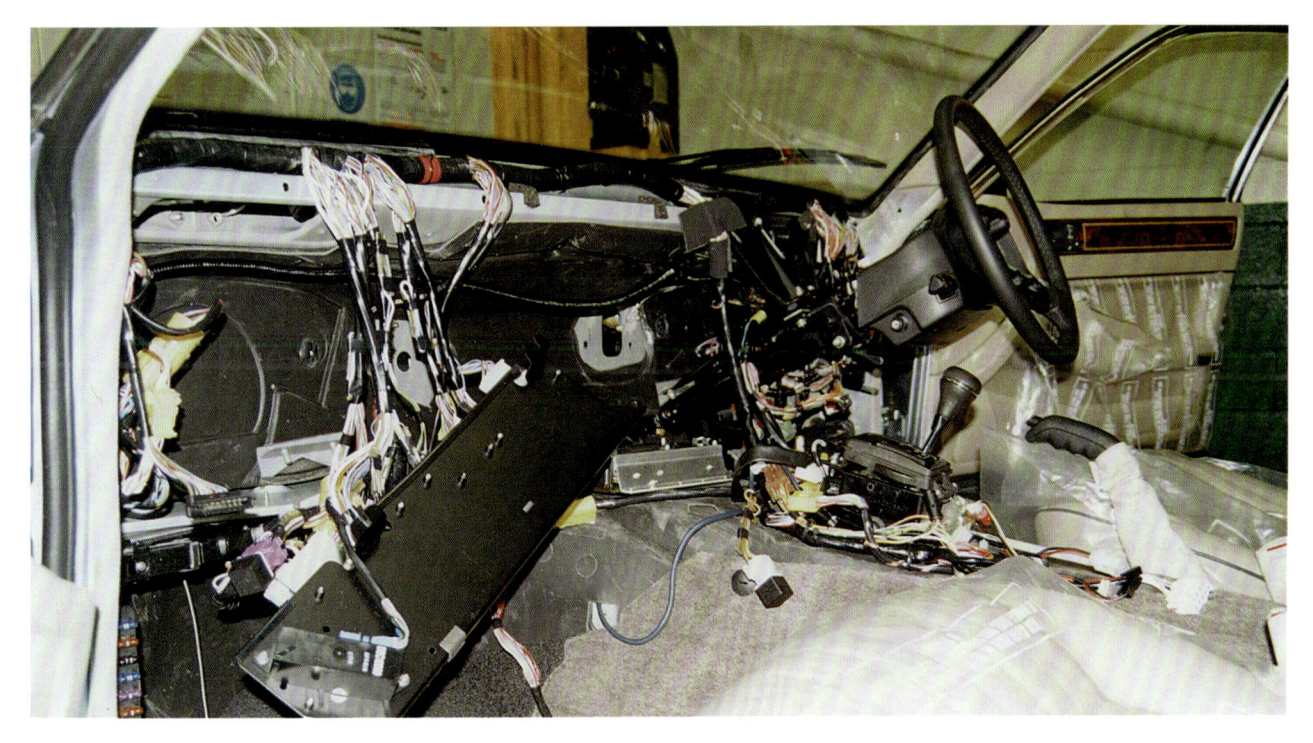

There are plenty of used and exhausted XJ40s around from which to find those elusive parts to upgrade your car, like these at EuroJags in the north-east of England.

they have great appeal and indeed, many XJ40s have been stripped just to get hold of the gearbox for racing purposes.

To change from an automatic transmission to manual gearbox is not such a daunting task although a new pedal box, hydraulics, flywheel (from the automatic transmission model) must also be fitted, along with ECU modifications.

Different steering racks can also tighten up the handling. Various types were fitted to different XJ40 models so a straight changeover is possible or you can purchase the JaguarSport type direct. It can also help to lower the suspension with slightly different road springs, and don't forget that if you have a car equipped with the self-levelling rear suspension, this certainly should now be decommissioned.

And finally, do you have the right tool kit with your car? On the left is the later tool kit from 1992, and on the right, the earlier type.

Appendix **A**

Specifications

Model	No of cyls	Engine cc	Bore mm	Stroke mm	Comp ratio	Bhp rpm	Torque lb ft @ rpm	Trans-mission	Final drive ratio	Wheel size	0–60 mph secs	Top speed mph	Ave mpg	Gross weight kg
XJ6 2.9	6	2919	91	74.8	12.6	165@5600	176@4000	Man	3.77	390x180mm TD	9.6	120	19.5	2140
Sovereign 2.9	6	2919	91	74.8	12.6	165@5600	176@4000	ZF Auto	4.08	390x180mm TD	10.8	118	19.8	2140
XJ6 3.6	6	3590	91	92	9.6	221@5000	249@4000	Man	3.58	390x180mm TD	7.4	136	18.6	2190
Sovereign 3.6	6	3590	91	92	9.6	221@5000	249@4000	ZF Auto	3.58	390x180mm TD	8.8	135	18.7	2190
Daimler 3.6	6	3590	91	92	9.6	221@5000	249@4000	ZF Auto	3.58	390x180mm TD	8.8	135	18.7	2190
XJR 3.6	6	3590	91	92	9.6	221@5000	249@4000	Man	3.58	390x180mm TD	7.4	136	18.7	2190
XJ6 3.2	6	3239	91	83	9.75	200@5250	220@4000	Man	3.77	7x15in	8.5	132	18.5	2250
XJ6 3.2 S	6	3239	91	83	9.75	200@5250	220@4000	ZF Auto	4.09	7x16in	9.5	131	19.2	2250
XJ6 Gold	6	3239	91	83	9.75	200@5250	220@4000	ZF Auto	4.09	7x16in	9.5	131	19.2	2250
XJ6 4.0	6	3980	91	102	9.5	235@4750	285@3850	Man	3.58	7x16in	7.6	140	16.4	2220
XJ6 4.0 S	6	3980	91	102	9.5	235@4750	285@3750	ZF Auto	3.58	7x16in	7.1	138	19.0	2290
Sovereign 4.0	6	3980	91	102	9.5	235@4750	285@3750	ZF Auto	3.58	7x16in	7.1	138	19.0	2290
Daimler 4.0	6	3980	91	102	9.5	235@4750	285@3750	ZF Auto	3.58	7x16in	8.1	138	18.6	2290
XJR 4.0	6	3980	91	102	9.75	248@5250	278@4000	Man	3.58	7x16in	7.2	145	15.9	2245
XJ12	12	5993	90	78.5	11	318@5400	342@3750	GM Auto	3.58	7x16in	6.8	155	12.9	2415
Daimler D6	12	5993	90	78.5	11	318@5400	342@3750	GM Auto	3.58	7x16in	6.9	155	12.9	2415

Appendix B

Model history

The following figures show the total production of XJ40 models from their inception, including known prototypes, many of which have been destroyed. The prototype figures include the special one-off Coupé and estate cars manufactured and now in the hands of the Jaguar Daimler Heritage Trust.

Notes on production figures

2.9 and 3.2-litre Standard/Daimler – The factory production records do not differentiate between the two different models, so the overall production totals are for both.

Federal models – Mainly US specification cars, many of which were sold under the Vanden Plas name, but not as Daimlers.

6.0-litre export models – Mainly US specification cars, mainly sold under the Vanden Plas name.

Majestic models – Stretched floorpan versions of the saloons built to special order.

Insignia models – Bespoke cars with differences in interior and exterior trim are included in the overall figures, and amount to approximately 200 vehicles in total.

Sport models – Aimed at a younger, sportier buyer with Sport Handling Pack, revised interior trim and some body colour coding.

Gold models – The last special edition models.

Many thanks to Jaguar Cars Limited and the Jaguar Daimler Heritage Trust for allowing access to, and the means to collate, the information included here.

Appendix C

Total production figures

Model	Prototype	1986	1987	1988	1989	1990	1991	1992	1993	1994	Totals
2.9 Std/Daimler	96	673	2613	3043	3575	1191	–	–	–	–	**11191**
2.9 Sovereign	4	453	817	834	548	301	–	–	–	–	**2957**
3.6 Standard	56	778	2213	4038	2262	–	–	–	–	–	**9347**
3.6 Sovereign	17	1615	19266	20743	8650	–	–	–	–	–	**50291**
3.6 Federal	–	24	4744	6002	2549	–	–	–	–	–	**13319**
3.6 Daimler	78	415	3411	4772	1638	–	–	–	–	–	**10314**
3.2 Std/Daimler	–	–	–	–	–	1936	3727	3733	3200	457	**13053**
3.2 Sport	–	–	–	–	–	–	–	–	1610	1507	**3117**
3.2 Gold	–	–	–	–	–	–	–	–	–	1499	**1499**
3.2 Sovereign	–	–	–	–	–	698	1042	1063	582	102	**3487**
4.0 Standard	–	–	–	–	3879	5383	1707	1429	928	250	**13576**
4.0 Sport	–	–	–	–	–	–	–	–	–	500	**500**
4.0 Gold	–	–	–	–	–	–	–	–	–	23	**23**
4.0 Sovereign	–	–	–	–	7767	14350	6781	5795	12179	3464	**50336**
4.0 Federal	–	–	–	–	1965	3514	2182	2116	1886	1201	**12864**
4.0 Daimler	–	–	–	–	–	3489	1751	1796	1380	462	**8878**
4.0 Majestic	–	–	–	–	–	–	–	1	73	47	**121**
6.0 Export	–	–	–	–	–	–	–	–	1121	400	**1521**
6.0 Jaguar	–	–	–	–	–	–	–	–	1087	156	**1243**
6.0 Daimler	–	–	–	–	–	–	–	–	864	121	**985**
6.0 Majestic	–	–	–	–	–	–	–	–	–	50	**50**
Misc prototypes	–	–	–	–	–	–	–	34	–	–	**34**
Totals	251	3,958	33,064	39,432	32,833	30,862	17,190	15,967	24,910	10,239	208,706

Appendix D

Factory options listing from 1986 to 1994

Colours (exterior)
Glacier White
Signal Red
Black
Westminster Blue
British Racing Green
Kingfisher Blue
Solent Blue
Diamond Blue
Platinum
Silver Frost

Oyster
Regency Red
Flamenco Red
Morocco Red
Jade Green
Gunmetal Grey
Rose Bronze
Sapphire Blue
Dorchester Grey
Isis Blue

Trim
Doeskin
Barley
Savile Grey
Isis Blue
Cream

Cherry Red
Charcoal
Parchment
Magnolia

Seat piping
Blue
Buckskin

Sage Green
Cherry Red

Gold only colours
British Racing Green
Regency Red
Gunmetal
Sapphire Blue

Westminster Blue
Morocco Red
Kingfisher Blue

S only colours
Flamenco Red
Kingfisher Blue
Diamond Blue

British Racing Green
Silver Frost
Black

Accessories
Side body moulding rubbing strips
Walnut/Rosewood gearknob
Sheepskin overrugs
Rear screen blinds
Child's booster cushion
Fire extinguisher for boot or under-seat location
Jaguar tyre pressure gauge
Snow chains
Electrically controlled boot-mounted cooler box
Basic two-bar carrier
Roof box
Cycle holder
Sail board holder
Tailored boot mat
Mud flaps
Towbar kit
CD auto-changer system
Cup holders
Ultrasonic intrusion security system
Tool kit (applicable to very late cars only)

Stainless door edge guards
Wind deflector for sunroof
Tailored over-carpets
Childs safety seat
First aid kit for boot area
Fog lamp kit
Jaguar warning triangle
Headlamp beam converters
Continental touring kit (spare parts, etc.)
Roof rack
Luggage frame
Luggage net
Ski holder
Mountain bike holder
Headlamp protector covers
Rubber carpet mats
Locking wheel nut set
Telephone kit
Heated front screen
Spacesaver spare wheel
Sports suspension system

Alloy wheel styles
16in lattice

15in lattice
16in five-spoke
15in radial
15in Roulette
15in Teardrop

16in JaguarSport Speedline (two types)
16in Diamond-turned 20-spoke
16in Aero
16in Diamond-turned/Silver Kiwi

156   Jaguar XJ40

Appendix E

Regular maintenance schedule

Procedure	7.5/10	15/20	30	60
Check condition of lower wishbone brushes	■	■	■	■
Check ball joints	■	■	■	■
Change engine oil	■	■	■	■
Change oil filter	■	■	■	■
Check heater return hose	■	■	■	■
Check front shock absorbers and springs	■	■	■	■
Check condition of front subframe	■	■	■	■
Grease top wishbone brushes (early cars), check condition of top wishbone brushes (late cars)	■	■	■	■
Check front wheel bearing for play	■	■	■	■
Remove and examine front wheel bearings/ grease and reassemble or replace			■	■
Check condition of front brake discs and pads	■	■	■	■
Remove and grease front caliper slides (Jurid brakes), check front calipers are free (Teves brakes)	■	■	■	■
Check oil drain plug is tight	■	■	■	■
Check condition of all drive belts	■	■	■	■
Change gearbox oil and filter plus O ring/ gaskets (autos)			■	■
Change gearbox oil (manuals)			■	■
Change fuel filter				■
Check condition of rear shock absorbers/ A frame bushes/rotoflex couplings	■	■	■	■
Free off handbrake lever pin	■	■	■	■
Check differential oil level	■	■		
Drain and refill differential oil			■	■
Grease universal joints	■	■	■	■
Check play in rear wheel bearings/output shaft bearings/trunnion bearings/ universal joints	■	■	■	■
Check condition of rear brake pads/discs	■	■	■	■
Grease rear caliper slides (Jurid), check rear calipers are free (Teves)	■	■	■	■
Strip and repack rear hub bearings				■

Procedure	7.5/10	15/20	30	60
Adjust handbrake shoes	■	■	■	■
Check remainder of handbrake linkage for seizure	■	■	■	■
Check rear bump stops	■	■	■	■
Wax all brake and fuel lines, including self-levelling lines	■	■	■	■
Wax front subframe	■	■	■	■
Bleed brakes	■	■	■	■
Check coolant level and concentration	■	■		
Change coolant			■	■
Change spark plugs			■	■
Check air filter	■			
Change air filter		■	■	■
Check engine breather cap and lines are clear (2.9 only)	■	■	■	■
Check brake fluid level	■	■		
Change brake and clutch fluids			■	■
Check PAS fluid level	■	■	■	■
Check mineral fluid level	■	■	■	■
Check distributor cap and rotor arm	■	■	■	■
Check viscous coupling on cooling fan	■	■	■	■
Top up screen wash	■	■	■	■
Change screen wiper blade	■	■	■	■
Check battery fluid level	■	■	■	■
Check tyre pressure and condition including spare	■	■	■	■
Check all lights	■	■	■	■
Check all drain/refill plugs are tight	■	■	■	■
Tighten wheel nuts to correct torque	■	■	■	■
Clean mast	■	■	■	■
Clean ash trays	■	■	■	■
Check screen wash and wiper park operations	■	■	■	■
Observe and comment on unusual items like corrosion, etc.	■	■	■	■
Clean off oil/finger prints from whole vehicle	■	■	■	■

Appendix F

Engine management system fault codes

The following does not apply to 2.9-litre engined models.

3.6-litre engines

1. Cranking signal failure. No crankshaft sensor signal detected after cranking engine for six seconds, or the cranking signal line at L12-8 is active above 2,000rpm.
2. Air flow meter failure. Either open circuit or short circuit to ground.
3. Coolant temperature sensor failure.
4. Feedback circuit failure (catalyst vehicles only).
5. Air flow meter failure. Low throttle potentiometer voltage with high air flow meter voltage.
6. Air flow meter failure. High throttle potentiometer voltage with low air flow meter voltage.
7. Idle fuel adjustment potentioneter failure.
8. Not allocated for use. Should this fault number be displayed, a 6.8 kilhm resistor fitted in place of a hot start sensor is faulty.

3.2-litre/4.0-litre engines

11. Throttle pot at idle or associated wiring. Throttle pot idle trim out of normal operating range.
12. Air flow meter or associated wiring. Air flow meter signal out of operating range.
14. Coolant thermistor or associated wiring. Coolant thermistor resistance out of range or static during engine warm up.
16. Air thermistor or associated wiring. Air thermistor resistance out of range.
17. Throttle pot or associated wiring. Throttle pot, resistance out of range.
18. Throttle pot/air flow meter calibration. Low throttle pot signal at high air flow.
19. Throttle pot/air flow meter calibration. High throttle pot signal at low air flow.
22. Fuel pump drive. ECU output to fuel pump relay.
23. Fuel supply. Poor feedback control in rich direction.
24. Ignition drive. ECU output to ignition amplifier module.
26. Air leak. Poor feedback control in lean direction.
29. ECU self check. Checks micro processor function.
33. Injector drive fault. Checks for ECU output to injectors.
34. Injector. Looks for injector dribble.
37. EGR drive. ECU output to EGR switching valve.
39. EGR check sensor. Look for correct operation of EGR.
44. Lambda sensor or associated wiring. Feedback out of control, rich or weak.
46. Idle speed control coil AB drive. ECU output to stepper motor driver.
47. Idle speed control coil CD drive. EDU output to stepper motor driver.
48. Idle speed control motor or valve. Looks for stepper motor being grossly out of position.
66. Air pump drive. ECU output to air pump relay.
68. Road speed sensor or associated wiring. Looks for road speed indicating less than 5km/h at high engine air flow.
69. Drive/Neutral switch or wiring. Looks for cranking in 'D' or high air flow in 'N' (automatic only).
89. Purge valve drive. ECU output for purge valve.

NOTES

UK and Middle East specification vehicles:
Fault codes 11, 12, 14, 16, 17, 18, 19 and 68 will illuminate the warning light. It will remain illuminated until the engine is switched off.

The ECU remembers the failure and when the ignition is switched on again the warning light will illuminate.

When the engine is started the light will extinguish if the fault has not reoccurred. If the fault is still apparent the light will remain on.

Catalyt (non Federal) and Australian specification vehicles:
The procedure is the same as that stated for the UK. In addition, fault codes 23, 26 and 44 will illuminate the warning light.

Federal specification vehicles:
All the fault codes above will illuminate the warning light which will remain illuminated when ever the ignition is on.

These fault codes are cleared via the serial link to the ECU or by disconnecting the battery supply to the ECU.

Index

Accessories 156
Air bags 16, 70–71, 86
Air conditioning 71, 77, 144–145
AJ6 engine 17, 19 26–29, 52, 56–57, 63–64, 69, 127–128, 135–138
AJ6 Engineering 151
Alfa Romeo 164 Cloverleaf 92
Arden 110–111
Audi 200 36
Austin 7 7
  Mini 36
Austin-Rover, Swindon 20, 22
Autocar magazine 53
Autocar and Motor magazine 65, 93
Autosport magazine 52

Bank of England 117
Beasley, Mike 12
Bentley Turbo R 116
Bertone 12
BMW 82
  5 Series 82
  7 Series 16, 35
  525i SEX 92
  530I 61, 64
  730i 91
  735i 65
Body design 20–23
Body kits 149–150
Braking system 31–32, 45, 57, 129, 140–141
British Leyland 8–9, 12, 15, 36
  LC40 10
Budget Rent-a-Car 77, 89
Buick engine 10

Cabriolet's International 106
Cadillac 35

Car magazine 53, 92
Car & Driver magazine 53
Catalytic converters 70
CD auto-changer 73, 79, 115
Central locking 55
Chasseur 104–106, 108
Citroën XM V6 92
Claims to fame 23
Clarion sound systems 43, 45, 53–54
Colour schemes 156
Concepts (styling) 11–14, 19
Corrosion 22–23, 121–126
Cost of ownership 36–37
Coupé 98–99, 111–112
Coventry Motor Museum 39
Cruise control changes 55
Custom Cabrios 149

Daimler 7, 29, 36, 45–49, 61–62
  DS420 107, 113
Dates in XJ40 development 12
Dealer network 36
Department of Transport 82
Diagnostics 34
Diana, Princess 116
Donington circuit 95
Door locks 57, 145
Door mirrors 55
Drag factor 21
Dunkeld Castle 38
Dunlop tyres 32, 86

Eagle limousine 112–113, 116–117
Earls Court Motor Show 19
Egan, John Sir 7, 10, 12, 15, 37, 63, 67
Electronics 33–34, 129, 137, 142–144

End of the line 93
Engine management fault codes 158
England, 'Lofty' 12
Ernest Hatfield, dealership 102–103
Estate cars 102–105, 109–110
EuroJags 152
European Touring Car Championship 19

Fault codes 158
Ferguson, Lady Sarah 117
Ferrari Testarossa 96
Fiat X1/9 116
Final assembly 34
Financial investment 20, 24
Fire tender 95
Fleet Motor Show 82
Fleet News magazine 63
Focus groups 16
Ford Motor Company 55, 63, 93
  Granada 36
  Scorpio 61, 92

Gaydon test track 94
Giamakva, Peter 89
Goodrich tyres 104
Guangdong Motor Show 74
Guild of Motoring Writers 12

Hall, David 114
Hayden, William 63, 67
Hilton Hotel, Park Lane 38
Humberstone 102–105, 109

Insignia 106–108, 113, 154
Institute of Mechanical Engineers 37–38
Ital Design 11–12

J-Day 37–38
Jaguar
  E-type 8, 10, 96
  Mark V 7
  Mark VII 7
  Mark X 7, 18
  XJ projects 7–8
  XJ6 (pre-XJ40) 7, 10
  XJ6 Gold 91–93, 119, 153–156
  XJ6 Sport 82–85, 154–155
  XJ6 (X-300) 93, 111, 113, 149
  XJ8 8, 113
  XJ220 55, 63
  XJ-S 8, 10–12, 14, 19, 26–29, 53, 97, 111, 116
  XJR 85, 88, 91, 95, 98, 100–102, 138–139
  XKR 66
Jaguar Daimler Heritage Trust 40, 93, 110, 112, 154
Jaguar Enthusiast magazine 130
Jaguar Enthusiasts' Club 118–120, 130, 136
JaguarSport 97–98, 100–102, 150, 152, 156
Janspeed 96–97
Just Jags 149

Kenwood sound system 115
Kiwi wheels 91, 147
Knight, Bob 12
Know Your Jaguar guide book 67

Lancia Sratos 116
Le Mans 24hr race 55, 63
Lexus 67, 76
Limousines 112–113, 116–117
Lincoln 35
Lister 106, 114–116
Loughborough University 26
Lucas 66
Lynx Engineering 102
Lyons, Sir William 9–10, 12, 37

Maintenance, general 130–139
Maintenance schedules 157
Majestic 61–63, 67, 85, 108
Making of the Forty (TV film) 39
Marketing strategy 35–36
Maserati Quattroporte 116
McCarthy, Mike 52
Mercedes-Benz 76
  E280 91

S Class 16, 35
S280 93
W123 82
280E 92
300 SE 61, 64
Metric tyres/wheels 32–33, 64
Michelin tyres 32, 115
Microprocessors 33
Mock ups 12, 15–16
Model history 154
Motor magazine 37, 52–53

National Exhibition Centre 38–39, 112
National Motor Show 97
Newcastle United FC 114–115

Optional equipment 50, 156

Paintwork 20, 23, 44, 50, 84, 98, 108, 156
Performance upgrades 151
Performance Car magazine 53, 66
Peugeot 605 92
Pilkington Glass 66
Pininfarina 11–13
Pirelli tyres 65, 69, 77, 86, 98
Police specification 94–95, 117
Popular Mechanics magazine 53
Pressed Steel Fisher 18
Project Aerospace 108
Prometheus 20 66
Production figures 155
Production line 88–90
Prototypes 18, 155

QCR Motors 149

RAC 24hr rescue service 90
Randle, Jim 18, 37, 66
Rapport 116
Renault 25 36
Road & Track magazine 53
Robinson, Geoffrey 12
Rolls-Royce 106
  Silver Spirit 13
Rover engine 15
Rover
  800 Sterling 64, 92
  827 SI 61

Saab 9000 CDE Turbo 92
Scheele, Nick 67, 89, 93

Security systems 71–72
Servicing package 90
Silverstone 82
Special Vehicle Operations Dept 98, 106–112
Specially Designated Vehicles 18
Specifications 153
Sports Handling Pack 64–65, 78, 85–86
SS Cars Limited 7
Standard Motor Company 7
Steering 31, 129
Styling concepts 11–14
Suspensions 29–31, 64–65, 129, 139, 141–142

Tebbitt, Norman 38
Television coverage 39, 81–82
Tool kits 152
Transmissions 28–29, 56–57, 69, 77, 129, 136
Triumph TR7 116
Turbo Technics Co. 104–105
TWR 97–98, 100, 138–139, 149–150
Tyres 32–33, 64, 69, 73, 77, 84, 86, 98, 146–147

Unipart/JDHT Classic Parts Scheme 150–151
Unleaded fuel 49

V12 engine 76–78, 132–135
Vanden Plas 36, 40 61–63, 67–69, 75, 88–89, 154
Vascar radar system 94
Vauxhall
  Cavalier 14
  Senator 36
Vehicle condition monitor 24
Volvo 760 36

Waeland, Derek 20
Walkinshaw, Tom 19, 97
Walmsley, William 7
What Car? magazine 65, 76, 82
Wheels 32–33, 64, 69, 73, 76, 84, 86, 98, 131, 146–147, 156
Whittaker, Charles 104
Wilcox limousines 112–113, 116–117
Williams, David 102
WP Automotive (see Lister)

Yokohama tyres 104